Road **Runner** Guide to **Cyberspace**

Quick Access

Internet Quick Tour 3
Rules of the Road: Netiquette 15
E-Commerce: Online Shopping 23
Internet Safety Overview 33
Road Runner Browser 45
Road Runner Internet E-Mail 63
Internet Newsgroups 77
Cool Web Sites 89
Locating Information: Web Searches 101
Internet Research Resources 113
Government Online 125
News, Business and Finance 137
Web Publishing 153
Web Graphics 167
Top 10 Electronic Copyright Myths 181
Windows Primer (Cool Tips) 189
Glossary of Internet Terms 203

Detailed Table of Contents on Page iv

Road
Runner
Guide to
Cyberspace

by **Ronald L. Wagner**

ISBN 0-9654604-6-0
Ninth Edition

Copyright © 1999 by Citapei Communications, Inc.

Distributed by
Road Runner Group
www.rr.com

Published by
Citapei Communications
www.citapei.com

Editors
  Lisa M. Kauffman
  Derrick Frost
  Sean Callahan

Technical Reviewer
  Jason Kuder

Technical Consultants
  Derrick Frost
  Michael Suhanovsky
  Jason Welz
  John Voelcker
  Josh Hartmann
  Mike Murphy
  Chris Broccoli
  Josh Greene
  Kurt Fennel
  Paul Hart
  Andy Haines
  Howard Pfeffer

Publishing Consultants
  Tim Evard
  Randy Roswell
  Rusty Pickard
  Bobby Benya
  Robert S. Rusak

Cover and Art Design
  Ron Wagner

Production
  David Prentice

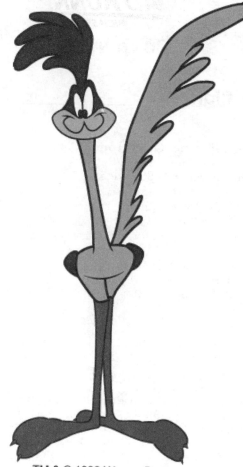

"Beep! Beep!"

CONTENTS

Phase 1: Preflight   2

Chapter 1
Ground School: Internet Quick Tour   3
> internet versus The Internet (3)
> How the Internet Got Started (5)
> There's Really No Control? (6)
> How You Got Invited (6)
> Who Is The Internet? (7)
> What's Out There for Me? (7)
> Web Principles (10)
> We All Are One (11)
> Cable Internet Access (11)
> About All The Jargon (12)

Chapter 2
Rules of the Road: Netiquette   15
> New Communication Tools (15)
> Flaming Words (16)
> Business Netiquette (17)
> Electronic Elements of Style (19)
> Emoticon Lexicon (20)
> Miscellaneous Netiquette (21)

Chapter 3
E-Commerce: Online Shopping   23
> The Truth about Credit Card Purchases (24)
> Tolls on the Information Highway (26)
> Internet Commerce Systems (27)

Chapter 4
Online Privacy: Internet Security   33
> Sniffers and Snoopers (34)
> Anti-Virus Protection (36)
> Top 10 Internet Security Problems (37)
> Web Browser Security (39)

Phase 2: The Launch   44

Chapter 5

Countdown: Road Runner Browser 45
Marking Your Trails (47)
Creating Some On-Screen Elbow-Room (50)
Finding What You Need (51)
Using The Information You Find (52)
Right Mouse Button Bonuses (55)
Favorites Folders (56)
Online Audio (58)
Online Video (60)

Chapter 6

Earth-to-Cyberspace: E-Mail 63
Internet E-Mail Applications (64)
Send E-Mail (66)
Read Messages (69)
Response Options (70)
Attachments (73)

Chapter 7

A Global Community: Newsgroups 77
Getting Started (78)
Nine Keys to Newsgroup Success (84)

Phase 3: Cyberspace   88

Chapter 8
What to See First: Cool Web Sites 89
Site Sampler (89)
Games and Programs (92)
Family Sites (95)
Miscellaneous (97)

Chapter 9
Finding Your Way: Internet Searches 101
Search Engine Principles (101)
Helping Others Find Your Page (104)
Web Search Engines (105)

Chapter 10
Cyber-Info: Research Resources 113
Bookstores (113)
Virtual Libraries (116)
Real Libraries (118)
Electronic Reference Sources (121)

Chapter 11
For the People: Government Online 125
Federal Government (126)
State Governments (131)
Local Governments (132)

Chapter 12
Making It Pay: News, Business and Finance 137
General News (137)
Investment Management (141)
Marketing Sites (142)
Consumer Information (144)
Selling Your House (146)

Phase 4: Web Publishing   152

Chapter 13
Your Cyber-Spacestation: Web Publishing 153
   Tools, Tools, and More Tools (154)
   Word Processors (154)
   Stand-Alone HTML Editors (157)
   Graphics Software (159)
   Common Gateway Interface Tools (159)
   Java and JavaScript (160)
   Testing Your Web Site (160)
   Decisions, Decisions... So Many Choices (162)

Chapter 14
Pictures in Cyber-Space: Web Graphics 167
   Web Graphics Primer (168)
   Graphic Drawing Packages (173)
   Image Scanning (176)

Chapter 15
Cyberspace Copyrights: Top 10 Myths 181
   Copyright Myths (182)
   Copyright Summary (185)

Chapter 16
Boosting Efficiency: Windows Primer 189

INTRODUCTION

> "Once a photograph of the Earth, taken from the outside, is available... a new idea as powerful as any in history will let loose."
>
> **Sir Fred Hoyle, 1948**

Twenty years after Sir Fred Hoyle made this prediction, an "earthrise" was seen for the first time when Apollo 8 orbited the moon on Christmas Eve, 1968. Many of the people who saw that earthrise were building a global computer networking system that today brings you the Internet.

Certainly the Internet qualifies as Sir Fred's new idea. It is as powerful as any idea in history and it's no coincidence that the Internet was created by the first generation to see an earthrise. That historic celestial event illustrated the concept that we all are joined in global unity—and the Internet has turned this into reality.

Now, through your Road Runner high speed online service, you are hooked up to participate in this sweeping, global communications revolution—*the waiting is over!*

Not your everyday Internet service

Your Road Runner high speed online service brings you much more than what most Internet service customers get today. In addition to basic services such as Web browsing, electronic mail and Internet news, we bring you:

❖ **Road Runner, an information service exclusive to cable:** Road Runner is an online service which links to Internet sites. By merely double-clicking the Road Runner icon on your computer, you'll be able to jump to local news and weather, global news, sports, and entertainment, as well as sites dedicated to hobbies, pets, schools and a host of other engaging topics.

❖ **Great content and incredible speed:** The biggest problem on the Internet today is it's too slow. That's because most home users access the Internet through a telephone line connection. Telephone lines are not designed to carry stereo sound, graphics, and video clips—but cable television systems are! With Road Runner, you won't nod off waiting for things to happen on your computer screen.

❖ **Parental access control:** We recognize that some areas of the Web may not be suitable for young people, so we've built into the system controls that let the master account holder (the person who subscribes to the service) assign sub-accounts to each member of the family. The master account holder can restrict a child's access to just the local content and local Discussion Boards. The child will have a unique e-mail address that can send and receive mail from anywhere on the Internet, but access to newsgroups, file transfers and anything else on the Internet is at the sole discretion of the parent.

❖ **The Road Runner Guide to Cyberspace:** Most Internet services simply give you access and leave you on your own. But you're not on your own with us because we give you the *Road Runner Guide to Cyberspace*. You need more than simple Internet access, and this book will walk the novice cyber-naut through cyberspace and show you a few thousand good reasons to use Road Runner.

What's in the book?

We thought you might ask, so here's an overview of what we've included:

❖ **Phase 1 - Preflight:** This is the ground school for your cyber-journey, which includes a quick tour of the Internet and some help with Internet etiquette and cyberspace security issues.

❖ **Phase 2 - The Launch:** Here's where you actually lift-off and go into cyberspace as we show you how to use the Web to explore cyberspace on your own.

❖ **Phase 3 - Cyberspace:** This is a tour guide of what's out there in cyberspace. As you explore this treasure trove of valuable Web sites and services, you'll be thrilled that you became a cyber-naut.

❖ **Phase 4 - Web Publishing:** Here's where we help you handle the "what's next?" question by showing you how to create your own little place in cyberspace—a Web site of your own. It also includes copyright information and a mini-lesson on Windows—in case you're new to computers and need a quick lesson to get up and running fast.

❖ **Appendix:** We wrap up this book with a two-part appendix: 1) a glossary of Internet, Web and computer terms; 2) and an index.

A closing note: Internet access speed

You subscribed to Road Runner for its blazing speed. And you've made the right choice because we can deliver the Internet to you faster than any other available service provider. But getting the Road Runner service into the back of your computer isn't the total solution to fast Internet access. There are many other performance factors that can mask the high-speed Internet capability you have on tap.

If you're not happy with the speed of your system, ask a reliable, local computer store to evaluate your video card, monitor, processor power, RAM memory and hard drive. You might need to upgrade some components to enjoy the full power that the Road Runner system can deliver. But that's enough build-up. Turn now to **Phase 1: Preflight** and then off to ground school!

NOTES

Phase 1

Phase 1: Preflight

Winston Churchill said, "I love learning. But I hate being taught." Believing that you might agree with Churchill, we have strived in this book to create opportunities for you to enjoy something you love—the pleasures of learning something new. This book is not constrained to the technical nuts-and-bolts. After all, volumes of technical computer tomes already crowd computer store bookshelves.

Of course we'll give you some technical material, but we'll do so in a way that will help you integrate your technical needs with your human needs. But this book is different from any you can buy in the stores because it's targeted toward Road Runner customers. You'll get the information you need to get the most from your high-speed cable Internet access.

Reading the first four chapters here in Phase 1 before going online, will prepare you for the dramatic transformation that Road Runner will bring to your life. The changes will be unprecedented. After you've prepared yourself by learning the basics about the Internet, you'll move into Phase 2 for our "Step-by-Step" exercises that will walk you through the most important functions of most of the Internet software you'll use.

After you've finished these chapters, you'll be all set to explore the Web and learn how it can serve as a powerful enhancement to your daily work and to your personal and family life at home.

❖ **Chapter 1** gives you an **Internet quick tour** and a map of your new online environment so you'll know the lay of this new cyber-land before you jump in. It's an easy-reading overview that will introduce you to the basic technical aspects of the Internet.

❖ **Chapter 2** gives you the highlights of **netiquette** (Internet etiquette) that will help you steer clear of a serious electronic faux pas. The Internet is a revolutionary communication tool and you need to know the rules of the road to keep from being blasted out of cyberspace by irate fellow travelers.

❖ **Chapter 3** There's been some negative hype about the safety of conducting electronic **financial transactions** via the Internet. But we'll show you that most of the news is good and that the Internet is as safe a place for your financial transactions as anywhere else.

❖ **Chapter 4** will put you at peace with **Internet security**. You may have heard horror stories about Internet security problems, but there's little danger that your data will be compromised or your computer system damaged by Internet hackers. We've included many safety tips in this chapter that can directly enhance the safety of your own Internet activity.

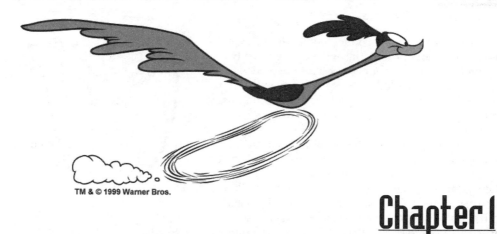

Chapter 1

Ground School: Internet Quick Tour

To get you started in the wonderful new world of the Internet, we've included a quick overview of that famous *information superhighway*. This chapter gives you enough of the Internet's origin, history and current status so that you can chat about the Internet and basically understand what's going on out there in cyberspace. And we'll do it without swamping you with technical details.

The end of this chapter lists some Internet sites that can guide you toward learning even more about the Internet. So, if you enjoy details, after you read this chapter you'll know how to find out more about the Internet from the Internet itself.

But let's not worry about details now, we're just out for a scenic tour. So, we'll begin by defining an important term—the term "internet" itself.

internet versus The Internet

There are internets and then there is *The Internet*. A small "I" internet could be any two computer *networks* that are interconnected so that users on both networks can share resources on either network. A network is at least two computers connected locally to each

Figure 1 A basic internet

other—but some networks have thousands of computers. An internet is at least two connected networks—regardless of the size of either one. Here, we've depicted two connected networks as icons and have labeled them Network A and Network B (see Figure 1). This is the simplest internet possible.

More networks can be connected, but in the simplest form of an internet, they all must be directly connected to each other (see Figure 2). Notice that each network, labeled Networks A, B, C and D, has a direct connection to every other network on this internet.

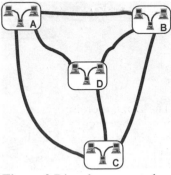

Figure 2 Directly connected internet

It's easy to see that directly connecting each computer would limit the size and area that an internet could cover. Linking them in series would reduce the number of lines (see Figure 3) but Network A is not connected to Network D. For A and D to exchange information, the middle networks, labeled Networks B and C, must act as relays for the outerlying networks.

Networks that act as relays include devices called routers. In Figure 4, for example, Network B and Network E are not directly connected, so they can communicate only via the routers in intermediary networks. If Network A has a router, then data traffic could be routed from Network B through Network A to Network E. If Network A does not have routing capability, but Network C and Network D do, then Network B still could communicate with Network E through Networks C and D. Routers are what makes the global Internet possible.

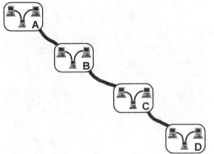

Figure 3 Linear internet

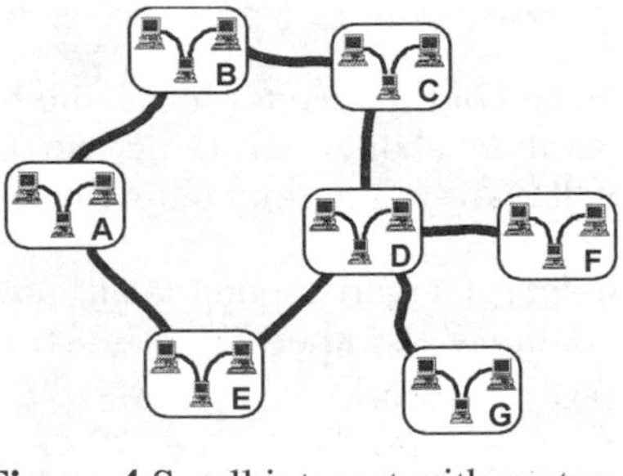

Figure 4 Small internet with routers

The Internet

Imagine if one of the above-depicted network models grew to connect millions of computers around the world. That's the capital "I" Internet, the master of all internets. It's growing explosively and has become practically a living entity. No one knows how many networks the Internet connects. The number of computers connected via the Internet increases daily, approximately doubling every six months. Some Internet gurus predict that the number of Internet users could reach 500 million by 2001.

The bottom line is that the Internet is a vast, global entity of literally countless computers, networks, routers and data lines. If you really want to know the latest estimates, check out some of the addresses listed at the end of this chapter.

How the Internet Got Started

The Internet started at the U.S. Department of Defense (DoD). In the Cold War era, the DoD needed to create a research network to link computers in universities, research labs and government centers all across the country. The DoD donated a lot of money to universities and helped universities get connected to each other.

The DoD, therefore, accidentally did us all a wonderful favor. They planted the seed for the Internet by sponsoring the development of the basic "genetic-coding"—called network protocols—and then they set it free. From this early research sprang the TCP/IP network protocols (Transmission Control Protocol/Internet Protocol) that handle the global data transfers that race across today's Internet. The government's hands-off approach worked in your favor because it left the Internet to grow without the burdens and restraints of being accountable to an office of bureaucrats.

The Internet was designed and built in a totally free environment by the people who knew best how to build it. It's so vast and uses such a varied collection of computers and connections that it can't be destroyed without destroying the nerve centers of every developed nation. And that was the DoD's plan, illustrated by this quotation from RFC1462 that says the Internet was born "...trying to connect together a U.S. Defense Department network called the ARPANET and various other radio and satellite networks. The ARPANET was an experimental network designed to support military research—in particular, research about how to build networks that could withstand partial outages (like bomb attacks) and still function."

So, while the U.S. Government was the parent, no group has ever controlled the Internet. And now it's too big for anyone to even try to control.

Why the Internet is so popular

Personal computers have been consumer products for more than 20 years, since the Apple II launched the PC revolution in 1974. During that time, most people avoided computers completely. Many of those who used PCs did so because they needed to use PCS at work—even though many would have been happy to have never touched a PC. So why is it that—after so much avoidance—there's such a massive rush to get online?

> "A human being is a part of the whole, called by us 'Universe,' a part limited in time and space. We experience ourselves, our thoughts and our feelings as something separated from the rest—a kind of optical delusion of our consciousness. This delusion is a kind of prison for us, restricting us to our personal desires and to affection for a few persons nearest to us.
>
> Our task must be to free ourselves from this prison by widening our circle of compassion to embrace all living creatures and the whole of nature in its beauty."
> **Albert Einstein**

Einstein understood that one day we would, collectively, begin to see through this optical delusion of separateness. The Internet is the first tangible evidence that humankind can truly be interconnected and can widen "our circle of compassion to embrace all living creatures." Cyberspace is the planetary space from where we finally can see beyond the limitations of our personal desires and realize the vast benefits to global unity.

There's Really No Control?

That's right!

Practically speaking, of course, no complex system would function smoothly without some central coordination. But coordination is not control. The Internet's central coordination is provided by the Internet Architecture Board (IAB) that *ratifies* the communications standards on the Internet.

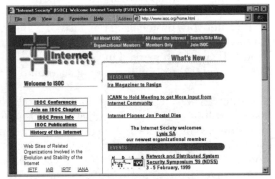

The IAB heads a group of volunteers called the Internet Society (ISOC) that fosters the Internet and promotes Internet

Figure 5 The ISOC home page

usage. The ISOC is based in Reston, Virginia, has branch groups around the world and hosts an annual, global conference (see Figure 5). The ISOC's first president, Dr. Vinton Cerf, is the co-creator of the basic programming codes—called TCP/IP (Transmission Control Protocol/Internet Protocol)—that you will use as you "surf" through cyberspace.

Another group of volunteers—no more groups after this, we promise—called the Internet Engineering Task Force (IETF) develops standards and resolves Internet technical and operational issues. The IETF functions as a public forum that organizes workgroups that explore ways to keep the Internet abreast of technology changes.

How You Got Invited

During the Internet's first 20 years or so, the people who were building and using it did not allow any commercial or personal usage. Its construction had been funded by a vast conglomeration of organizations and was used primarily for technical communications between those who built it.

The first major step toward you being invited to the cyberspace party occurred in the late 1980s when the National Science Foundation (NSF) established its own network, the NSFNET, to connect five supercomputers that it owned. The NSF realized that these supercomputers had the potential to be a national treasure if they were interconnected and made available to other computer systems across the U.S. Wisely, the NSF set up a national network modeled after the existing Internet. This provided regular Internet connections and access across the U.S.

> ### Cyberspace
> Cyberspace has become a generic term that represents the total universe of all interconnected computers. The term was created by science fiction author William Gibson. In Gibson's books, cyberspace is a computer network called "The Matrix." His books foretell of a cold and forbidding future that suffers from too many people and too many computers. Mere fiction, right?

The dissolution of the Communist Party in the Soviet Union triggered some vast changes in the lifestyles of former Soviet citizens. But the collapse of the Soviet Union had a far-reaching impact on us all and the Internet may be a highly visible sign of the sweeping, global changes that have followed.

With the Cold War threat gone, the defense-related purposes of the Internet all but evaporated. Blessedly for all of humankind, the people who held the reins of this potential military machine recognized its value as a tool for the growth of global peace and international harmony. Commercial Internet traffic no longer was considered to be inappropriate usage and restrictions on Internet connection requirements were lifted—and now anyone can join in the fun.

Who Is The Internet?

You are. And so are your friends. And so is Road Runner.

And *where* is the Internet? It's your computer, every other computer connected to the Internet, plus millions of miles of copper wire, fiber optic cable, microwave channels and satellite links. It's similar to the air you breathe; no one owns it or controls it and it's everywhere.

Isn't it wonderful that the Internet, with its roots tied to the DoD, has now become a thriving, open system? It seems to fulfill an ancient prophesy that said, "They will beat their swords into plowshares and their spears into pruning hooks." Of course we're only talking about virtual swords and virtual plowshares, but the result is that the Internet is now yours, too. So jump into your virtual spaceship, and let's blast-off!

What's Out There for Me?

You have probably heard a lot lately about the Internet. Most of what you've heard is about one function of the Internet that's called the World Wide Web. You'll often see it written in shorthand—Web, WWW and W3. There are several other functions on the Internet, but the importance of some of them is waning rapidly. Still, we'll give you a short rundown of each basic function, with the popular functions listed first.

World Wide Web (Web)
As with many inventions, the World Wide Web has become more than anyone ever dreamed. The Internet created the basic connections to join us all into a single inter-related system, but the Web merged the old Internet with modern graphics, colorful screens, sound and animation. The Web made the Internet user-friendly by employing technology called *hypertext*. Hypertext, as used on the Web, makes the Internet almost universally accessible because you can access information with simple mouse clicks instead of arcane computer commands.

Jargon Cutter
World Wide Web - An Internet-based system, created at the CERN laboratory in Switzerland in 1991, that lets you access documents that are linked together with the Hypertext Markup Language (HTML). It's called a Web because all of its documents are woven together into what is essentially a single system, even though it's made up of documents from millions of sources.

When information is written in hypertext, key words and graphic images can be highlighted and linked to related text. The reader merely clicks on a highlighted word to jump to the linked, related text.

Think of the end of an article in an encyclopedia that has a list of "Related Topics." How many times have you actually dragged out all the additional volumes that would be required to see those related topics? How about never?

But in a hypertext encyclopedia (CD-ROM encyclopedias use hypertext), you simply click on the titles of the related topics to jump to the follow-on article. How many times will you actually click on a hypertext link to see a related topic? How about constantly? Hypertext is a charismatic attraction—it's an electronic black hole that can pull you ever deeper into interesting areas in cyberspace—and that attraction is why you may have heard so much about the Web.

E-Mail
The bulk of Internet traffic is electronic mail (e-mail). E-mail enables you to swap messages with anyone on the Internet anywhere in the world. The best part is that e-mail is free through your Road Runner service—there are no distance-based or per-message charges for e-mail. A few online services still charge a per message rate, but you don't have to worry about that. E-mail will completely change the way you conduct much of your communication.

We've included a full chapter on Internet e-mail in Phase 2. It's got plenty of details that will help you master the Internet e-mail that comes with Road Runner.

Chat Rooms
Chat rooms are "virtual rooms" in which you electronically meet and chat with other Internet users. Any number of people, from anywhere in the world, can join a chat room at once. Chat rooms are "live," meaning that you see each message in real-time as it is entered. Users will join and drop out as they wish, which means that you'll never know who will be on at any one time. Most chat rooms use your Web browser and similar to many other Web pages you've seen.

One area of a chat room screen will display the online "nickname" of each user who has joined. Another area will display all of the messages that are exchanged between the various users—the messages scroll across the screen in the order they are entered by each user. Another area of a chat screen lets you input and send messages to the group. You can send messages that will be seen by all users and you can target individual members with whom you can exchange private messages.

Newsgroups

Newsgroups—sometimes referred to as the Usenet—are electronic discussion forums. Newsgroups are akin to community bulletin boards upon which people can post notices, but they serve the global community and have no formal membership requirements—anyone on the Internet can read and post messages. They perform a similar function to chat rooms, except that messages are stored and can be read at any time by anyone who chooses to peruse the currently-posted messages.

No one can accurately count their number, but we've counted more than 30,000 public newsgroups. There also are private newsgroups but counting them would be impossible. We go into newsgroups in detail in Phase 2.

FTP (File Transfer Protocol)

The title pretty much explains its usage—you can use the File Transfer Protocol (FTP) to transfer computer files between your computer and other computers on the Internet. You will use this mostly to transfer files into your computer from larger computer systems (download or receive), though you also can transfer files from your computer to others (upload or send). What can you get using FTP? Just about anything you can imagine that can be stored on a computer: software, documents, spreadsheets, maps, photos, a copy of the Constitution, audio sound clips and even video clips. The Internet has thousands of FTP sites and millions of files.

Perhaps you'll use the FTP directly sometime, but you will encounter it primarily as a hidden part of the Web. You can use your Web browser to access FTP sites and to download files, but you cannot upload files with your Web browser. You'll find more coverage of FTP, including Step-by-Step exercises, in Phase 2.

Mailing Lists

Here's a terrific tool to stay informed on a vast array of topics. The best feature about getting information from this system is that—unlike most of the Internet—it comes to you. Instead of providing a repository of information that can be searched and down-loaded, mailing lists send automated e-mail to users who subscribe to the list.

When you subscribe to a mailing list, you join an informal, electronic community. The core of any mailing list is a software application called a *list server* that runs the list. When any member sends a message to the mailing list (actually to the designated list server) that message is redistributed to all members of the group. In a large group with lots of traffic, the In box in your e-mail application can fill in a few hours.

Some mailing lists are *moderated*, which means that someone reads the incoming messages and decides which ones to redistribute to the entire group. Depending on your point of view, you'll regard the moderator either as a meddling censor or as a thankless saint doing you an enormous favor.

Golden Oldies

Many aspects of the Internet already have become passé, but that doesn't mean they're old—it just means that life in cyberspace moves pretty fast and yesterday's hot technology is today's "Remember when..." The vinyl records of the Internet are Gopher, Veronica, Archie, Jughead, Finger, Telnet and WAIS. Of all of these, you might use Telnet sometime to contact a library. The others simply have been over-taken by the much more versatile and powerful World Wide Web. Since almost all of your Internet work will involve the Web, let's close your Internet tour with a little more information about it.

Web Principles

While the Web is vast and it may seem complicated, the Web's underlying principles are surprisingly simple. The task of implementing those simple principles across a dizzying array of incompatible computer systems, however, has not been simple. Our hats are off to the talented people who invented and created the Web. It required a lot of detailed planning and work, but the core principles remain simple.

The Web is built around computer documents. That is basically it! Using any Web browser on the Web basically resembles loading documents into your word processor. As you most likely are aware, your Windows word processor can display embedded graphic images and play embedded sound files. So can the Road Runner Browser, but it can't edit the files it loads. So, you can think of your Web browser as a "read-only" word processor.

Beep! Beep!

Your Road Runner browser has an **Edit, Page** command that lets you edit Web documents. The read-only principle remains the same, however, because you can't save the edited version of the page on the original Web server.

HYPERTEXT

If you are becoming confused by the term "hypertext," don't be dismayed. It's not your fault that hypertext isn't hypertext anymore.

The term was created as a definition for a word or phrase within a text document that provides a link to other text documents. In an electronic encyclopedia, for example, you merely click on any of the "Related Topics" and you see the related article—that's hypertext.

Your first exposure to using hypertext, however, might be to click on a graphic image that jumps to another graphic image. Or you might click on a graphic image that downloads a sound file. "Why," you might ask, "is a button called *hypertext*?"

Sorry about the confusion. But a long, long time ago—way back in 1991—no one had any idea that hypertext would become what it is today. Obviously the people who coined the term hypertext were better computer programmers than seers. That's not a complaint, though, because no one saw this coming. If the term were to be coined today, it might be called "hyperlink."

The bottom line is that hypertext is on-screen magic. It is revolutionizing communication. You'll be able to click on words, buttons or graphic images and be swept off to any region within cyberspace that the author wanted you to see—other documents, images, sound clips, video clips, forms, software and tables of data. And you easily will be able to create your own hyperlinked documents, thus being able to jump your readers off to any region within cyberspace that you'd like them to see.

We All Are One

We all want to be connected—it's a natural part of human nature because, truly, "We all are one." The hyperlinks on the World Wide Web are rapidly creating a physical manifestation of our longing for unity—to become one.

> "In a real sense all life is inter-related. All persons are caught in an inescapable network of mutuality, tied in a single garment of destiny. Whatever affects one directly, affects all indirectly... I can never be what I ought to be until you are what you ought to be, and you can never be what you ought to be until I am what I ought to be. This is the inter-related structure of reality."
> **Martin Luther King, Jr.**

King probably wasn't thinking of the Internet when he wrote about the "network of mutuality," but it's possible—the Internet had been born. Whether or not he knew it then, today we have an unsurpassed network of mutuality that has joined together everyone on this planet. The World Wide Web has given us the ability to transform humanity into a single living organism.

Cable Internet Access

And where, might you ask, does your cable television company fit into the Internet? You thought that television was television, right? Well, it still is, but the Internet is something extra—and no one is better equipped to bring it to you. It's all about a technical term called "bandwidth."

Jargon Cutter

Bandwidth - A term that represents the amount of data that can flow through an electronic cable. You could equate it to the number of lanes in a road system. As the number of lanes increases, more traffic can flow. As bandwidth increases, more data can flow. Internet bandwidth is expressed in bits per second. Data can flow no faster than the slowest area bandwidth through which it passes.

Before you got cable Internet service, you may have used a 14.4 modem or a 28.8 modem. If so, your modem was the weakest link in the chain of electronics that brought Internet service into your computer. Think of a traditional phone-line modem as a section of narrow, farm road in what otherwise is a superhighway. Most of the Internet has plenty of bandwidth, but you were missing it because data had to go the last few feet of its journey through a telephone line and a telephone modem.

Today, however, your system provider is no longer the weak link in the chain. Cable television has an enormous bandwidth capacity—thousands of times faster than some telephone modems. In fact, your Road Runner service provider can transmit information to its customers much faster than most PCs can process it. As you upgrade your PC in the coming years, the service will get even faster!

Does this also mean that everything you do on the Internet now will be blazing fast? No, not at all. Your cable system gets its Internet traffic via a wide highway and then it delivers it to you via a wide highway, but much of the Internet still suffers from serious bandwidth limitations. If a Web site you visit has a slower Internet connection than yours, you'll receive data from it no faster than it can send data. Now, since your system is so fast, the weakest link is going to be the Web sites you visit. The speed at which data loads into your system now depends mostly on the speed of the Internet connection that those Web sites have.

Until cable Internet service made its debut in your community, only very large Internet service providers or very large companies could afford to get high-speed service from the telephone company. So, for a while, your service is going to be the fastest thing in cyberspace.

Internet information travels through a lot of different systems and cables before it reaches our Road Runner facilities. You may need some patience with other folks throughout the Web who don't have the capabilities of cable modem technology.

About All The Jargon

The glossary at the end of this book gives you the basic jargon you need. You'll encounter a lot of jargon on the Internet, but with this handy guide next to your computer you'll always be able to look it up.

We've used in this book as few technical terms as we could, but the Internet involves a lot of technical jargon. Learning it can bewilder an Internet beginner. In fact, there's even jargon for an Internet beginner. The term is "Newbie," and, as you soon shall see in the Orbiting In Cyberspace section at the end of this chapter, there's a whole Internet site dedicated to helping newbies.

Jargon Cutter

Jargon Cutter - Throughout the book, we'll use these little inserts to buzzsaw through some of the techno-confusion when we need to spring a new term on you. And, there's always the glossary in the back of this book, or one of the many glossaries that you can find on the Web.

Jargon is an integral part of the Internet, so please learn the essential jargon before the Step-by-Step lessons. Jargon is useful, of course, because once you understand the terms, its shorthand will save time when communicating about the Internet. Besides, you're going to see it everywhere so you might as well learn it now. To help you, we've assembled in the "Orbiting in Cyberspace" section some valuable Internet sites that will keep you abreast of the rapidly-changing world of the Internet.

ORBITING IN CYBERSPACE

The Internet Society
http://www.isoc.org

The Internet Society (ISOC) is the non-governmental, international organization for global cooperation and coordination for the Internet and its internetworking technologies and applications. Its members, both individual and organizational, have a common goal of maintaining the viability and the global scaling of the Internet.

> For individual membership: membership@isoc.org
> For organization membership: organization-membership@isoc.org
> Fax: 703-648-9887
> Voice: 703-648-9888
> Mail: 12020 Sunrise Valley Drive, Suite 210
>   Reston, Virginia, 20191-3429, USA.

Electronic Frontier Foundation
http://www.eff.org

The Electronic Frontier Foundation (EFF) is a non-profit civil liberties organization that works in the public interest to protect privacy, free expression, and access to public resources and information online, as well as to promote responsibility in news media. Click on the Net Guide link on their home page for a list of links to download a copy of their *Guide to the Internet*. It's even available in English, Italian, Polish, Russian and Japanese—we told you the Internet is global! If you plan to post information to the Web, be sure to check out their Intellectual Property Archive.

Cyber Course
http://www.newbie.net/CyberCourse

Here's a permanent, on-going training site on the Web, designed especially for new Internet users (newbies). It's an extremely well-done treasure trove of information and it's free (see Figure 6). It includes a section called Cyber Course and another called Newbie Newz. The course has several sections that can walk you through learning Internet basics. The Newbie Newz is a mailing list that will help you learn about the Internet.

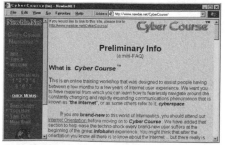

Figure 6 The Internet teaches itself

Computer Literacy Bookshops
http://www.clbooks.com

Here's a Web page that was designed with functionality, not glitz, as the highest priority. It serves its purpose well and you won't waste time browsing through unnecessary graphics. Use their search feature to locate books by topic or by author. You even can use this page to order Internet books for your friends and colleagues who aren't lucky enough to have the Internet book that came with your Road Runner service.

Boardwatch Magazine
http://www.boardwatch.com

Originally a magazine for the Bulletin Board System (BBS) community, Boardwatch magazine (see Figure 7) now covers the Internet and commercial online services as well. This Web site has the full text of back issues, dating back to October 1994. The articles deal with trends, legal and social issues and technology. Luckily, they avoid much of the hype that plagues a lot of Internet sites. It's a great site if you want to know all of the latest Internet developments.

Figure 7 An Internet staple: Boardwatch Magazine

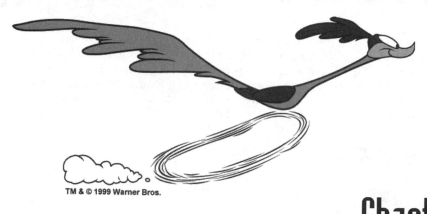

Chapter 2

Rules of the Road: Netiquette

Every land has its own language and culture. Cyberspace has both of those, plus a whole new psychological demeanor. It's a good thing, too, because the Internet itself consists of computers and a few million humming, blinking electrical boxes that would be too cold, ugly and boring for humans to tolerate. In this chapter, we're going to help you understand all three aspects of the land of cyberspace: language, culture and psychological demeanor. This discussion introduces yet another bit of Internet jargon: netiquette—Internet etiquette.

Proper netiquette—the special rules of Internet social consideration—will improve the quality of your relationships and smooth the complicated process of communication. The detached nature of Internet communication presents some serious limitations to expression and understanding that require special care.

Sociologists say that between 70 percent to 90 percent of human communication is conveyed through body language and tone of voice—only 10 percent to 30 percent is conveyed through words.

Mailed letters have expressive abilities because you can communicate a lot with your choice of paper, letterhead design, how the envelope is addressed, font size and style, your signature, plus embellishments such as color, bold, italics, pictures, charts and even enclosures. The telephone lets you use tone of voice and pauses, but its role in both business and personal communication is waning. Thus, much of your communication is at risk of becoming impersonal because the Internet reduces our messages to nothing but plain text.

New Communication Tools

Since few traditional communication tools convey across the Internet, we'll show you some replacements. These tools include examples of popular "emoticons"—icons that emulate emotions—that can prevent misunderstandings by letting people experience the emotional context behind the text on the screen.

We also will give you some tips on writing for the Internet. The timbre of language is different from written business or personal letters of the past and that results in more misunderstandings. Our "Electronic elements of style" section later in this chapter can spare your fingers a few keystrokes because rules of grammar are less rigid and time-saving acronyms abound. We'll give you enough tools so that you'll be able to understand the ones you read and quickly shed the status of "Newbie."

Flaming Words

We present these tools because misunderstandings abound on the Internet. The result often is something called a flame war—the Internet equivalent of a shouting match. The heated messages that are flung back and forth in a flame war are called flames. Sending flames is called flaming.

When you eventually encounter a flame war—we hope only as an observer of someone else's battle—be prepared to witness a return to the grade school playground. No, it's worse than that. Grade school kids have better things to do than to devote as much time to getting in the last word as some Internet users spend. Flame wars are a tremendous waste of Internet resources and totally unnecessary.

Apologies R painless

Often, good netiquette on the part of either correspondent will stop a flame war before it starts. You can do your part to keep the peace in cyberspace. If something you send or post earns a hostile reply message, instead of firing back the first barb that comes to mind, perhaps you could reread your original message.

Did you leave open the possibility for an alternate interpretation? Remember that if the other person *feels* they've been flamed then there's no question about it—they have been flamed. Even if you're completely perplexed by their interpretation, the best course is to acknowledge the results and accept responsibility for the harm.

> ## The Bright Side
> Here's a high note, in case reading all of these negative things about communicating in cyberspace is making you jittery. Not being able to see the other person has its benefits. There are countless excellent relationships on the Internet between people who wouldn't engage each other in person. In cyberspace, bigots can't be biased. Age and gender barriers don't exist. Accents don't impede comprehension. And no one will criticize what you're wearing.
> When you feel that the impersonal realm of cyberspace has cost you the good will of a relationship, think of how many relationships have been created that never would have blossomed F2F (face to face).

You will step on a few toes in any crowd, and in cyberspace newsgroups, for example, you can stomp on a lot of them fast. When you do, you'll do yourself a favor to simply reply with something like, "Sorry. Your reply showed me that I hit a sensitive spot. I didn't phrase it carefully at all. Will you accept my apology and can you accept a rephrased version of what I meant to convey?"

It's amazing, though, how a few people never can apologize or accept responsibility for their actions even across the anonymous reaches of cyberspace. The Internet gives you the ability to insult thousands—perhaps millions—of people at the speed of light. The good news, though, is that it also gives you a fast and almost painless way to apologize and make amends—and doing so is excellent netiquette.

Let it be

Finally, consider the other side of the flame war alliance: Help prevent flame wars by being slow to come to a boil.

Few people send intentional insults, so someone may be taken aback if you blast off an immediate, flaming retort. They may feel that you have thrown the first punch and blast you back when you were certain you'd receive a humble apology. So you nail them for being so silly as to think that you flamed them and—voilà—a flame war has been launched.

The Internet may well trample your feelings if you are sensitive to every perceived wrong. Instead of being quick on the flamethrower trigger, give the benefit of the doubt to your e-mailing friends, family and business colleagues by assuming the best of their intentions and let most things slide.

There's one other good reason to let things slide. Some newsgroups are haunted by "trollers," people who troll through the Internet fishing for a flame war. Their motives, often politically-based, are to start flame wars that will disrupt communications and distract other users from accomplishing their planned goals. As with most activities, when you're on the Internet, stay focused. Ask yourself if responding to flames will help you accomplish your goals. If not, then avoid the distraction, disruption and wasted time of a flame war. If, however, your goals are to "scream" at people, then go ahead and jump into the fray—but remember, some trollers may be laughing because they tricked you into wasting time on a contrived fight.

Business Netiquette

Practicing good netiquette is even more important for you if you have a home-based business. A private flame war is annoying, but a business-related flame war—even between just two individuals—can tarnish the reputation of your entire organization. Countless programs—called "sniffers"—roam the Internet and sample text in message traffic and alert people to read messages that contain "interesting" words. Any sensitive topic might be considered interesting by someone who owns a sniffer—and they'll be excited that their sniffer made a catch. Anything you say in Internet e-mail could be on the front page of The New York Times or your local paper tomorrow.

Your trusty old telephone creates fewer opportunities for misunderstanding because you can hear each other's tone of voice. Tone of voice works to head-off trouble from both ends of a conversation. You may hear words that might have sounded offensive in a transcript of the call, but on the phone you don't take offense because the tone of voice clearly signals a light-hearted context. Conversely, if you accidentally offend someone on the phone, you can sense by a change in their tone of voice that you've touched a sensitive area. You have time to recover.

The Internet brings to you the burden of double-trouble: not only does it make you more easily misunderstood, it leaves documented proof of what you say that can span the globe in a few minutes. So, not only can your communication quickly insult vast reaches of humanity, it can create evidence for a lawsuit.

SPAMMING

Practicing good netiquette will do more than create good relations. It can keep you from being thrown off the Internet. Sending spam—the act is called spamming—is a sure-fire shortcut to getting your Internet plug pulled. Spam is universally hated and you surely will join the crowd when you first see it. So what is spam?

The Hormel Company, who for years have produced the commercial meat product Spam, probably aren't happy that their trade name has been appropriated by the Internet community and used in a negative context. Nonetheless, on the Net, "spam" (lowercase) refers to a message or document that nobody wants. The Internet usage actually comes from a Monty Python comedy bit in which every item on a restaurant menu was made of Spam.

Most often spam refers to inappropriate usage of newsgroups. It comes from entrepreneurs who believe that they've got the hottest product or service ever created. Their messages usually have a title similar to, "$$$ MAKE REAL MONEY FAST $$$." So the spammer writes some breathless hype and posts it to unrelated newsgroups, often hundreds of them and sometimes thousands.

Advertising in newsgroups is not considered to be good netiquette. So spam annoys people who log onto a newsgroup for some news on their favorite topic. And, in groups where ads are appropriate, the ads you see are related to the newsgroup's topic. They are well-written and they convey exactly the type of information that the group's readers are seeking—which is **not** spam!

People who spam are likely to have their messages canceled from the Internet and may find *themselves* canceled from the Internet. Some spammers cry that this infringes on their free speech rights, but the U.S. 1st Amendment doesn't cover disturbing the peace. People have a right to express their opinions in the proper forum, but society doesn't tolerate screaming and bombarding everyone with the same message—neither does the Internet. Gross offenders usually are reported to their Internet providers and find their Internet account quickly canceled.

To learn more about spam and how you can help alleviate the problem, visit the Web site of the Coalition Against Unsolicited Commercial E-Mail at *www.cauce.org*.

Beep! Beep!

Be sure to read the chapter in Phase 2 that covers newsgroups. We include a good background on newsgroups and give you some tips that will help you get along well with your fellow Interneters.

To reduce your Newbie status, you can benefit from learning the rules of the electronic road that make up the rest of this chapter. Let's start with some handy acronyms. These widely-accepted Internet shortcuts can save you typing time and help convey what you really mean to say.

Electronic Elements of Style

So here, in alphabetical order is a glossary of helpful and well-known Internet acronyms.

ADN	Any Day Now
AFAIK	As Far As I Know
B4N	Bye for Now
BBS	Bulletin Board System
BL	Belly Laughing!
BTA	But Then Again
BTDT	Been There, Done That
BTW	By The Way
CUL	See You Later
CUL8R	See You Later
DTP	Desktop Publishing
F2F	Face to Face
FAQ	Frequently Asked Questions
FB	Flame Bait
FLAME OFF	Off limits for flaming
FLAME ON	Normal flaming rules restored
FUD	Fear, Uncertainty and Doubt
FWIW	For What It's Worth
FYI	For Your Information
<G>	Grin
GAL	Get A Life
GIGO	Garbage In, Garbage Out
GIWIST	Gee, I Wish I'd Said That
GMTA	Great Minds Think Alike
IAC	In Any Case
IC	I See
IDTT	I'll Drink To That
IME	In My Experience
IMO	In My Opinion
IMHO	In My Humble Opinion
IOW	In Other Words
IRL	In Real Life
JIC	Just In Case
LOL	Laughing Out Loud
OTOH	On The Other Hand
::POOF::	I'm gone
POV	Point Of View
PTB	Powers That Be
RE	Regarding
SYSOP	System Operator
TAFN	That's All For Now
TIA	Thanks In Advance
TNTL	Trying Not To Laugh
WRT	With Regard To

Emoticon Lexicon

The Internet has embraced a shorthand language called *emoticons* or *smileys* that help remedy its inability to convey tone of voice. The name smiley comes from the first emoticon, which was a little smiley-face. :-) Smileys since have evolved well beyond their simple origin and now convey a wide range of emotions.

These little electronic writing aids are so widely used that entire books have been written about them. If you want to keep a more complete reference guide by your computer, check your local computer book store for an emoticon book—they have more smileys than you can use. Or is that *should* use? Smileys, however, are not widely used, so if you use a smiley that is found only in emoticon books, will it convey anything other than a confused, "What?"

Here's a brief listing of some of the most widely understood emoticons or smileys. The key to understanding them lies in your perspective: look at them sideways.

Positive emotions

:-)	The original smiley, conveys friendliness or kidding
:->	A surprised smiley
:-D	Delighted smiley
:'-)	Tears of joy
:-}	Sarcastic grin
:-]	Goofy grin
:-x	Kiss
[]	Hug

Negative emotions

:-(	Frown, sadness
:-P	Sticking out your tongue
%-(	Confused and sad
:-O	Shocked or screaming
>:-|	Frowning
>:-<	Frowning and very angry
:-<	Dejected
:-C	Very unhappy
:'-(	Crying
:-{}	Blabbermouth who won't shut up

Mixed emotions, etc.

:-\	Mixed feelings leaning toward happy
:-/	Mixed feelings leaning toward sad
:-|	Neutral
:-J	Tongue in cheek
:-@	Screaming out loud
:-$	Put your money where your mouth is
'-)	Wink

Miscellaneous Netiquette

We'll close this chapter with a few comments on general netiquette that can help us all get along better in our new global, cyber-community.

Use mixed case

PLEASE DON'T EVER POST OR MAIL ANYTHING IN ALL CAPS. IT'S ANNOYING TO READ, ISN'T IT?

All caps definitely rate as poor netiquette; it's the equivalent of screaming all the time and it's harder to read than normal mixed case text. Save the ALL CAPS only for an occasional SPECIAL EMPHASIS when needed unless you want the whole message to be ignored.

Bold, italics and underlining

Most likely your e-mail message window won't accept any of the standard font attributes such as bold, italics and underlining. Even if it does, expect the codes to be scrambled for your readers. Keep an eye out for changes in this area because they're coming fast. Expect to soon be able to send fully formatted e-mail messages with bold, italics, underlining and a selection of fonts, perhaps all of your installed Windows True Type fonts! For now, however, if your reader needs a document with all the formatting codes intact, then create a document in your word processor and attach the file to a short e-mail message.

Nonetheless, some typing standards have emerged on the Internet that enable you to use regular characters to represent both underlining and italics. You'll find underlining represented by bracketing a text string with underscore characters, perhaps using it to emphasize something _that is really important_. Similarly, asterisks are used to bracket text that should be italicized such as a book title, *Gone With The Wind*.

ORBITING IN CYBERSPACE

Arlene Rinaldi's Netiquette home page
http://www.fau.edu/rinaldi/netiquette.html

This site includes a lot of Internet netiquette tips and guidelines. It includes links to many other Internet sites on the same topic. Also, as you browse through Arlene's site, you'll encounter information on subscribing to many mailing lists that cover a variety of Internet topics.

A Parents' Guide to the Internet
http://www.familyguidebook.com/netiquette.html

This site includes links to discussions of classroom netiquette, network netiquette and e-mail netiquette. There are links dedicated to online safety for kids, teens, college students, parents, teachers, librarians and law enforcement officers. Another good link on this page takes you to Sophie's Safe Surfing Club. And, if you're a newbie you'll appreciate the If You're New Link as well as Comparing Filtering Software Programs.

Netiquette
http://www.albion.com/bookNetiquette/TOC0963702513.html

This is the home page of an Internet book on netiquette by Virginia Shay. The site includes a complete table of contents of the book that links you to excerpts from each chapter so you can sample the content of the printed book. In addition to netiquette, the book and this Web site also include discussions of cyberspace copyright issues.

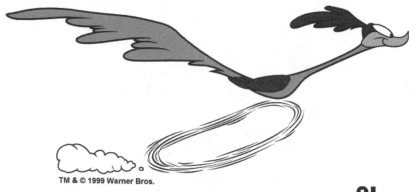

Chapter 3

E•Commerce: Online Shopping

Money makes the cyber-world go 'round, just as it does in the real world. But why not? These days money is mostly just electronic energy zipping around between people and financial institutions, so the Internet is a natural tool for some of that zipping. We will need money in the cyberspace world, just as in the real world, especially as the distinctions between the two merge. This chapter deals with cyber-space money issues. You'll find a mixture here, however, of security issues and finan-cial issues, because on the Internet—as in real life—the two are closely related.

The key to making online financial transactions possible has been the development of technology that keeps messages secure while they fly through cyberspace—sort of like electronic lock boxes. But there are other uses for secure technology than protecting just financial transactions.

USE YOUR OWN JUDGMENT

These are heady times on the Web as stock prices for Internet-related stocks have made everybody think that cyberspace is the gold rush of the new millen-nium. But just how are we going to get all that gold out in cyberspace back to earth when everything is only 1s and 0s in computer code? The whole area of interactive commerce is still in its experimental phase and new approaches are emerging daily. The technology for secure transactions—the ability for you to electronically transfer funds out of your bank to a seller of goods, or to use your credit card to make a purchase online—contains some risk at the moment.

Road Runner, therefore, does not endorse any existing methodology for electronic commerce nor does it guarantee the security of any transaction that may pass through its system. While Road Runner takes all reasonable pre-cautions to protect the integrity of its system, it assumes no liability for financial transactions that may occur between Road Runner users and others. The following information and Web site are provided for your information only.

By using security documents, merchants of all sizes now can use the Internet to conduct electronic commerce transactions anywhere in the world via the Web. A few examples of what's being done with secure documents:

❖ Cyberspace retailers can sell everything from computer software to astrology reports to flowers.

❖ Financial merchants can offer online banking and stock trades online or can accept credit card applications.

❖ Internet travel services can let customers make their own reservations and buy airline tickets.

❖ Non-profit organizations can accept membership applications online.

❖ Publishers can offer subscriptions to online versions of their publications.

These security measures are not restricted to financial transactions, of course. Many other uses are appearing on the Internet:

❖ Circulating confidential business marketing plans, product announcements and private personnel information.

❖ Survey data and customer questionnaires can be collected because organizations can protect the privacy of its Web users by using secure documents.

❖ Geographically diverse organizations can exchange sensitive company financial data, market reports, research data and new product ideas and designs.

But that's enough digression—the main focus here is on money issues. We'll begin with income by giving you an overview of how money moves around in cyberspace. Then we'll cover some expense issues that will help you plan and implement a Web site for personal use, for a home office or for work.

The Truth about Credit Card Purchases

The security of making credit card purchases is a major topic of concern among new Internet users. Most people are reluctant to use their credit card for Internet purchases. Most of these fears are unfounded and are based on some over-blown anecdotes that people have read or heard about Internet credit card security risks.

Most likely you, too, have read some bad news about Internet credit card security. Credit card transactions are but one aspect of exchanging funds on the Internet. There are other options, but credit card transactions are easy to understand and they're related to something we all know and they've been a hot topic in the press.

If you give someone a credit card number on the Internet, you can't be sure where the information will travel and who might copy it while it's en route. Because conventional data transfer on the Internet isn't encrypted, an experienced computer hacker might create a program that grabs and saves for later analysis any data that looks like #### #### #### #### ##/##, the sequence usually used for credit card numbers. The hacker then could build a database of credit card numbers and, supposedly, use them to buy things or fence the numbers to professional credit card thieves. But credit card security problems didn't originate on the Internet.

Unsafe at any speed

Unfortunately, the Internet isn't the only place where you can't be sure where your credit card information will travel and who might copy the information. Internet credit card number theft certainly is possible, and occurs occasionally, but it's no more of a threat than any other credit card transaction and is safer than most.

Consider other credit card transactions and you'll realize that there are plenty of easy ways for people to collect and sell credit card numbers without needing the technical expertise, the tools and the access required to hack the Internet. When you make a mail-order purchase or even hand your credit card to a waiter, you are risking theft by people who need far fewer skills than experienced computer professionals. It's far more likely that you'll be the victim of traditional credit card fraud than someone will intercept an Internet purchase you might make.

Internet technology actually makes credit card transactions safer than handing your card to a waiter. The basic technology is called "public-key cryptography," the foundation of "secure" Web documents. Secure documents are encrypted, which means they are scrambled by the sender and unscrambled by the receiver. A secure document can't be read without a "key" that is used during the unscrambling process.

Beep! Beep!

For more information about public-key cryptography, visit the Web site of the Internet security masters at www.rsa.com. They created the Secure Sockets Layer (SSL) encryption technology that's used by your Road Runner Browser.

```
┌─ Sausage Software Secure Server - On Line Orde... - ┐
│ File  Edit  View  Go  Favorites  Help               │
│ [e]                                                 │
│ Address │https://secure.rucc.net.au/sausage/register.htm│ │
```

Figure 1 A secure URL

When you access a secure Web document, your Web browser may warn you before that document is transferred to your system. This may only occur on the first secure document you encounter because the warning will include an option to stop all such warnings in the future. If you mark the option as checked, you'll not see a warning on future secure documents, but you can change back at any time by changing your preferences settings. Whenever you accept a secure document with a public key, the site certificate is added to your browser's certificate list.

It may seem dangerous to deactivate the automatic secure document warning feature, but there are several other ways to recognize a secure document. With or without a warning you will see two other clues that tell you you're viewing a secure document:

❖ The status bar will display a padlock.

❖ The document's URL automatically changes from "*http://*" to "*https://*" even if you entered it manually without adding the "s" on the end (see Figure 1).

Public-key cryptography scrambles numbers and other personal or corporate data before it's sent, then enables the receiver to unscramble the original information. New technology planned by credit card companies will let buyers pay by credit card without merchants ever knowing the buyer's card number.

Tolls on the Information Highway

The real challenge to the Internet and the information age is how to get very small payments to creators of intellectual property without making everyone on the information superhighway run through countless electronic toll booths. It can be done and we'll discuss later some emerging technology that will make possible very small payments (micropayments).

One toll-collecting method would be to employ advertising as in other electronic media. This is a rapidly growing phenomenon. You'll see Web pages sprinkled with logos that advertise "site sponsors" who help the site owner cover the costs of maintaining a database, a newsletter or a search engine. In exchange, the sponsors get to place a link on the site—often a graphic image of their logo—so that visitors can quickly get information on the sponsor's product.

If you maintain a Web site, you may be able to help finance your Internet costs by selling space to sponsors. And you may be able to increase traffic at your site by sponsoring well-done, related sites that already have high traffic. Site sponsoring could be a quick way to draw attention to a new home-based business you've just begun.

> ## COMMERCIAL WEB SITES
> Road Runner is a consumer information service created for cable customers' use in their homes. The system is designed for home use by the average family. If you anticipate running a business from your home using Road Runner, contact your cable company's Road Runner Business Manager for more information. A special connection may be required.

Another option is to dispense Internet cash that can be collected in small amounts any time you get a piece of information. Internet cash also has the benefit of being able to keep all transactions private. When paying by Internet cash, even the merchant you pay may not know who made the purchase. Cybercash (*www.cybercash.com*) is a typical company that offers an online payment plan (see Figure 2).

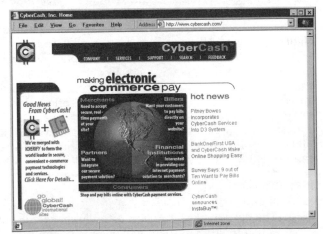

Figure 2 CyberCash security payments

The other side of privacy

Privacy cuts two ways, though. Criminals are eager for new ways to hide and launder income from illegal activities. Terrorists want to eliminate money trails that can lead authorities to them or their sponsors. The U.S. Government is exploring ways to monitor transactions, but Internet privacy systems—especially secure data-encryption and digital cash—would make their mission much more difficult. No one knows how this conflict will play out, or whether an acceptable compromise can be found between Big Brother and anarchy. Meanwhile, as the government ponders options, the Internet is rapidly creating its own monetary system—let's learn more about this phenomenon.

Beep! Beep!

You might be surprised to find that the U.S. Government is interested in Internet security, and that some security technology faces import restrictions. If you intend to use international commerce transactions via the Internet, then you'll need a security system that's certified for export outside the United States and Canada.

Internet Commerce Systems

Many potential merchants are anxious to sell information, search services, software and audio or video clips on the Internet. When these merchants begin to sell on the Internet, they'll find an eager cadre of potential clients and customers. But turning those into paying clients and customers is going to take some consumer education because today most things on the Internet are free. Under the present system, owners of intellectual property have little incentive to make their valuable "information goods" accessible through the Web. This will improve as Internet collection systems become more secure, reliable and inexpensive.

Free Internet products abound today because Internet commerce is only a small percentage of sales for most companies that distribute products via the Internet. As the balance shifts in favor of the Internet, companies will be less able to subsidize their Internet service sales with traditional sales.

For example, let's look at the cost of obtaining an upgraded software driver for a printer. For years we all expected to be charged a few dollars to cover the company's cost of producing and mailing a diskette that contained the updated files. Today, however, you can download updated files free directly from a company's Web site. But this can't continue. Companies bear some distribution costs even when they use the Internet for file updates. The good news is that they will be able to cover their Internet distribution costs for far less than it costs to cover mail distribution of diskettes. Few of us would mind being charged fifty cents or a dollar for instant delivery of a file update. But for now, there is a gap in what buyers expect to pay and what sellers need to charge.

Countless entrepreneurial groups are developing Internet commerce mechanisms that will bridge this gap between sellers and buyers by creating a common and inexpensive Internet marketplace. Let's consider some of the features that these groups may employ in the commerce systems that are being developed.

Micropayments

The Internet marketplace will explode when it is able to support *micropayments*. Micropayments will enable merchants to profitably sell information for as little as 10 cents. But for *micromerchants* to flourish, the Internet needs to offer extremely low cost accounting and billing. Transaction costs need to be as little as one cent for a 10-cent item—now you'll be able to sell your best jokes or even family recipes.

Internet commerce systems that support micropayments will enhance the quality and variety of information products sold and bought on the Web. Those selling the information—even micromerchants selling a single page of information—will receive fair compensation for their products and will be able to remain in business.

Beep! Beep!
To learn more about how micropayments may impact your life, check out the Web site of Dr. Brad J. Cox, Ph.D. at *www.virtualschool.edu/mon/TTEF.html*. Brad's a professor at George Mason University in Fairfax, Virginia and this site is the home page for his book *Superdistribution: Objects as Property on the Electronic Frontier* (Addison-Wesley, 1995).

Security

Internet commerce systems have to provide secure transactions for both your family's needs and your business' needs. When you sell products via the Internet, you'll need assurance that hackers cannot sniff through your e-mail for passwords that will enable them to download products without paying. We all want assurances that our credit card information will remain a private matter.

In client/server systems such as the Internet, transaction security is a two-way street. Both your system (the client) and the merchant's system (server) must use software that includes security features. Your Web browser has built-in security features, so you already have the required software. This means that, in effect, Internet security is now a one-way street, with the responsibility falling to the merchant to create a secure service that uses your Web browser's security features.

Certified delivery

Another Internet commerce requirement is for "certified delivery" of online transactions. Certified delivery protects both sellers and buyers, especially when the product's value is time-sensitive. The seller needs to be able to prove that the buyer got the product on-time, while the product had the value for which the buyer paid. Sellers also need to know that when they transmit their information, they will get paid.

The same system also gives buyers assurance that they will not be charged if some system problem prevents delivery. Buyers do not want to be charged just because the seller's system transmitted the information. This requires an information exchange between seller and buyer that verifies that a delivery can be accomplished and that payment can be made. The seller's system will transmit electronic products only after the availability of a valid payment is confirmed. At the same time, certified delivery also means that you are charged only when the information is actually received. It's a tricky "Catch 22" situation, but system developers have created programs that protect both sides of the seller-to-buyer partnership.

Automated flexible pricing

Few businesses charge the same price for the same product to all buyers. Because a lot of factors can affect pricing, a merchant's Internet commerce services might need to offer discounts and handle premium-pricing. Here are some pricing factors that some advanced Internet commerce systems can handle:

❖ Prepaid, subscription-type sales that track your balance of available funds, sending information to you without charge if you have a balance and requiring additional payments if you've depleted your balance.

❖ Discounts—perhaps even free copies—if you are a member of a site license group that has paid a flat rate.

❖ Volume discounts if you're a member of a pre-registered consumer group, user group or government agency.

❖ Volume discounts if you're a single buyer who is a frequent customer.

❖ Premium surcharges for purchases made during peak-hour access and discounts for off-peak access.

❖ Time-sensitive charges that could invoke a premium for information downloaded today, discount that same information tomorrow and perhaps offer it to you next week as a free sample.

❖ Price quotations for when you are shopping, but not ready to buy. The best systems can store quotations with your database record so there won't be price confusion when you return to complete the sale.

A typical commerce group

Let's look in-depth at a company that describes itself as a business model for a commerce server. The NetBill project (*www.netbill.com*) has teamed with strategic business partners, Visa International and Mellon Bank Corporation. NetBill research, however, is funded in part by a grant from the National Science Foundation (NSF). While NetBill has a growing full-time and part-time staff—drawn mainly from the ranks of Carnegie Mellon University (CMU)—much of its development has been completed by students in project courses taken as part of CMU's graduate program in Information Networking.

Beep! Beep!
The National Science Foundation (NSF) has been funding Internet development for a long time. NetBill is another example of how they've helped us all enjoy the incredible power of the Internet. Now they're helping to make it more secure.

A commerce server is a set of standards and the software that implements those standards so buyers can pay merchants online. A typical commerce group—such as NetBill—maintains commerce servers that link you and the organizations with which you'll conduct Internet business. These links not only handle the actual financial transaction, but they certify the delivery of both product and payment. NetBill's project group handles both sides of certified delivery (see Figure 3).

NetBill uses a financial transaction protocol that supports flexible pricing and can calculate customized quotes for individual buyers and handle pricing approvals. It uses digital signature technology to provide account security on both sides of transactions. Buyers can sign orders digitally using a key that is never revealed to the merchant, so eavesdroppers cannot intercept credit card numbers and approval authorizations.

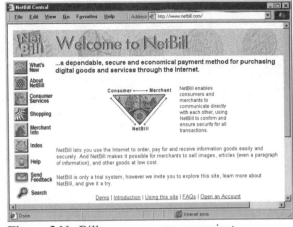

Figure 3 NetBill commerce server project

THE INS-AND-OUTS OF COMMERCE SERVER TRANSACTION

When a buyer requests an electronic product from a merchant, the buyer's client software sends a digitally-verified purchase request to the merchant's server. The electronic product is transmitted to the buyer in an encrypted format. Encryption transforms data into a format that is unreadable by anyone without a secret decryption key that will "unlock" the information and restore it to a readable format.

The merchant's information server computes a cryptographic checksum—a series of arithmetic operations that detect whether a file has been damaged or modified—on the encrypted message. After transmitting the product to the buyer, the merchant's server then sends an electronic payment order (EPO). At this point, the buyer has the goods—but does not have the key required to decrypt the goods—and the buyer has not yet been charged.

The buyer's system calculates a checksum and sends a reply to the merchant's server. When the server receives the EPO reply it compares its checksum against the one computed by the client library. If the checksums match, the server knows that the buyer received the encrypted goods without error.

After this verification, the merchant creates a digitally-verified invoice that includes the price, the checksum and the decryption key for the product. The merchant sends both the EPO and the invoice to a commerce server, which verifies that the product identifiers, prices and checksums all match.

The commerce server debits the buyer's account (which was pre-funded) and credits the merchant's account, logs the transaction and saves a copy of the decryption key. It then sends the merchant a digitally-verified message with either an approval code, or an error code if the transaction failed.

Finally, the merchant forwards the commerce server's reply and the decryption key to the buyer's client software, which enables the buyer's software to decrypt the information product.

This probably sounds ridiculously complicated, but computers handle the whole process in a few seconds.

Multiple users and accounts

NetBill supports "many-to-many" relationships between consumers and accounts. This means that a single corporate or academic account may authorize many users to charge against it and obtain special pricing. Also, individual consumers may maintain multiple personal accounts. One user on every multiple-user account must be designated as the account owner, and someone must be designated as the account administrator. An authorized administrator can use a standard Web browser to open an account, view and change an account profile, authorize funds transfers into the account and view current statements of account transactions and balances. Account information checks by administrators are handled as regular financial transactions to ensure authentication and security.

Account creation is one of the largest costs associated with traditional credit card and bank accounts. The automatic account creation features of commerce servers help to limit costs for both consumers and merchants. Low-cost account creation is going to be a key contributor toward developing widespread micropayment systems.

Account types

A commerce account currently comes in two basic flavors:

❖ Debit model (pre-paid);

❖ Credit model (post-paid).

In the debit model—used by DigiCash and CyberCash, for example—buyers must deposit into a commerce account sufficient funds to cover anticipated purchases. Buyers first would deposit real money (via check or credit card) with DigiCash or CyberCash and then go surf the net with electronic money.

In the credit model—patterned after traditional credit card vendors—transactions are accumulated and billed to the buyer's commerce account at the end of a billing period. These accounts, again like credit cards, have a pre-established dollar limit for each buyer. Both models give both merchants and consumers instant online access to transaction status and statement activity.

Other uses for commerce servers

So far, we've focused only on the sale and purchase of electronic goods and information. But there are plenty of non-electronic products to sell, and a good commerce model will support the purchase of traditional goods and services. Let's consider a few possibilities:

❖ Ticketing for entertainment events and for airline reservations. Airlines are setting the stage for this as they develop ticketless flights. Your ticket might be no more than a confirmation—printed from a Web page—with a code number that agents would match with their computer when you check in.

❖ Utility payments, such as for electric bills, phone service, gas bills, tax payments and perhaps even lottery sales.

❖ Products that currently are sold via traditional mail order catalogs.

❖ Contributions to charitable organizations or political campaigns.

❖ Online video and audio, although at the present time, this conflicts with the safeguards in certified delivery.

❖ Software application rental. Software could incorporate the client library in any application. Periodically, the software would ask users to approve another purchase to get the next month's activity or "issue" of new software.

While many of the information exchanges on the Internet may continue to be provided by merchants for free, commerce systems will increase the incentive of creators and producers of information goods to supply more and better products. And we all benefit from the improved quality and increased quantity of new goods available via the Internet.

Summary of money issues

Never rely, however, on a single source for security or commerce information for your business. Be sure to cross-check information you read on the Web and get second opinions from professionals you interview.

The Road Runner Browser chapter in Phase 2 covers more on handling secure Web documents, including tips to help you configure your Web browser the way you want.

ORBITING IN CYBERSPACE

NetBill
http://www.netbill.com

Here's the Web site for Carnegie-Mellon's NetBill commerce server project that we profiled earlier in this chapter. NetBill's research is funded in part by a grant from the National Science Foundation (NSF), one of the founders of the Internet.

CyberCash
http://www.cybercash.com

CyberCash offers consumers, banks and merchants the Secure Internet Payment Service (SIPS™). SIPS protects credit card numbers used for shopping on the Web and lets merchants safely process Internet credit card transactions. In 1996, SIPS began to let consumers use their own money for Internet payments. Check out this Web site for details on how you can use their system. CyberCash encryption software has been approved for worldwide export by the U.S. Government.

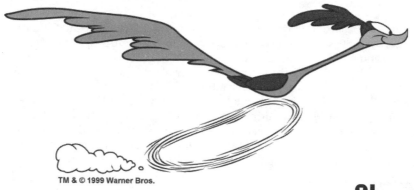

Chapter 4

Online Privacy: Internet Security

Computer thieves use high-tech tools that let them break into corporate information systems all over the world in a single night—all while sipping a soda and listening to background music. Skilled computer thieves can earn a living without leaving the comforts of home—or their college dorm room. Actually, it's not all that bad. A few simple precautions will deter all but the most diligent computer hacker. Besides, ever since the early 1990s, it seems the watchword of our society has been precaution. You take security precautions in almost everything you do. Now you need to extend those practices to your Internet adventures.

HOME-bASED LOCAL AREA NETWORK SECURITY

If you have a local area network (LAN) in your home, you need to protect your data from unauthorized access. Most likely, your home-based LAN is set up with *File and Print Sharing* enabled. The Road Runner installation checklist includes an item to disable this feature. If you set up a LAN after we have installed Road Runner, or if you performed the installation yourself, *please verify* that you have disabled *File and Print Sharing*.

Why is this so important? Through Road Runner, your computer will be connected to the Internet whenever it is on. Whenever a LAN is connected to the Internet, any files or printers that are shared on the LAN are also shared on the larger network. Thus, anyone on the Internet could, potentially, access your files. Disabling *File and Print Sharing* blocks such access.

Don't worry. Even if your *File and Print Sharing* were enabled, there are millions of computers on the Internet, so the odds are very low that your network would be targeted by a hacker. Besides, most hackers are out to make a buck and, unless you have information on your LAN that can be sold, your home system is unlikely to be of interest to hackers.

Don't take this personally—hackers aren't after you in particular. They're out surfing the Net very much as you do, but with a different purpose in mind. And, like you, they usually get interested in whatever appears to be easy. If you encounter a complicated Web site that's hard to understand, you will quickly move on because there are plenty of user-friendly sites. Same with hackers—only for them "user-friendly" has a different meaning.

Hackers sometimes play a game called "door rattling." It's the equivalent of snooping through a neighborhood and rattling doorknobs to see if anyone forgot to lock up. So, a user-friendly system for hackers would be a business computer system that pops open when the door is rattled—which means an easily-guessed password, or no password protection at all. Door rattling thieves aren't after any system in particular—just the ones that easily open and hold valuable business information.

Passwords

Easily-broken passwords are among the top security problems on the Internet. If a hacker can get a foothold in your network—either by guessing a password or by using low-security public access—they can search for words that could be used as passwords by users with high-security access.

Passwords that are found in dictionaries, or that are used in documents, e-mail or Web pages are ready prey for hackers. Passwords like "TOPP$DOG," which can't be found in a dictionary, but are still easy to remember, are a safer choice.

Consider combining the case-sensitivity of network passwords and the diversity of languages other than English to further enhance your password security. For example, your mail password could be as simple as "coRReo," the Spanish word for mail. Even if you had a Spanish surname and a hacker used that as a clue to try Spanish words, he still would have to test thousands of upper-case and lower-case combinations or the word correo.

If you have valuable, sensitive business information, you have to make it secure. You may be surprised at how little you need to do—often a simple encryption system is sufficient—because most Internet bandits are in for the quick buck. There are plenty of easy targets and unprotected data floating around the Internet.

Sniffers and Snoopers

Have you ever wondered how hackers can break into a system? The simplest technique is to obtain the login ID and password of a system administrator.

But that's secure information, right? So, how can a hacker get a login and password?

You may be surprised how often hackers use inside sources who sell computer security information. The rampant waves of corporate downsizing that are sweeping the U.S. has bred a whole generation of employees who do not hold a high degree of loyalty to large corporations. Selling a key login ID and a password may bring a disgruntled employee the severance pay he or she believes is fair compensation for being dumped.

Or, hackers may use their snoopers and sniffers to find passwords that can gain them entrance onto a system where the system administrator's password may be found. A sniffer is an Internet program that monitors Internet traffic looking for data that it suspects might contain login IDs or passwords used to log onto its targeted systems.

Jargon Cutter

Sniffers and snoopers - Internet programs that monitor Internet traffic looking for data that they suspect might contain login IDs or passwords used to log onto targeted systems. They're automatic and work around the clock, saving Internet messages for a hacker to browse through at his convenience.

If you send a lot of unencrypted messages that contain secure keywords, then your system will be user-friendly to a hacker. Of course, hackers are mostly interested in information with a profit potential. Ordinary e-mail is at no more risk of being intercepted than an ordinary phone conversation is of being taped by a wire tapper.

When you log in to a remote host using Telnet or FTP, your login ID and password travel across the Internet unencrypted. Most e-mail also can be monitored as well. Any sniffer that has targeted your organization's Internet traffic can pick out login IDs from e-mail. If you e-mail a password to a colleague or business associate, you may also be inviting in a host of hackers.

Spoofing

Hackers can pretend to be a trusted user by changing their host login IP address to match someone else's. They then force their data to take a particular path through the Internet using "source routing," so that the last link in the route is the trusted system. Data sent back to the trusted user's host is rerouted to the hacker's system. Such masquerades—as well as the creation of bogus messages—is called "spoofing."

Jargon Cutter

IP Address - Every computer on the Internet has a unique number called an IP address. An IP address is something like a telephone number. This number travels with e-mail and other Internet traffic to keep everything going to the right places—that's the good news. The bad news is that hackers can slip in fake IP addresses to make mail appear it's from another source.

Thus, even if you receive a direct e-mailed request from someone you trust, you have to consider that the message could be a spoof. Before you e-mail sensitive data, at the very least, be certain that the trusted individual actually sent the message. For maximum Internet security, never send any sensitive data without encryption.

SECURITY SOLUTIONS FOR SMALL OR HOME-BASED BUSINESSES

Large corporations have large computer budgets and a staff of computer experts that can implement security measures and data encryption. But what can you do if you're a small business or a home-based business that needs to transmit secure, private information across the Internet?

Fortunately, there are some simple and inexpensive solutions that will stop all but the most ferocious and well-armed hacker. One good example is the Eudora e-mail application. Their package now includes free PGP (Pretty Good Privacy) message encrypting.

PGP will protect sensitive items, such as e-mail and file attachments with the strongest encryption available commercially to individuals. Sending unencrypted e-mail and attachments is similar to mailing a postcard. Like a postcard, unprotected e-mail has no sealed envelope and can be read by anyone who handles it.

Of course your messages normally are not handled manually. But it could happen. For example, if you ran a small business that contracted to do sensitive work for a large company, a hacker might target your e-mail in hopes of picking up something of value to sell.

PGP encryption means that your e-mail messages can't be "cracked." The NSA (National Security Agency) has estimated that it would take all of the personal computers in the world today (that is more than a quarter billion PCs) working for 12 million times the age of the universe to crack a PGP-encrypted message. Any hacker who is targeting data to try to make money is going to move on to softer targets once he discovers that your messages are encrypted.

You can learn more about PGP by visiting *www.pgp.com* (see Figure 1).

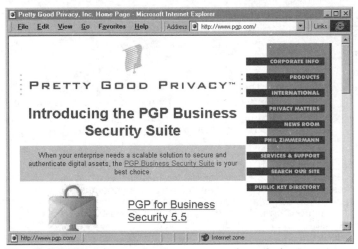

Figure 1 PGP - Inexpensive Internet security solutions

Anti-Virus Protection

There's more—even with the best security measures, *you* could do yourself in via a computer virus. A computer virus is a self-replicating program that damages computer operating systems or data files. Remember the Trojan Horse fable in which the victims brought in the "gift" that led to their destruction? Computer viruses often are disguised as electronic Trojan Horses—programs that are interesting or useful but whose true purpose is to damage your system. The Internet will entice you to pull in lots of outside files. If your system lacks anti-virus protection, you're running on the edge. If it does, don't short-circuit the safeguards to save a few minutes.

Fortunately, there are many anti-virus protection options available, including Trend-Micro (*www.antivirus.com*). Of course Internet anti-virus technology is changing rapidly because new computer viruses are being created almost every day. So, your best source for up-to-date information is to keep up with anti-virus Web sites (see Figure 2), as well as the Microsoft and Netscape Web sites to see their latest offerings and anti-virus news. There, you can expect to find links that will connect you to the anti-virus Web sites with which they partner.

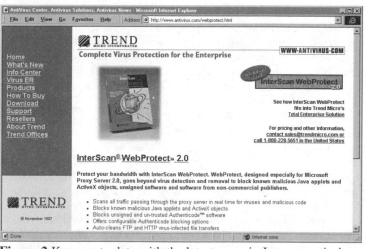

Figure 2 Keep up to date with the latest news in Internet anti-virus

Top 10 Internet Security Problems

Believe it or not, many computer security problems are internal. For all the media hype about hackers and computer theft, the criminals can't compare to what we all, collectively, do to ourselves. Here, in approximate order of occurrence are the Top 10 Internet security problems.

Number 10 - Government agents

So far this has been rare, but in a few cases the FBI has raided computer sites and confiscated all computer equipment. Can't happen to you, right? Are you sure you know everything that everybody is doing on your system? If someone posts secret information on the Internet, then you could hear a knock on the door anytime and see a band of Federal agents with moving vans and warrants to remove your equipment. Of course it's rarely enforced, but just beware of the risks.

Number 9 - Sniffers and snoopers

Unless your system contains sensitive data, you're not likely to be a target for sniffers and snoopers. But any research-oriented organization could attract eavesdroppers. Budget cuts have forced many companies to slash R&D funding—but a few dollars spent on hackers could replace a competitor's shut-down research laboratory. The good news is that data encryption will give you simple and highly-effective protection against the effects of criminals using sniffers and snoopers.

Number 8 - Credit card fraud

Most horror stories of online credit card fraud are unfounded. First, people don't need the Internet to steal credit card numbers. Remember when you used to tear up all your credit card carbons? Today, trash bins behind strip shopping malls once again have plenty of credit card numbers and no one can backtrack to find out who got them. Besides, there simply are very, very few reports of credit card numbers being ripped off across the Internet. And the thieves who do operate online can leave trails that can lead authorities right to them.

Number 7 - Youthful hackers

Kids enjoy a challenge and your system might be an inviting target. Kids, however, rarely are out to steal your data and usually lack the fencing contacts if they did download something sensitive. They have, however, reformatted a lot of hard drives and deleted a lot of files. A simple tape backup system will protect you against most of them. And, disabling *File and Print Sharing* will keep them out in the first place.

Number 6 - Professional hackers

This is a computer security problem without borders. In 1995, a group of Russian computer hackers was accused of stealing more than $10 million from Citibank accounts in the U.S. Professional computer hackers not only enjoy their work, but they also enjoy the potential for enormous rewards. And if they're smart and are willing to work on the run, they're extremely hard to catch. We've been lucky so far because a lot of hackers have relied too heavily on their genius-level brains and not enough on running—it's amazing how many times law enforcement officials simply drive to the home of a suspect and pick him up while he's still online.

Number 5 - Internal credit card fraud

This is a problem for any business and it probably will grow—but it didn't start with the Internet. The advent of the Internet and the expansion of credit card usage in lieu of bank checks has created a ripe environment for people to obtain and sell credit card numbers. Encryption will prevent outsiders from getting your credit card number when you shop online. Look for electronic commerce systems that support secure transactions—your Road Runner browser supports these secure shopping sites.

Number 4 - Inside jobs

With a few mouse clicks in an FTP application, an employee can circumvent the best of firewalls and do the work of legions of hackers. Former employees, too, may have left with sensitive secrets or with passwords to use to come back in later. In this era of downsizing and outsourcing, businesses need to focus security efforts on employees whose jobs may soon be eliminated because they might take security information when they leave—especially if they helped create it.

Number 3 - Viruses

The presence of computer viruses causes a lot of damage, but not for the reason you might suspect. Computer viruses actually cause little direct data loss. Countless people, however, have spent vast sums on virus prevention, monitoring and cleaning. The cure usually is far more costly than the problem. Nonetheless, it is a necessary expense, because if you don't spend the money to protect your system from virus intrusion, you will one day lose some data to a computer virus—it's almost certain. But good virus protection and tape backups will ensure that viruses cost you only time and inconvenience and don't cost you a lot of money.

Number 2 - Hardware theft, fire and failure

This problem far outstrips all the others we've listed so far. Many companies have been dropped to their corporate knees by theft, fire and hardware failures. These security risks are not just threats, nor are they theories—they are real and they happen every day. A regular routine of simple tape backups and off-site storage of the data tapes will protect your important data. Unfortunately, human nature and the laws of metaphysics have proven that the Friday when someone is too rushed to run a backup and take the tape off-site is the same weekend his computer is stolen. This has happened many times—be diligent with your backups!

Number 1 - Computer users

And the number one cause of computer losses is—computer users. And they employ a wide range of tools: bad password choices and compromised passwords; accidental reformatting; unintentional file deletions; mistakes with software that publicly post sensitive data instead of sending it securely to one site; flame wars by employees that generate negative attention or law suits; failure to run regular backups (see Number 2); and intentionally circumventing firewalls or other security measures because someone is in a hurry. So, for the most part, computer users are their own worst enemy. In a way it's comforting because at least it is something that you can control.

Tape Backup Tips

Now that you're really getting into the cyberspace mode, you are at some risk of experiencing a computer data loss. For example, losing the mailbox and address book files from your e-mail application or losing your Favorite Folders list could be costly because they may be your only record of important business contacts. And, if you track your finances and manage your securities and retirement portfolios online, imagine what would happen if your hard drive suddenly disappeared and was never seen again!

There are scores of true computer-data horror stories that all could have been prevented by tape backups. In fact, in most cases tape backup systems were in place, but using them had become a forgotten task.

On a corporate network, many people think the network administrator handles all important backups. While that's true for normal data files, you'll find that by default many e-mail programs use the application's program directory, or drive, to store its mailbox files and address book. If these applications are installed on a local hard drive, then those mailbox files are not being backed up with normal data. If a local hard drive suffers a failure, the e-mail contact data would be lost.

If you don't work on a network, you can partition your hard drive into a C: drive and a D: drive, then keep all data files on D: and backup D: at the end of each session. Some e-mail programs let you specify the location of mailbox and address book files, so keep these on D:, too, because they are, after all, *data files* and not *program files*. Or, specify a network drive that gets backed up with everything else.

Finally, buy extra backup tapes and keep a recent set of tapes *off-site*. Get into a pattern of rotating your latest backup with the off-site tapes. A backup tape that's left inserted in the drive slot won't do you any good if your computer is stolen or destroyed by fire or natural disaster.

Web Browser Security

Today's Web browsers have Internet security built into them. They employ several different security methods, so you'll need to choose the method that suits your computing needs.

Site Certificates

A Web site can have a site certificate that guarantees that the site is run by a legitimate company and that its data is secure. The certificate ensures that no one can spoof the site and assume the site's identity. A Web browser verifies the information in the site's certificate, which includes the site's real Internet address. These site certificates are dated, so the browser also confirms that the certificate is current.

You've probably noticed that if you attempt to download software from a Web site, your browser will ask you to confirm that you want the files. But when you download software from a Web site that has a site certificate, your browser will download it without asking you.

You can get a "personal" site certificate that enables a Web site to verify that the only person who can contact them on your behalf really is you. The certificate will contain your name and a password, and is also dated.

A personal certificate binds your identity to a pair of electronic keys that can be used to encrypt and sign digital information. A certificate makes it possible to verify someone's claim that he or she has the right to use a given key, helping to prevent people from using phony keys to impersonate other users, as we mentioned earlier in this chapter. Used in conjunction with encryption, certificates provide a complete security solution, assuring the identity of all parties involved in a transaction and assuring that the data being sent cannot be intercepted along the way.

Setting Security Options

Your Internet Explorer browser has a lot of security options. To check your current certificates, or to manage the list, click **View, Internet Options, Content**. From that tab, you can view or edit either your **Personal** certificates, **Authorities** (trusted sites), or **Publishers** (sites that publish downloadable software), which already includes the Microsoft Web site.

Beep! Beep!
You can get a personal certificate using your Outlook Express e-mail application. Click **Tools, Options, Security**, then click the **Get Digital ID...** button. This will connect you to a security information page on the Microsoft Web site. This page gives you a detailed explanation of certificates and has a list of links from which you can obtain a certificate.

VeriSign

VeriSign is a leader in Internet security technology and issues site certificates, personal certificates, server security and electronic commerce security. Your Internet Explorer browser relies primarily on VeriSign for site certificates. It comes preconfigured with several site certificates in place. For example, this is almost too obvious, but the Microsoft Web site has a site certificate. So, when you download software from Microsoft, you can rely on it not containing malicious code.

You can see their complete line of security solutions, or apply for a personal certificate by visiting their Web site at *www.verisign.com* (see Figure 3).

Figure 3 VeriSign - a leader in Internet security

An introduction to firewalls
http://www.soscorp.com

Be sure and check out the link on this page entitled <u>Introduction to Firewalls</u> that is produced by SOS Corporation, a New York City-based Unix systems management company. SOS can provide experts in computer security, systems programming, network administration and systems management. They produce an Internet security application called Brimstone, a full-featured Internet firewall. They also produce Freestone, a freeware firewall application that includes parts of Brimstone.

Computer security resource clearinghouse
http://www.first.org

This is a Web page maintained by the National Institute of Standards and Technology in Gaithersburg, Maryland near Washington, DC. There's a link on the home page called <u>Training</u> that brings up a page entitled, "Training, Awareness and Resource

Publications" that is a directory of a variety of resource material for the computer security professional or trainer.

Computer security newsgroups
comp.security.announce

comp.security.misc

comp.security.unix

You can access the Usenet newsgroups on computer security information and read security solutions posted by the Computer Emergency Response Team (CERT).

Phase 2

Phase 2: The Launch

Congratulations on finishing ground school. You've completed Phase 1 and you're ready to actually venture into cyberspace—so that's where we're taking you next.

These chapters feature hands-on exercises that we call "Step-By-Step," because they literally walk you through the different topics one step at a time. We'd like to lay a little groundwork for this phase before you start.

Each Step-By-Step exercise starts with a Goal, so you'll know what you are going to achieve. Each step begins with a checkmark. Many of the steps have brief messages after them that clarify either the step you just performed, or let you know if you need the next step or if you should skip it.

Beep! Beep!

We've written the exercises with some assumptions about your basic skills in Windows, so here's a little test. If terms such as dialog box, scroll bar, radio button, menu, double-click, or right-click, sound unfamiliar to you, then read the Windows Primer chapter in Phase 4 (see page 189) before you tackle these exercises. Plus, it shows you many helpful tips that will boost your efficiency when using the Internet.

So, if you're already a whiz with Windows, let's get started.. Here's what you'll get in the chapters in Phase 2:

❖ **Chapter 5** introduces basic Web surfing techniques and teaches you how to use the **Road Runner Browser** as a powerful information tool. You'll learn about using the Road Runner Browser to play audio and video clips over the Internet. And you'll learn about the exciting developments in animation and interactive features that are quickly bringing the Internet to life.

❖ **Chapter 6** covers Internet **electronic mail** (e-mail). E-mail has absolutely revolutionized global communications and most likely will revolutionize your personal communications. This is hard to believe at first, but you can send as many messages as you want—anywhere in the world—and it won't cost you any extra above your basic Internet service charge!

❖ **Chapter 7** shows you how to use one of the most popular areas of the Internet: **newsgroups**. Newsgroups are akin to community bulletin boards, but they're electronic and the community is the planet. They're organized by topics and the topics are organized into larger categories. Now, are you sitting down? Okay. This may be hard to believe, but there are more than 30,000 Internet newsgroups! There ought to be a topic in there somewhere that interests you, and we'll show you how to find it.

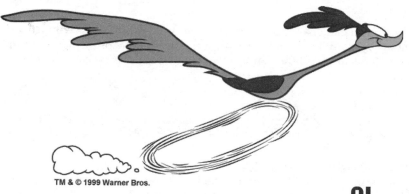

TM & © 1999 Warner Bros.

Chapter 5

Countdown: Road Runner Browser

Most of the time you spend on the Internet you'll be surfing the World Wide Web. It's an awesome experience and there seems to be, literally, no end to how much you can see and do on the Web. This chapter will give you an overview of how to surf the Web with a software application called a "Web browser." And this chapter includes hands-on work that we call "Step-By-Step" exercises.

The Web browser we provided you is a tailored version of the Microsoft Internet Explorer. You may have heard of other browsers, but there's no reason to use anything else. Even if you don't use the Road Runner Browser, though, much of the information in this chapter will be beneficial anyway because you're going to get a lot of concepts that apply to all Web browsers.

Why did we choose Explorer for the Road Runner Browser? The Road Runner Browser has been customized with a wealth of "extensions" that have been added to the normal Web browser functions—many of which are not yet supported by other Web browsers. These extensions increase its ability to bring you exciting, user-friendly Web pages. Today, millions of people are navigating the Web with the Microsoft Internet Explorer. And our version is even better because it's tailored for our special system features.

We also selected Microsoft's browser because it works seamlessly with Windows 95. For example, the Favorites Folders feature—a feature that permits you to store the addresses of your favorite Web sites—works the same as all other folder functions in all Windows 95 applications so that there's nothing new to learn.

Beep! Beep!
The "Favorites Folder" feature provides the same function as the bookmark feature in Netscape. If you've been using Netscape as your Web browser, you may be concerned that switching to the Road Runner Browser will force you to give up your priceless collection of bookmarks. Good news! Your Road Runner Browser will capture your existing Netscape bookmarks and put them in a folder called "Imported Bookmarks." You'll then build from there and you'll never miss Netscape.

You'll soon discover that the basics of using the Road Runner Browser are similar to using Windows 95 itself. But we want you to progress beyond the browsing basics and the exercises in this chapter will transform you into an efficient, power-user of the Road Runner Browser.

> ### Beep! Beep!
> You don't need to type "http://" at the beginning of a Web address. Your Road Runner Browser assumes you want a Web site and will fill in the protocol tag for you.

Road Runner Browser help menu

The Road Runner Browser itself has a pretty good selection of built-in online resources. You'll find them under the **Help** menu at the top of the screen. With this menu, you'll never have to hunt for *something* to do with your Road Runner Browser. Experiment with the items on that menu because you'll discover lots of useful, up-to-date information.

Surfing one Web page

When you see a screen on the Web, the process that puts it there is similar to when you open a document with a word processor. Thus the "Web pages" you see are pages in opened documents that are available via the Web. While Web surfing is akin to viewing documents in a word processor, you can't edit them—Web documents are read-only.

> ### Beep! Beep!
> Here's an important concept: Web documents don't really have "pages" as do documents in your word processor. Web documents are continuous, like a scroll. When you go to another "page" you're actually getting another document or jumping to another spot on the current scroll.

Besides being read-only, the Road Runner Browser differs from your word processor in another important way: It can open documents from computers all over the world. Your word processor only opens documents that are on your hard drive or your network. The Road Runner Browser has the ability to communicate with the Internet via a language called TCP/IP (Transmission Control Protocol/Internet Protocol). This is the basic programming foundation that carries computer information around the globe via the Internet.

So, Web pages are no more than computer documents. Okay, sure, they're usually spiffed up with color and graphics. And, increasingly, they also include sound, video or even animation. But the basic principle remains the same: the Web is just a network system that loads documents into a reader called a Web browser.

Since Web pages are no more than documents, let's review some shortcuts to moving around within a single Web document. You'll need to be as efficient at surfing individual Web documents as you are at surfing the entire Web. To learn these time-saving steps, open a Web page that has plenty of text.

Step-By-Step

GOAL: Learn to surf one Web page

✔ Press **DOWN ARROW** to scroll down through a Web page.

✔ Press **UP ARROW** to scroll up through this document.

✔ Press the **SPACE BAR** to scroll down one screen-worth at a time.

✔ Press **SHIFT+SPACEBAR** to scroll up one screen-worth at a time.

✔ Use your mouse on the scroll bar on the right of the screen.

> Use the arrow at the top or the bottom to scroll up or down. Or, grab the elevator button (square box) on the scroll bar and drag it up or down to more quickly scroll long distances.

✔ Press **CTRL+END** to jump to the bottom of this document.

✔ Press **CTRL+HOME** to jump to the top of this document.

✔ Press **PG DN** a couple of times.

✔ Press **PG UP** a couple of times.

> Remember these keystrokes throughout all of your Web surfing. When your computer is pushing the limits, using the mouse places a strain on your Windows resources. If the mouse acts sluggish or skittery, try using these keystrokes instead. Besides, the keystrokes are faster anyway.

Marking Your Trails

It's easy to wander off into cyberspace and get yourself lost. You'll be jumping from one hypertext link to another, ever more deeply probing the depths of cyberspace and then you'll decide you want to return to a screen you saw earlier. But you'll have no idea how to find it again because you never actually saw or typed the URL—it was just the result of choosing one of the dozens of hypertext jumps you've made. All you've got is a memory of how the screen looked, and now you want to see it again.

Jargon Cutter

URL - Just in case you've missed it earlier, a URL is a Uniform Resource Locator. It's somewhat equivalent to having the telephone number of someone you want to call. URLs specify the type of resource first (http, ftp, or gopher), followed by a colon and two slashes (://) and then the actual name of the resource.

Fortunately, the browser programmers experienced this lost feeling enough times so that they created some tools that you can use to mark your trail through cyberspace. Some are permanent markers and some just track where you've been today. Let's see how the Road Runner Browser can help you quickly return to screens you've seen before.

Back and forward

The simplest trail-marking features are Back and Forward. Your browser includes four methods to activate these two features. You can't experience these features unless you've been visiting a series of Web pages. So, practice these sometime after you've surfed through a number of sites.

Step-By-Step

GOAL: Activate the Back and Forward features

✔ Click the button at the top of the screen that's labeled **Back.**

> This returns you to the previous page you were viewing. It comes up quickly because your browser temporarily stores pages while you're online, so they don't have to be downloaded again into your computer from the Internet.

✔ Click the **Forward** button.

✔ Press **ALT+LEFT ARROW**.

> This is the keystroke equivalent of the **Back** button. If you'll press the **ALT** key with the thumb on your right hand you can activate the left or right arrow keys with your little finger and quickly jump back and forth through Web pages.

✔ Press **ALT+RIGHT ARROW**.

✔ Click **Go, Back** to surf using the menus.

✔ Click **Go, Forward**.

✔ Press **BACKSPACE** to see even *another* way to go back.

✔ Press **SHIFT+BACKSPACE** to go forward again.

> Okay, how many of these things are you supposed to remember anyway? Well, there are only four, but you just have to remember the ones you like. The menus are the slowest method, and the **Backspace** key is a bit awkward. The **ALT** key with the arrows is the fastest, but using the mouse on the Toolbar buttons is nice when you're just browsing around.

View history

If the document to which you want to return is a long way back, these techniques may become tedious navigation tools, although you can jump back very rapidly using the **ALT+LEFT ARROW** keystroke. Still, there are more direct routes back to pages you have previously viewed—without having to revisit everything else along the way. These steps may vary somewhat with different versions of the browser, but all versions will have a way to access your most recently visited pages. From that list you'll be able to rearrange the list by date visited or by site name.

Road Runner Browser caching

When you go back to revisit a previously-viewed page, you may notice that the page loads more quickly than it did originally. That's because the Road Runner Browser stores downloaded screens (called "caching" in computer talk—pronounced "cashing" in people talk) so that it doesn't have to download them from the Internet again if you decide to return. The larger the cache size, the more screens the Road Runner Browser can hold and the faster your system will respond to Back and Forward.

The default cache sizes that are set in the Road Runner Browser are compromises to accommodate computers that may have little free memory. If you have a large hard drive and plenty of RAM memory, you can increase your cache size to improve speed by changing your browser's preferences. The exact steps will vary between versions, but look through the tabs on your preferences dialog box until you see the caching options, then increase them.

Switching applications

What if you need to use another application while you're surfing? Remember that Windows has full multi-tasking ability—it can perform more than one function at a time. This means that you don't have to keep track of where you left off on the Web if you need to use another application for a while. Instead, you can switch to another application then come right back to the Road Runner Browser and pick up where you left off. Everything will be preserved, including your cache and history. Here are two time-saving techniques to keep in mind when you're surfing the Net.

You can switch to other open Windows applications by cycling through them with the **ALT+TAB** key or by clicking on the Taskbar to select any currently running applications. This is particularly valuable when you hit a Web site during peak hours that uses extensive graphics. You can **ALT+TAB** to another application and get a little work done or write a letter while the Road Runner Browser continues to download. For example, you could jump to your e-mail application and compose a message. It's not much, but at least you can save a little time instead of watching the hourglass.

Run multiple Road Runner Browser sessions

Here's another little treat that will solve some problems of having too many sites to see. You can open multiple Road Runner Browser sessions, although this certainly is not a solution to Internet bandwidth problems. But it permits you to see two Web pages at once—or three Web pages, or more! When you create multiple Road Runner Browser sessions each occurrence is a separate Windows task that will appear on the Taskbar and you can switch between them using **ALT+TAB**. The title of each currently open Web site will appear on the **ALT+TAB** dialog box or on the button on the Taskbar. Follow these steps to open an additional Road Runner Browser window (see Figure 1).

Step-By-Step

GOAL: Learn to open multiple Road Runner Browser windows

✔ Click **File, New Window** or press **CTRL+N**.

This opens a new browser window. You can set each of them to different URLs. If you can see both sessions, you can use your mouse to switch back and forth. If not, then switch between them with **ALT+TAB**. Perform the next step **only** if the current browser window is not already maximized.

✔ Double-click in the title bar of the new browser window.

Activate the Taskbar to see them both. The icons are the same, but the title of the current pages appears before the words "Road Runner Browser."

✔ Click on the first Road Runner Browser session you had open.

✔ Press **ALT+TAB** once to return to the new Road Runner Browser window.

Note that this menu also lists in square brackets the name of each window's current document.

✔ Press **ALT+TAB** once again to return to the first window.

✔ Press **ALT+TAB** once to return to the new Road Runner Browser window.

Of course you don't have to run these windows maximized. You might want to use the Restore command (the middle icon in the upper-right corner) and then size them so that you can see both Web pages at the same time, perhaps to compare two Web sites.

✔ Click **File, Close** to close the new Web browser.

Notice that this closes only the current window. Closing the new one will not affect the contents within the first window.

Creating Some On-Screen Elbow-Room

Most Web pages are too large to fit into the Road Runner Browser main screen all at once, including the one you've been using so far. Usually, then, you'll need to scroll the screen to see everything available, but you'll still want to see as much as possible at one time. There's a lot you can do to eliminate unnecessary screen clutter. Check out the viewing preferences and experiment with resizing and rearranging your Toolbars to get the look you want.

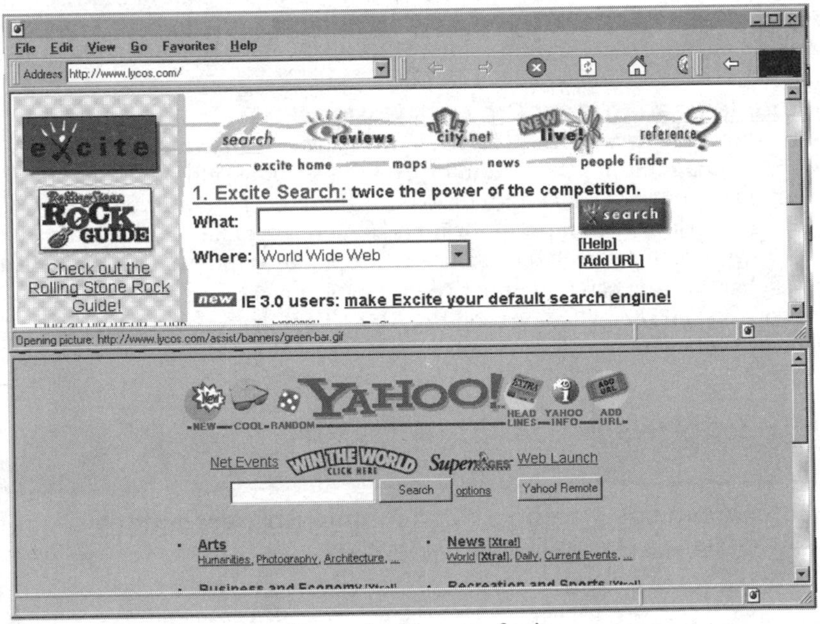

Figure 1 Double your surfing—double your fun!

Figure 2 Compact Toolbar for maximum viewing area

Once you've reduced the size of the Toolbar (see Figure 2), you'll enjoy the increased viewing area. Of course you also can eliminate the entire Toolbar, but that also eliminates the Address bar, a crucial navigation tool that you most likely will prefer to keep. The next table lists simple keystroke replacements for the Toolbar buttons in case you decide to hide them.

Toolbar Button	Replacement Command
Back	**ALT+LEFT ARROW** or **Go, Back** Goes back to the previous Web site you visited.
Forward	**ALT+RIGHT ARROW** or **Go, Forward** Goes forward after you've used the Back command.
Start page	Click **Go, Start Page** Jumps to your designated start page.
Refresh	**CTRL+R** or **View, Refresh** Forces the current page to download from the Internet again—highly useful for incomplete images or for Java applets (see the next chapter) that get stuck.
Open	**CTRL+O** or **File, Open...** Opens a Web site or a file on your local system.
Print	**CTRL+P** or **File, Print...** Prints the current Web page
Find	**CTRL+F** or **Edit, Find...** Searches the *current Web page* for keywords you enter.
Save	**CTRL+S** or **File, Save As...** Saves the current Web page on your local system.
Stop	**ESCAPE** or **Go, Stop Loading** Stops loading a page that's taking too long to load, if you get tired of waiting.

Finding What You Need on The Web

All the power that's built into your Road Runner Browser would be nearly useless if it weren't for the existence of a wide variety of Web search engines. The result is that you have a vast array of fast, powerful and comprehensive search engines that will help you locate nearly any topic in cyberspace.

Beep! Beep!

Search engines - Software applications that help you find information within computer information files are called search engines. They have two basic functions. The first is to run through the information files word-by-word and build an index of the words it finds—much like the index in the back of this book. The second function is a user interface that accepts keyword input that the search engine uses to locate your search request. Later, in Phase 3, you'll find a whole chapter on Web searching.

Explorer's Web search engine

You've got some Web searching ability built into the menu system of the Road Runner Browser. Try our tailored search pages by typing in a keyword that interests you and clicking the button to submit your search. You'll get many more examples in the search engine chapter. You most likely will add an array of search engine URLs to your Favorites Folders so you always will have them handy to answer your research demands. Search engines are just about the most valuable resource on the Internet.

Use the Road Runner Browser Find command

Many of the hypertext Web pages that you'll view include jumps to other spots in the same document. These jumps don't load a new page, they just scroll through the current page and find a mark, called a "target." You'll be able to tell if you've jumped to a target within the same page because the URL will not change except for the very end, onto which will be appended a pound sign (#) and the target name.

But what you want to read might not have a targeted link, forcing you to do a lot of scrolling to find a particular phrase or keyword. Fortunately, the Road Runner Browser lets you search the full text of the current Web page with the Find feature, just press **CTRL+F** and try finding a keyword on any Web page that has text.

Using The Information You Find

Finding information for a school report, tracking down an important business lead, picking up a tip or an idea are all exciting things to accomplish on the Web. Finding some obscure material you've been seeking can be a huge relief. Discovering exciting information on the Web that you never knew existed is exhilarating. But once you find something, you need to know how to transfer it elsewhere within your system so that you have it in a useful format. There are numerous options and you probably will use them all depending on the information you've found and on how you plan to use the information later.

Copying and pasting Web pages

Probably the quickest and simplest option for transferring Web text is with the clipboard and the Copy and Paste commands. If you can see the information on your screen, you usually can paste it into your word processor. After the transfer, you can reshape and reformat the text, embellish it with nice fonts and print it as part of a larger document. Let's try an exercise to illustrate this principle.

Step-By-Step

GOAL: Learn to transfer Web text into your word processor

- ✔ Find your word processor icon and start the program.
- ✔ Use **ALT+TAB** to cycle back to Road Runner Browser.
- ✔ Drag your mouse to highlight some text on your screen.
- ✔ Press **CTRL+C** to Copy it to the Windows clipboard.

    Or, you can place the mouse over the selected text, click the right button and select **Copy**. You also can click **Edit, Copy**.

- ✔ Use **ALT+TAB** to cycle back to your word processor.
- ✔ Press **CTRL+V** to Paste the copied text into a blank document.

    You now could return to the Road Runner Browser and grab more text from the last document you accessed or get more from any Web document in the world!

You won't be able to grab all of the text you read on the Web because some text actually is part of a graphic image. In those cases, you'll know it's not regular text characters because as you drag your mouse, the text will not highlight.

> **Beep! Beep!**
> The Road Runner Browser has a command that will automatically select all of the text on a Web page. You can press **CTRL+A** or click **Edit, Select All**. Then use the normal Windows **CTRL+C** command to copy the selected text to the clipboard.

Printing in the Road Runner Browser

If you only need to read the document and don't need to use it in your word processor, you can print the document directly in the Road Runner Browser. The print function is great for information such as airline schedules and data tables, when you need a quick hard copy or when you need the graphics as well as the text.

When you print the document directly, you'll get all of the graphics as you see them on the screen. And, the Road Runner Browser offers optional embellishments for printed Web pages that include headers and footers with name, date and URL. Experiment with these page options if you're not satisfied with the default setup.

Saving Web documents

You can use the Road Runner Browser to save Web pages, but if you're not careful the file will be saved with all of the hypertext markup language (HTML) codes. If that happens, you'll need to clean out the HTML codes to get down to only the text you need. Fortunately, there is a Road Runner Browser option that cleans the HTML codes from the document as it saves.

Step-By-Step

GOAL: Learn to save a Web document

✔ Click **File, Save As File...**

The Road Runner Browser lets you enter a filename. If you skip the next step, the file will be saved in HTML format—the language of the Web. That's wonderful if you're learning to create your own Web pages and want to see all the codes that made this page possible. But if you just want the text itself, do the next step.

✔ Click on the **Save as Type** drop list.

✔ Change to **Plain Text (*.txt)**.

You don't have to actually use the *txt* extension—the document will be saved as plain text even if you keep the *htm* extension as long as the file type has been set correctly with this drop list.

✔ Use the normal **Save As** folder tools to set the desired path.

Put this document in a directory that you use for word processing because you'll open it later in this exercise. Please write down or remember the directory.

✔ Click **OK** to save the document.

✔ Use **ALT+TAB** to switch to your word processor.

If your word processor is not running, start it now.

✔ Click **File, Open...** or press **CTRL+O**.

Navigate to the saved Web document and double-click it to open it and display the conversion dialog box.

WordPerfect for Windows only: (see Figure 3).

✔ Click the drop-list arrow to get a list of formats.

✔ Select **HTML** and click **OK**.

✔ Click **File, Save** or press **CTRL+S** then click **OK**.

Microsoft Word for Windows only:

✔ Click **File, Save** or press **CTRL+S**.

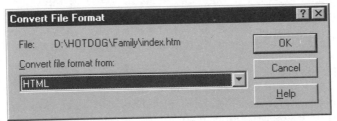

Figure 3 HTML files import into your word processor

At this point, the document you had in the Road Runner Browser now has been saved in the format of your word processor (see Figure 3). If you didn't switch to plain-text you'll see a lot of HTML codes. If you don't want the codes, you can clean up the file manually, or you can return to Road Runner Browser and save it again in the plain-text format.

Saving images

The last method you have for capturing Internet information is to save graphics files, and the Road Runner Browser makes this easy. All you have to do is click your right mouse button on any Web graphic and choose the correct save option. Let's do it.

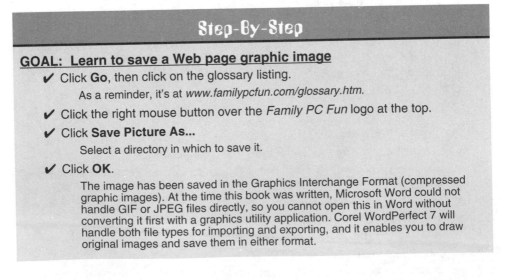

Step-By-Step

GOAL: Learn to save a Web page graphic image

✔ Click **Go**, then click on the glossary listing.

As a reminder, it's at *www.familypcfun.com/glossary.htm*.

✔ Click the right mouse button over the *Family PC Fun* logo at the top.

✔ Click **Save Picture As...**

Select a directory in which to save it.

✔ Click **OK**.

The image has been saved in the Graphics Interchange Format (compressed graphic images). At the time this book was written, Microsoft Word could not handle GIF or JPEG files directly, so you cannot open this in Word without converting it first with a graphics utility application. Corel WordPerfect 7 will handle both file types for importing and exporting, and it enables you to draw original images and save them in either format.

GETTING THE LATEST ROAD RUNNER BROWSER

We want you to use the latest version of the Road Runner Browser, so you'll be able to download free upgrades from our system. We'll notify you via e-mail when a new version is available and tell you how to get it. **Do not** download Internet Explorer upgrades from the Microsoft Web site because our tailored version includes features not found on the generic version. If you use Microsoft's generic version, you'll miss important features on our system.

Jargon Cutter

Beta test version - A version of a software product that has passed the initial in-company testing phase (Alpha test) and is ready to be tested by actual users, but is not considered reliable enough to release as a final product. Technical support is not available for Beta test versions. Once the Beta testing bugs have been fixed, the product is released as a full version.

Right Mouse Button Bonuses

If you used the right mouse button in the last exercise when you saved a graphic, then you may have noticed that the menu had several other shortcuts. We'll run through one of them with you now in case you missed them or didn't save a graphic. To see these commands actually function, you'll need a Web page that has a graphic image. Let's continue to use the same Web page.

Copy a link location

The Road Runner Browser also uses the right mouse button to let you copy the URL of a hypertext link into your Windows clipboard. You then may use **ALT+TAB** to cycle to your word processor and paste in the URL. As you've seen, some URLs are a real mess to retype, so this method may save you time, aggravation and mistakes.

Step-By-Step

GOAL: Save a link location to the Windows clipboard

✔ Start with the glossary page used earlier.

✔ Place the mouse over the **Home Page** link, but don't click.

Read the link's URL on the status line at the bottom of the screen. You don't want to type that, do you?

✔ Click the right mouse button and click **Copy Shortcut** .

The URL is now in the clipboard. You can switch to another application with **ALT+TAB**, then press **CTRL+V** to paste it.

If you click on **Copy** on this menu, the image itself will go in the clipboard and you can paste the image into nearly any Windows application.

Refresh the current document

Remember that if you use the Back command to cycle to a document you've already seen, you'll be getting a cached copy and the browser won't pull in a new copy from the Internet. Sometimes you'll need to force the Road Runner Browser to pull in a document from the Internet again. Why? There are a few examples:

❖ To update a live-action video camera, a stock report or a sports score. If you visit pages similar to these and then surf for a while, then return to the page, you'll get the old version. Refresh pulls in the latest page.

❖ To fix a Java applet that's locked up with an "exception" error. Reloading the page will get it going again.

❖ To thwart those Internet gremlins that sometimes—for completely unknown reasons—keep a page from loading correctly the first time you hit it. In fact, sometimes you'll get a message that the address is invalid, but a simple refresh command will load it correctly the second time.

To refresh a Web page, click the right mouse button, then click **Refresh**.

Favorites Folders

Favorites Folders let you save Web locations so you can easily return to them without having to write them down. Your Favorites Folders use a permanent file that saves the URL of Web documents and assigns them a plain-language name. You can drop-down your Favorites Folders any time and quickly jump to any of your favorite sites. We'll show you three different features: 1) adding Favorites Folders, 2) editing Favorites Folders and 3) modifying and arranging the list itself.

Adding Favorites

Adding a Favorite site is very simple. Whenever you see a site for which you want easy access, simply add it to the list. The current URL will be added to the main Favorites Folders list unless you click specify another folder. Let's try it.

Step-By-Step

GOAL: Add a Favorite site to your list

✔ Go to a Web site you'd like to save.

✔ Click **Favorites, Add Favorite**.

✔ Click **OK** to add it directly to the main list.

✔ Click **Favorites, Add Favorite**.

> You'll now see that the last Web site has been added to the main menu. Now let's add the same site again but we'll put it in a different folder. We'll come back to it later to delete it, so don't worry about having a duplicate.

✔ Click **Create in**, then click **New Folder**.

✔ Type *Practice* and click **OK**.

> This creates a folder under the main menu and adds the current site. Be sure to organize your folders carefully. Here are some suggested folders

> - Search Resources
> - Reference Resources
> - Corporations
> - Universities
> - Miscellaneous

Now let's learn how to delete a folder.

✔ Click **Favorites, Organize Favorites**.

✔ Click on the folder "Practice."

✔ Click **Delete** to delete the folder and the Web site that was in it.

Within this dialog box you can sort your Favorites by name or by date added. Click the **Details** button in the upper-right corner.

✔ Click **Name** to sort by name, click again to sort in reverse order.

✔ Click **Modified** to sort by date, click again to sort in reverse order.

✔ Click **Close**.

Editing existing Favorites

Sometimes a URL for which you've created a Favorite will change or you'll get some new information about a Favorite site that you'd like to add to the description. The Road Runner Browser makes editing your Favorites a snap.

Let's learn how to change the URL or the name of an existing Favorite. Changing names is a good way to force them to be sorted together in a manner that is logical to the way you'll use them. For example, let's say you were collecting Web sites that discussed flying topics. Most of these sites would have completely unrelated names and would not be next to each other when they were sorted. But you could rename them all to begin with "Flying:" and they would all end up organized in sequence.

Step-By-Step

GOAL: Learn to edit a Favorite

✔ Click **Favorites, Organize Favorites**.

✔ Open a folder if necessary so you can see an actual Favorite.

✔ Click on the Favorite, then click **Rename**.

If you need to change the URL to which the Favorite points, that's easy, too.

✔ Right-click any Favorite, then click **Properties, Internet Shortcut**.

✔ Make any necessary changes, then click **OK, Close**.

Saving your Favorites

Your Favorites Folders may become one of your most valuable cyberspace assets. It may contain links to your best friends or to crucial business partners from around the world. The Road Runner Browser keeps this valuable resource under the Windows program directory in a folder called Favorites. Many people do not regularly run a backup of their program directories. If your Road Runner Browser program directory isn't backed up frequently then you could lose valuable contacts.

To save your Favorites from accidental loss, periodically copy them to a floppy or to a directory on your PC or your network that is included in regular backup sessions. Don't trust this to chance—protect your Favorites file. If you need to move it to a directory that is regularly backed up on tape, follow these steps.

Step-By-Step

GOAL: Learn to move your Favorites Folders file

✔ Right-click the **Start** button, and then click **Explore**.

✔ In the left pane, open the **Windows** folder, if necessary.

✔ Drag your **Favorites** folder to the directory you want.

Be sure to include this directory in your regular backup routine.

Favorites summary

Favorites are an important feature of the Road Runner Browser because they will speed your work by enabling you to save any URL you find on the Internet. Please note that the Favorites are not limited to saving URLs of Web documents. You can use your Favorites to save the URL of anything on the Internet: FTP sites, Gopher sites, and newsgroups.

Also, the Favorites Folders will hold file names. This means that you even can create links to HTML documents on your own hard drive. And if you're connected to a network, you can include files from other computers and create an "Intranet" effect even if your network doesn't yet have a formal Intranet.

 ### Jargon Cutter

Intranet - An internal Web that runs on a network. The documents on an Intranet often are kept private and are not accessible on the World Wide Web, although they could be. An Intranet is a powerful productivity-enhancing tool that is sweeping through organizations of all sizes.

 # Online Audio

Online audio works by converting sound into digital information and storing that information in audio computer files. These files then can be transferred across the Internet and can be played on a wide variety of operating systems and computer platforms. You soon will see that sound files come in a lot of different formats and that each of these formats uses a proprietary compression scheme to reduce the size of the saved sound files they produce. File compression is crucial to the spread of Internet audio because sound files require very large file sizes in relation to the length of the sound clip. Don't be surprised to watch sound files grab 11K of disk space for every second of sound.

The use of online audio is increasing rapidly. Unfortunately, there isn't a uniform standard for digital audio formats, though the field is narrowing. Here are the more common types you'll encounter in a Windows environment:

❖ .WAV files (common SoundBlaster-type audio files);

❖ .AU files (common Internet audio files);

❖ .RA files (RealAudio files).

Wave audio

Wave is the native sound format for Microsoft Windows systems. The short musical segments you hear sprucing up your Windows activities are wave files. The wave format is the least efficient of the three listed here, requiring approximately 50 percent larger files than .AU sound files. It's main advantage lies in the huge number of wave files that are available—including lots of public domain clips. And, if you find a wave clip that you want to use, you can convert it to the efficient Sun format, .AU.

Sun audio

One of the most popular Internet sound file formats is the .AU format, also called the uLaw, NeXT, or Sun Audio format. This format can be used on most of the machines on the Internet that are equipped to play sound. It also produces reasonably small files that consume little bandwidth to transfer. It's a nice balance between audio quality and required transfer time. It definitely has sufficient audio quality for the typical sound clips you might offer, pretty much matching wave.

RealAudio

RealAudio is the name of a company that developed the .RA standard. It's become popular on the Internet because of its extremely small bandwidth demands. In fact, with a good connection, even a 28.8kbps modem can play .RA sound clips in real time. Of course, this isn't a concern for you because of your speedy cable Internet access, but you're still in a minority.

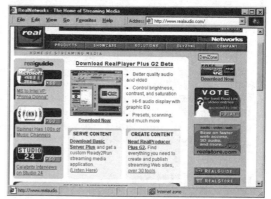

Figure 4 RealAudio - Web audio

The Road Runner Browser can't play sound files by itself. Instead, it hands off the files to a sound player application, such as the built-in Windows player. There are many players available and you can download others yourself on the Web. Some players are dedicated to playing only a single type, while others can play a variety of sound files. Whichever you choose, you can set it up under your browser options.

If you don't have a special audio player configured, then the Road Runner Browser will use the default Windows sound player—which includes the ability to save a sound file to disk. If your default Windows player won't handle RealAudio .RA files, you'll need to download and install the .RA sound player. Once the sound player is installed for that type of file the Road Runner Browser will handle future files of that type automatically. Your system, however, may already include the player you need.

Visit RealAudio's Web site at *www.realaudio.com* to download the latest version of the .RA player (see Figure 4). And if you plan to develop a Web site, check out their links to Web sites that use RealAudio so you can get some ideas on how to use it yourself. When you've completed the download, you'll need to run the installation.

Differences In File Formats

There are dramatic differences in file sizes and resulting download times. We did a comparison test to illustrate the real-life differences. It uses a clip from *Hollywood Online* (profiled later) that offers sound clips in multiple formats.

Bandwidth comparisons

The clip tested was from a scene in the film "American President," starring Michael Douglas and Charlie Sheen. The clip is 5.71 seconds long and goes like this:

Michael Douglas: "She didn't say anything about me?"
Charlie Sheen: "Well, no sir, but I can pass her a note before study hall."

Here's a comparison chart of the test:

Format	Size	Comments
.RA	5K	Music barely audible, voices not clear
.AU	44K	Music clear, voices excellent
.WAV	62K	Music clear, voices excellent

Even though you might not notice a difference in formats because you now have a cable Internet connection, keep in mind that other people may have slow modems. If you want to experiment with the various Internet audio formats, check out GoldWave at *www.goldwave.com*. If you offer sound clips on your Web site, you can provide a link to this site so that your visitors can get a sound player. GoldWave handles just about any computer audio format and can convert audio files between the different formats.

Online Video

Digital video standards have quickly been adopted by the Internet, and in particular by the World Wide Web. Because video fits so well with the expectations we all have developed for graphic displays on the Web, you'll see a rapid increase in Web video. Three formats are commonly used by PCs for video on the Web: .MPEG, ,MOV files and .AVI files.

MPEG

The MPEG (Moving Pictures Experts Group) is a group of people that meet under the ISO (International Standards Organization) to generate standards for the compression of digital video and audio. The MPEG conducts approximately four one-week meetings each year. Between meetings members work on topics discussed at the meetings.

Specifically, the MPEG defines a compression standard that reduces the storage space needed by digital video. The compression standard ensures that, much like video cassette standards, we all can use each other's digital video files. The technical details, however, are not defined. That's left to individual vendors and that is where proprietary advantage is obtained, even though MPEG is a publicly available standard.

Jargon Cutter

MPEG - The MPEG video files that are used on the Internet have a file extension of either .MPEG or .MPG. The MPEG core technology used in these files includes many different patents from different companies and individuals worldwide. Since the MPEG committee only sets the technical standards without dealing with patents and intellectual property issues, there are differences in the performance of video files from one vendor to the next, even though they use the same file extension.

Quicktime

Quicktime video files sometimes have a file extension of .QT, but most often you'll see the .MOV extension. Some video sources will give you a choice of formats. A good example is *Hollywood Online* (see Figure 5), where you'll find a wide assortment of video clips. The Windows file formats listed there are .AVI and .MOV, so you'll need a Quicktime video player for .MOV files. Check them out at *www.hollywood.com*.

You may need to install a Quicktime helper application in your Web browser. If so, do a Web search for "Quicktime Player" and download one from one of the links you find.

After the Quicktime files are on your system, run the installation program so that your browser will be able to handle the files. If you're interested in more information about digital multimedia files, check out the following sidebar. From it you can learn more details, find more sources and keep up with the latest industry changes such as player upgrades.

Figure 5 Hollywood - trailer videos

Multimedia File Formats on The Web

For even more coverage on these topics, check out this informative Web site: *www.lib.rochester.edu/multimed/contents.htm*, maintained by Allison Zhang. Our thanks go to Allison for creating such an informative site and sharing it with all of us on the Web. Her home page is entitled, "Multimedia File Formats on the Internet: A Beginner's Guide for PC Users." Check out the Table of Contents to see all the topics offered. She also maintains a helpful FAQs file that can be a ready reference source as you learn Web multimedia.

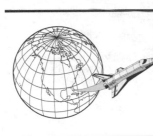

ORBITING IN CYBERSPACE

WWW FAQs
http://www.boutell.com/faq

With so much cyberspace to surf, where do you start? Start here. This online Frequently Asked Questions (FAQs) site is an excellent site for new Web users. Most of the other sites listed here are information-searching resources, so you might want to try this site first to get a better overview of what's out there waiting for you in cyberspace.

Point Communications Top 5%
http://point.lycos.com/categories

These folks scour the Web searching for the best sites. They award their logo badge to the winners, then list them by category so you can find the best sites quickly and easily. In addition to listing top Web sites, they have Internet news, general news, hot topics and even politics. Be sure to put this site on your Favorites Folders list and check it often to help you stay abreast of the latest Web developments.

Quicktime video player
http://www.apple.com/quicktime

Here's one source for a Quicktime video player and it includes some small video demonstration clips. You'll also find information about the technology, such as how it works and how you can add your own video clips to your Web site.

Ear-Chives
http://www.5g.com/earchives

The audio clips on this site are taken from popular movies and television shows (see Figure 6). All files are in .WAV format and have been digitally reprocessed to enhance quality. Use these files to attach your favorite sounds or sayings to Windows events, objects or dialog boxes, using the Windows Sound System. The collection increases constantly, so check back often and enjoy! Be sure to read the chapter in this book on copyright issues before offering these clips on your Web site.

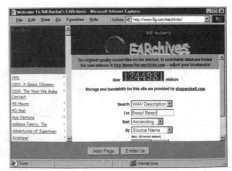

Figure 6 Earchives - sound clips

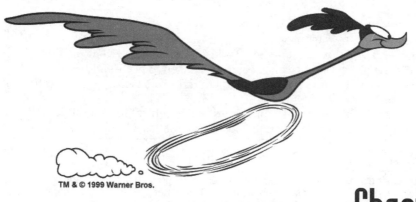

TM & © 1999 Warner Bros.

Chapter 6

Earth•to•Cyberspace: E•Mail

Internet electronic mail (e-mail) is a powerful and exciting new communication tool. The world rapidly is becoming a global community and e-mail is the perfect answer to communicating in this emerging, global environment. World-wide, overnight package delivery and fax machines certainly had a major impact on communications, but faxing even a short message overseas is quite costly. Internet e-mail has turbocharged the emergence of a global community by drastically reducing the cost of international communication—you pay the same monthly rates, no matter how many e-mail messages you send or how far they go.

In this chapter, you'll learn e-mail basics as well as some special features. A key role of this chapter is to help you see Internet mail as more than a substitute for the standard letter or fax. E-mail technology has improved to the point that your messages can now include text formatting such as large headings for emphasis, color fonts, bold, italics, and imbedded graphic images. These new features combine with instant delivery to make e-mail a better communication system than regular mail. And you don't need to buy a postage stamp or trek to a mailbox!

Using graphic screen images and sample messages, we'll make sure you know the basics of Internet e-mail. And, since Internet mail is not perfect, we also will show you what happens to e-mail between here and there, why mail sometimes gets lost and how to protect yourself.

THE FIRST INTERNATIONAL E-MAIL MESSAGE

In September, 1973, the U.S. Government's ARPANET (an international network project launched by the U.S. Department of Defense in 1969) held a conference to set up a temporary computer link via satellite from Los Angeles to Brighton, England. This link was used for an international experiment in data packet transmission between computers.

Len Kleinrock, a computer scientist at UCLA, had attended the conference in Brighton, but returned home a day before the conference ended. As he unpacked, he noticed that he had left behind his electric razor. Knowing that the link was still operating, Kleinrock logged on and linked to his friend Larry Roberts in England. Kleinrock asked Roberts to retrieve his razor and Roberts replied, "Sure. No problem."

Roberts asked Danny Cohen, a mutual friend, to return the razor to Kleinrock. The razor arrived the next day and *voilá*, electronic mail was an instant hit.

Beep! Beep!
If you skipped the netiquette chapter, you'll benefit by going back and reading it now. There's a unique social order to e-mail and you'll find that your Internet communications will go more smoothly for you if you follow common netiquette guidelines.

Internet E-Mail Applications

For this chapter's Step-By-Step exercises and screen images (see Figure 1), we'll use Microsoft Internet Mail, which is included with many Road Runner installation packages. (**NOTE:** This software is subject to upgrading. The application you have will depend on the city in which you live. We also distribute IE 4.0, which includes Outlook Express e-mail.). Fortunately, the principles and the screens are quite similar for nearly all e-mail applications. In fact, some of the steps are identical.

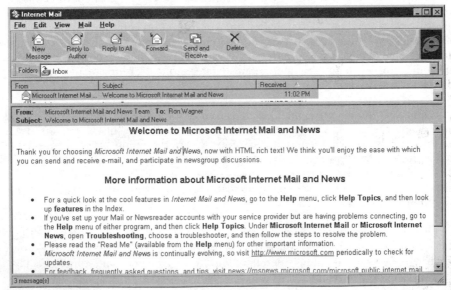

Figure 1 Internet e-mail - typical basic screen

Almost all Internet e-mail applications provide the same services but with different user interfaces. We'll cover the basic services that your application provides, but there isn't enough space here to cover everything that your software can do. Here's a list of the services that you'll find within your application:

❖ Send—Compose, edit and send messages.

❖ Read—Check mail, open In box and read messages.

❖ Response options—Reply to, forward or redirect received messages.

❖ Attachments—Include computer files that "tag along" with messages.

❖ Housekeeping—Delete messages, create tailored mailboxes and transfer messages between mailboxes.

❖ Signature files—Create a block of text that is automatically attached to the end of all messages you send.

❖ Address book—Create a list of frequently used e-mail addresses and assign a plain-language nickname.

❖ Multiple recipients—Send Carbon Copies (CC) and Blind Copies (BC) of messages.

❖ Print—Print the contents of any e-mail message.

❖ Save—Save the contents of any e-mail message for inclusion in other documents.

Your application, of course, has all of these features, and more. For example, you can specify the font in which your messages will display and you can control the color of the various mailboxes. In fact, you can even specify to send your messages in HTML format like Web pages.

E-Mail Addresses

Most likely you already have seen Internet e-mail addresses. In case you're wondering how to decipher the codes, we'll help you with a typical example:

isatest@internet.com

The special symbol in an Internet address (@) is called the "AT" symbol. To pronounce this e-mail address, you would say "isatest AT internet DOT com." And it's actually pretty much what it sounds like. The user "isatest" is "at" the Internet location called "internet dot com." The part of the address before the @ is the user and the part after the @ is the user's Internet domain name.

What does the "com" represent? It's called the *first level domain* and identifies the broad category of the user's cyberspace domain. The first level domain give you an idea of the type of organization in which the user is based. There are six commonly used first-level domains in the U.S.:

com	commercial	**edu**	educational
gov	government only	**mil**	military only
net	networks	**org**	organizations

Outside the U.S., other countries have their own first level domain name. These are too numerous to list here, but some common ones you'll see are:

ca	Canada	**de**	Germany
fr	France	**uk**	United Kingdom
au	Australia	**il**	Israel
mx	Mexico	**jp**	Japan
ru	Russia	**hk**	Hong Kong
it	Italy	**be**	Belgium
se	Sweden	**no**	Norway

Internet addresses are used backwards, from right to left. Each step up the chain narrows down the path to the user. Let's examine an example:

jsmith@library.utulsa.edu

Starting with the right segment, "edu," you see that this domain is an educational institution. The next step up is "utulsa" which represents the University of Tulsa. Those two together are called the second-level domain. The next step indicates the library server within the utulsa second-level domain. Finally, the user, "jsmith" AT "library.utulsa.edu" is pinpointed. Later in this chapter we'll tell you how the Internet uses these plain-language addresses and how to get one tailored to use your own domain name.

Send E-Mail

The first thing we'll do with e-mail is send a practice message to yourself that we'll use in later lessons. But before you send your first e-mail message, you've got to create one. So, we'll walk you through the three basic phases of sending an e-mail message: composing a new message, editing it and then sending it.

Creating a new message

Here's a Step-By-Step exercise that shows the basics of creating an e-mail message. Your e-mail works through your cable TCP/IP connection, which gives it the ability to communicate with any computer in the world that's connected to the Internet.

Step-By-Step

GOAL: Learn to compose an e-mail message

- ✔ Start the Road Runner Browser.
- ✔ Click **Go, Read Mail**.
- ✔ Click the **New Message** button.
    The insertion point is flashing on the **To:** line.
- ✔ Type your own Internet e-mail address then press **TAB** twice to move the insertion point to the **Subject:**
- ✔ Type *E-Mail Exercise 1* then press **TAB** to move the insertion point to the body of the message.

✔ Type a salutation then press **ENTER** twice.

Press **ENTER** only to end a paragraph or for blank lines, because you'll want the program to handle the word-wrapping automatically as in your word processor.

✔ Type a message, then press **ENTER** twice.

✔ Type a closing.

Edit a message

You easily can edit your message anytime before you send it. Use the normal editing commands that you use with your favorite word processor. Here's a quick summary of some of the most useful keys:

❖ Cut (**CTRL+X**), Copy (**CTRL+C**), and Paste (**CTRL+V**)

❖ Top of document (**CTRL+HOME**), bottom of document (**CTRL+END**)

❖ Word right or word left (**CTRL+RIGHT ARROW/LEFT ARROW**)

Remember that you can size a window by dragging its borders. Touch the borders in any corner with the mouse to get a diagonal mouse arrow so you can drag both horizontally and vertically with one move. Resizing the window may help you compose your message (see Figure 2). Notice that the message automatically includes your signature at the bottom of the message window. You'll need to configure your application to include your personalized signature block.

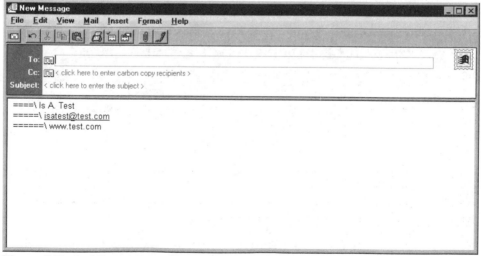

Figure 2 Typical Internet e-mail new message window

Send a message

Now let's send the message you just created.

Step-By-Step

GOAL: Learn to send e-mail

✔ Click on the **Send** button.

> The Send button is the first button at the top-left of the message window, just below the menu item, **File**. When you clicked on **Send**, your message was sent instantly.

✔ Close e-mail if desired, or keep it active for the next exercise.

This e-mail message has now been launched on its journey through cyberspace. Your Internet post office knows how to forward the message to the next computer in the delivery chain, as does each computer along the chain. Eventually—usually within a few seconds—the message has found the recipient's mail server and is stored on a hard drive waiting for them to check their mail. This delivery chain may baffle human logic, but it makes perfect sense to computers.

Beep! Beep!

Just as with real mail—affectionately called "snail mail" in cyberspace—there's no way to predict how quickly your message will reach its destination. It may be seconds. But then, it may be days, if there are problems along the way. Normally, however, if your message doesn't go through right away, you'll get a returned mail notification so you'll know the message didn't arrive. You can try sending again immediately, unless the return message says how long to wait.

How Do I Lookup Someone's E-Mail Address?

Someday you easily will be able to find almost anyone on the Internet. But that day hasn't yet come. The Internet today is like an early rural telephone system. If you've grown accustomed to instant directory telephone assistance and you are using a CD-ROM telephone book that can locate nearly anyone in the country, Internet directory services may be a disappointment because the coverage on e-mail addresses is not as widespread. Check out some of our Internet directory references in this chapter's Orbiting in Cyberspace section.

Currently, information only is available for individuals who are registered with these directories. Other Internet lookup tools are experiencing explosive growth, so look well beyond what you read in this book.

What about people who are searching for your e-mail address? Help your friends, family, clients, customers and associates find you by registering yourself in as many directory services as you can find. It will take a bit of work, but if you begin with the resources listed at the end of this chapter, you'll increase your chances of being found. Since you're joining us here in cyberspace, you might as well let us all know how to find you!

Read Messages

Before you actually can read any e-mail messages, you must get it from your mail server by checking your mail. After you've received an e-mail message, you can read it and then perform a wide variety of follow-up actions. In this section we'll cover receiving, opening and reading messages as well as basic reply actions.

Jargon Cutter

Mail Server - A computer at an Internet service provider that acts as a 24-hour-a-day cyberspace post office. All mail transactions are processed by such computers. They send out-going messages across the Internet and store incoming messages until they are retrieved at the recipient's convenience. Incoming mail servers are called *POP* (Post Office Protocol) and outgoing mail servers are called *SMTP* (Simple Mail Transfer Protocol).

Receive, open and read messages

After starting your e-mail application, you'll need to activate the Check Mail function. Depending on how you set your options, you may not need to check mail manually. But, even if your setup checks mail for you, we'll show you here how to check mail manually anytime you need an immediate update.

Step-By-Step

GOAL: Learn to check mail

✔ Click on **Send and Receive** or press **CTRL+M**.

Your mail will be checked immediately and any messages you've received will be placed in the **Inbox**. If you performed the previous exercise, you should have at least one right now.

✔ Select the **Inbox** from the **Folders** drop-list.

✔ Click on **E-Mail Exercise 1** to see it in the message window.

You can scroll through the message with your mouse or with **Page Up** and **Page Down**. If you have more messages, you can jump to the next message on the list by clicking on them.

What Happens Between Here and There?

Your e-mail messages do not traverse the Internet in a straight line or even as a single unit. Messages are broken up into digital units called packets. Your mail server then performs some very fast magic on the packets that will carry the pieces of your e-mail.

Your mail server begins by checking its own directory of Internet addresses to see if it knows how to get your message to the destination address. If you've e-mailed before to this addressee, your mail server knows the address and the message begins its journey. If not, then your mail server hasn't a clue about how to locate the addressee and must go for help.

When a mail server doesn't know domain name, it contacts the InterNIC domain name registry in Reston, Virginia. The InterNIC is the central Internet location for all domain names—they convert a domain name into computer-coded numbers. Your mail server will store that number for future reference so it won't need to return to the InterNIC if you use that same domain again.

Once the plain-language address you typed has been converted into a computer-coded address that the Internet understands, your e-mail can be sent. Messages are broken up into packets and each packet is tagged with the address as well as being numbered so they can be reassembled.

The Transmission Control Protocol/Internet Protocol (TCP/IP) that the Internet uses to handle traffic always checks for the quickest route for each packet. Each packet in your message could, theoretically, take a different route to its destination, though this is unlikely. Once the packets arrive at the destination, they are reassembled by the recipient's mail server and saved as a single computer file.

Response Options

Naturally, you'll have a response to most of the e-mail you receive. That's why the Internet is so busy—everyone is responding to everyone else in an ever-increasing cascade of e-mail messages. But quick responses are part of the value of the Internet, so let's learn how to reply and how to use some of the options. We'll cover replying, forwarding, redirecting and requesting a return receipt.

What's This Gibberish At The Top of My Messages?

The top of your e-mail contains several lines of text before the actual message. These extra lines are just above the body of the message and they identify the sender, give the date of the message plus its subject, and show the priority that the sender assigned to the message. But there's more.

In Microsoft Internet Mail, you can click **View, Preview Pane, Header Information** to see even more details about your message. In Outlook Express, you can click **File, Properties, Details** to see more information and, if that's not enough, you can click **Message Source** to see highly technical details.

All the extra text you see with these features—it's sometimes called "cruft"—traces the path the message followed to reach you and can help sort out—with the aid of an expert—any problems you might have with a message that is undeliverable. Fortunately, the e-mail applications we have given you hide the cruft so that you see cleaner messages.

Internet e-mail simplifies the task of replying to messages by automatically addressing the new message to the sender, entering your address and the subject, using the original subject as a pattern. You'll see at the top of the window the date and time of the original message, followed by the actual text of the message—marked off to stand out—and you'll be ready to type the reply message.

You'll be able to blend your reply into the original message. This makes it easy for the sender to follow your reply comments in context with the original. It's definitely different from replying to a traditional snail mail letter. Let's perform another Step-By-Step exercise now to learn how to reply.

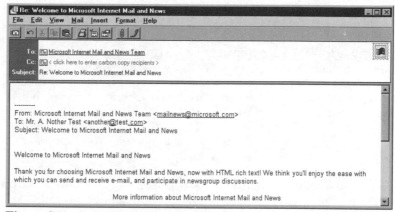

Figure 3 Reply window - the original message can be included

Step-By-Step

GOAL: Learn to reply to an e-mail message

✔ Click **Reply to Author**, or click **Mail, Reply to Author**.

✔ Review the **To:**, **From:** and **Subject:** lines (see Figure 3).

✔ Use your mouse to select text you want to cut then press **DELETE** or **CTRL+X**.

> Don't return the entire contents of the original message to your sender, this is extremely annoying unless it was no more than a couple of lines. Instead, leave just enough to provide a lead-in to your reply.

✔ Add blank lines between sections of the reduced message.

✔ Type your responses to each topic in turn (see Figure 4).

✔ Click **Send**.

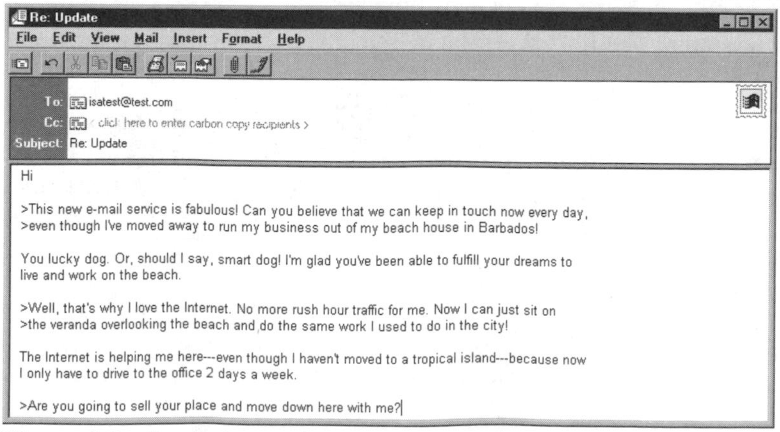

Figure 4 Reply window - after you've entered your responses

Frequently Asked E-Mail Questions

What if my addressee's computer isn't running right now?

Internet e-mail does not pass directly between the computers of its sender and its recipient. E-mail goes through a routing process similar to that of a regular, mailed letter. Instead of being handled by a series of people, however, e-mail is handled by a series of computers across the Internet until it ends up at the local post office—the mail server—of the recipient. Mail server computers run 24 hours a day so they can receive mail continuously. Your computer doesn't need to be running for you to receive e-mail any more than you need to be present at your local post office when a letter for you arrives on a mail truck.

E-mail is like regular mail that goes to a general delivery address: No postal carrier delivers the message from the post office. E-mail remains at the post office—on the mail server—until you go to get it. Fortunately, you can do that without leaving home.

E-mail software uses the Internet to ask the mail server if it's holding any mail for the recipient. If the mail server has any messages, it transfers them to the In box of your e-mail application where the mail can be read.

All those computers—can anyone else read my messages?

Yes, they can. Internet e-mail is not secure at all. This doesn't mean that anyone *will* read your mail. Do you imagine that a lot of postal workers read postcards that travel via regular mail? And what harm would be done anyway, even if someone did read it? Well, that depends on what you're saying, doesn't it! If you need to send secure messages, be sure to read the chapter on security.

How often should I check my mail?

You probably will check e-mail much more frequently than the postal carrier brings regular mail, but don't overdo it. An informal poll we took for this book revealed that some users spend up to two hours a day reading and replying to Internet e-mail. If you're expecting an important message, you can check more frequently, of course, otherwise a couple of times a day is customary.

Is there a limit to the size of an e-mail message?

Generally, the maximum file size allowed for Internet e-mail is 2 megabytes. If you're sending text files, that's enough to hold three or four full-length books. Graphics, sound files and video files, however, easily can exceed the limit. If you need to send files larger than 2 megabytes, have your service provider set up an FTP site for you. You can put up files of nearly any size, then send e-mail to the recipient with the URL, directory and filename so they can download the file when it's convenient for them and *after* they've determined they have enough free space on their computer.

Forward a message

Instead of replying to a message, you may want to forward it to another recipient. Perhaps if the message didn't interest you, but you know a friend would want to read it, you could forward it to her or him. The entire original message will be transferred and you probably should leave it intact, perhaps adding a comment of your own.

Step-By-Step

GOAL: Learn to forward an e-mail message

- ✔ Click **E-Mail Exercise 1** to see it in the message window.
- ✔ Click **Mail, Forward** or press **CTRL+F**.

    You also can click on the **Forward** button on the Toolbar.
- ✔ Type the new recipient's address.
- ✔ Review the **From:** and **Subject:** lines.

    Your name has been inserted as the sender, so the forwarded message will appear to the recipient to have come from you.
- ✔ Enter the addressee's information in the **To:** line.
- ✔ Press **TAB** until you reach the body of the message if you want to make any changes or additions to the text, then make the changes.
- ✔ Click **Send**.

Attachments

Any computer file can be sent along with an e-mail message as an "attachment." Attachments ride along across the Internet with e-mail messages and enable you to send word processing documents, spreadsheets, programs, configuration files, full-color drawings, photographs, charts and graphs, sound clips and video clips. The recipient gets the e-mail message in his or her normal In box and the attachment file or files are transferred into a designated "download" directory.

Attachments are easy to include and greatly expand the value of e-mail. Attachments can be a lot of fun. For example, you could attach a scanned, digitized photo to an e-mail message you send to a friend or family member.

Binary file attachments

The best format for sending attachments is the binary file option. If you choose the ASCII option, only plain, unformatted text can be sent. But with the binary option, you can send any computer file. Thus if you use binary to send a WordPerfect file to a friend or associate, the file will contain every graphic image, table and formatting command. If the recipient has the same version of WordPerfect, they'll see the file exactly as you created it. Let's learn to send an attachment, then learn to open an attachment you've received.

Step-By-Step

GOAL: Learn how to include with e-mail an attachment

- ✔ Start a new message to yourself.
- ✔ Type your own address on the **To:** line and press **TAB** twice.
- ✔ Type *E-Mail Exercise 2* and press **TAB**.
- ✔ Click **Insert, File Attachment**.

✔ Double-click on the **c:** folder to go to your root directory.

✔ Click on **autoexec.bat**, then click on **Attach**.

> The type, size and description will appear in the **Attachments** status bar at the bottom of the message. You can include multiple files within a message.

✔ Type in the body of the message *Practice e-mail with attachment*.

✔ Click **Send and Receive**.

The e-mail message will now be delivered via normal channels, but it will include the file you specified as an attachment. You might notice a slight increase in the time it takes for a message to be sent, especially if you send a very large file, such as a graphic image, a program or an audio/video clip.

TRANSMISSION TIMES

Transmitting a normal e-mail message does not place a major burden on Internet bandwidth. The transmission time is almost insignificant and no one has to wait and watch the file download anyway because mail is delivered to mailboxes even while the user isn't logged onto his or her mail server.

Attachments, however, bring the possibility of significant transmission time because you can include nearly any computer file. Still, even moderate-size graphics images won't encounter a noticeable delay in transmission. Nonetheless, quite a lot of Internet bandwidth is being squandered these days by people attaching huge graphics images to e-mail just to show a picture to a friend.

Finally—regardless of Internet bandwidth issues—before you attach a large file, you may want to verify that your recipient has enough free hard disk capacity to store files you plan to send as e-mail attachments.

Receiving an attachment

Your mail server now should have received the attachment practice document and we can retrieve it. Use the same steps outlined earlier because attachments do not require any special efforts on the part of the recipient. Retrieve it now.

The e-mail message itself will be in your normal In box and you'll see the attachment as an icon after you double-click on the message to open it.

So now let's look at the copy of your autoexec file. What happens in the next exercise, however, depends on how your system is set up. Your e-mail application is going to use your Win file associations to select an application to open the file. Most likely, this will be the Windows Notepad. The normal messages you receive probably will use your word processor, spreadsheet program, graphics software, or audio/video player.

Step-By-Step

GOAL: Verify the download of an attachment file

✔ Click the message with the attachment to display it.

✔ Right-click the attachment icon and then select an option from the menu. To save it, click **Save As. . .** then select a drive and directory.

If you're on a network, you can save the file anywhere on the network.

Attachments always create complete copies of all original files, so this is an exact copy of your autoexec.bat file. Your original file is never transmitted.

WinZip

Even though you've got a blazing fast connection to the Internet through your cable access service, most of the Internet still struggles with serious speed problems. And you won't be immune to those problems because Internet speed is like a chain—it's no better than its weakest link.

If you want to send large files as attachments to e-mail, you'll help everyone on the Internet if you'll compress your files so that they require less Internet bandwidth. File compression reduces the wasted space inside files so that they become smaller. They're not usable in their compressed form, but once they're uncompressed, they're perfectly restored.

The compression process is called "zipping" and the uncompressing process is called "unzipping." Zipping a file produces a second, smaller version—leaving the original completely intact on your system—that is anywhere from 10% to 90% smaller than the original. That could save a lot of Internet bandwidth.

You can download a nice utility called WinZip that will give you a highly user-friendly way in which to compress and uncompress files. The Win 95/98 version becomes a part of your Windows Explorer so you can compress files with a simple drag-and-drop operation.

WinZip is available online as shareware at *www.winzip.com*. After you install WinZip, register it via e-mail.

The next time you need to give someone a large file as an e-mail attachment, zip it up before you send it. Of course, they'll need an unzip program but if they don't have one you can tell them where you got yours.

Advanced Features

That completes our coverage of the basic e-mail features. The software you have does much more than the basic services we've shown, but the steps vary too much to show you in a book. Check out the Help file in your e-mail application if you want to become a "power user." Try out some of the resources listed below, too.

ORBITING IN CYBERSPACE

Four11 directory services
http://www.four11.com

Here's a Web page with links to several good directory services. Of course, the main feature is the Four11 Internet Mail Directory itself (see Figure 5). It's also got listings for Internet Web telephone addresses. This is a commercial service of the SLED Corporation, but they provide free basic listings for all Internet users as well as free searches. Of course they hope you'll sign up for their premium services.

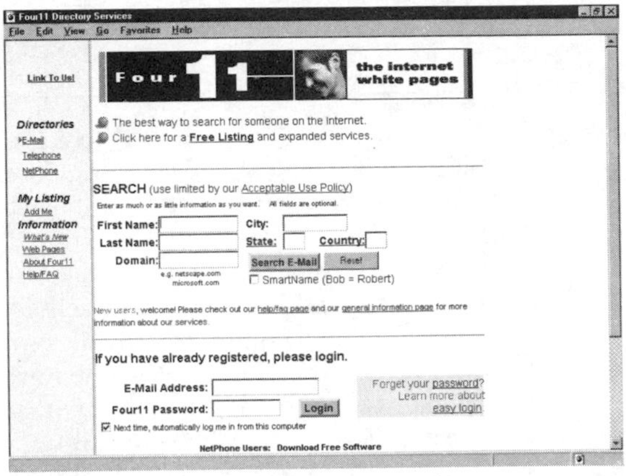

Figure 5 Four 11 Internet e-mail directory

Cool signature file ideas
http://www.coolsign.com

Want a new e-mail signature file? Something fun? Here's the place. Coolsig is the biggest signature collection on the Net. They have hundreds of files and ideas, grouped by category with a separate link for each: Students, Work, Religion, Politics, Quotations and many, many more.

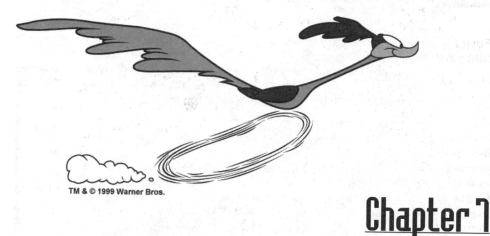

TM & © 1999 Warner Bros.

Chapter 7

A Global Community: Newsgroups

Newsgroups are global, electronic "bulletin boards," and each newsgroup serves as a central location for messages on one targeted topic. Related messages are "posted" in each newsgroup and anyone who looks at a newsgroup will see all the messages that have been posted to that group by other users. Theoretically anyone can access any newsgroup from anywhere in the world.

All of the Internet newsgroups, collectively, are called the Usenet and they are booming at an unprecedented growth rate. What's the attraction? Through newsgroups, everyone on the Internet can have a say in any topic that interests him or her and can read what others have to say on the subject. Because users can post questions to an entire group and get answers from all over the world, newsgroups have enhanced our sense of living in a global community. Through newsgroups, the Internet truly delivers "something for everybody."

There are thousands of newsgroups, and tracking them all would be a huge task. Actually, it would be impossible. Fortunately, your system includes an excellent newsreader that enables you to select—from the master list of all the groups on Road Runner—only the groups you choose to view on your computer.

The process of selecting newsgroups to view is called subscribing, although your system always has full access even to the newsgroups to which you are not subscribed. That probably sounds confusing right now, so we'll put it another way: subscribing and unsubscribing to newsgroups uses a process that is handled internally by your Microsoft News or Outlook Express newsreader. You cannot control the number or the subject matter of the groups that Road Runner sends you, but you can control the groups that are displayed on your computer.

Jargon Cutter

News server - A computer that receives Usenet newsgroups and makes them available via an Internet connection. News server use the Network News Transfer Protocol (NNTP) that let all types of computers enjoy access to newsgroups.

Any time you want to see a newsgroup to which you don't subscribe, you can subscribe and see the group's postings. There's no delay because all of the groups are available to you all the time and you control the ones you see. Similarly, if you unsubscribe to a group, your newsreader merely stops displaying that newsgroups's postings and that group remains available for resubscription.

How Many Newsgroups Are There?

How many can you stand?

As we researched this book, we found more than 30,000 public newsgroups. How many will you find? Well, there's no way to tell. It varies by system and we've only been counting the public newsgroups—it would be impossible to count them all because there are thousands of private newsgroups.

How many do you need? Road Runner delivers all of the major, well-known newsgroups available today—and we're adding new ones all the time. If you learn of a newsgroup that is not available to you, contact Road Runner and request that the group be added.

Jargon Cutter

Private newsgroups - Many organizations start their own newsgroup and restrict usage to people within the organization. These newsgroups can be used to coordinate projects and to exchange ideas between offices scattered all over the world. We'll have more information on starting a newsgroup later in this chapter.

Remember, if a newsgroup is available to you on your news server, then subscribing merely means that your newsreader automatically checks that group for new messages when you start your newsreader. We'll cover the actual steps to subscribe later, because we're first going to show you how to get the master list of all newsgroups and how to read a single newsgroup message.

Getting Started

Before you can read newsgroups, you'll have to download the master list of newsgroups that your news server provides. We'll give you a Step-By-Step exercise that will download the list and then another that will show you how to read the messages within the newsgroups that are on the list.

You'll find three basic components to your newsreader: the menus, the toolbar and the message window. If you've never opened your newsreader, the master list will be very short and only will contain the names of the lists that are provided as a default. Normally this is only one group, called *news.announce.newusers*. Don't worry, you'll soon see more newsgroups than you could ever use, so let's go get them now.

The first Step-By-Step newsgroups exercise will download the list of newsgroups that are on your news server. You should first start your newsreader. (NOTE: These software applications are subject to upgrading. Check your User Services Page for the latest version of the browser currently being supported by your cable company.) You will use either the Microsoft Mail Reader or Microsoft Outlook Express, depending on the system in use in your city. The procedures are very similar for both, and all of the screen images are taken from Microsoft Mail Reader.

Step-By-Step

GOAL: Learn to browse your newsgroups list

✔ Start your Road Runner Browser.

✔ Click **Go, Read News**.

✔ Click **News, Newsgroups** to get the list of current groups.

> There may be a delay the first time you do this as the reader downloads the list of groups. Double-click the title bar to maximize the size of the reader.

✔ Make sure the insertion point is in the top text entry box.

✔ Type **alt.quotations**.

> Listings that end with an asterisk lead to sub-topics. Clicking on a sub-topic expands the listing to increasingly specific levels. Some headers, such as **alt.***, have a lot of sub-topics and might require some time to download.

✔ Click on **alt.quotations** in the **All** box.

✔ Click **Subscribe** to subscribe, click **OK**.

> Click on the group list to see the number of unread messages in each group to which you have subscribed.

✔ To see the articles in the group, click on them and they'll appear in the lower window.

✔ Read the message.

Once you've subscribed to one or more groups, your newsreader will check those groups for new articles each time it starts. The results will be listed and you then can select any of the groups within which you want to see articles.

After you select a group, you'll see all of that group's current articles. The icon on the left margin shows whether or not you've opened that article. The name of the article's author also appears. And, the "thread" information shows you whether the article is an original, or is a response to an original by another author.

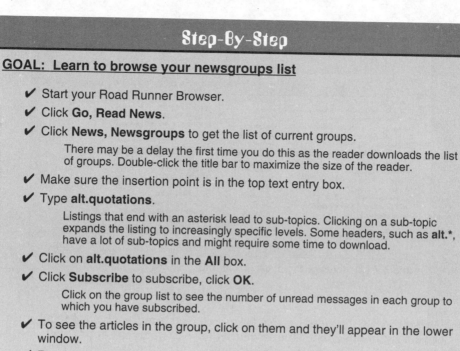

Figure 1 Subscribed groups example

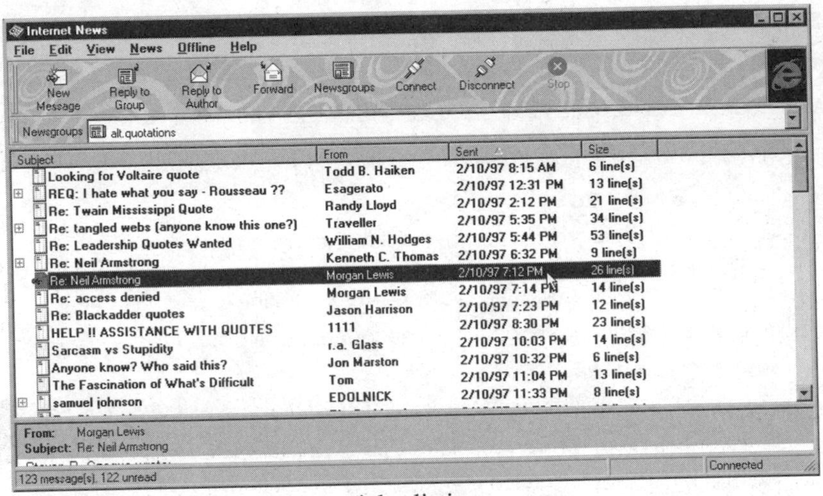

Figure 2 Typical newsgroup articles listing

In Microsoft News, the messages that have been read turn from bold to regular text. To see your list of subscribed groups, return to the list of groups by pressing **CTRL+W** or clicking on **News, Newsgroups**.

If someone replies to a reply, that article will be shown indented yet another level, etc. This hierarchical listing system creates a focused series of related messages. Threads help you easily track a newsgroup discussion.

Beep! Beep!

After you've downloaded the master list, every time you start your newsreader, it checks for new groups and adds them to the list. If you'd like to stop this from occurring automatically, you can change your settings.

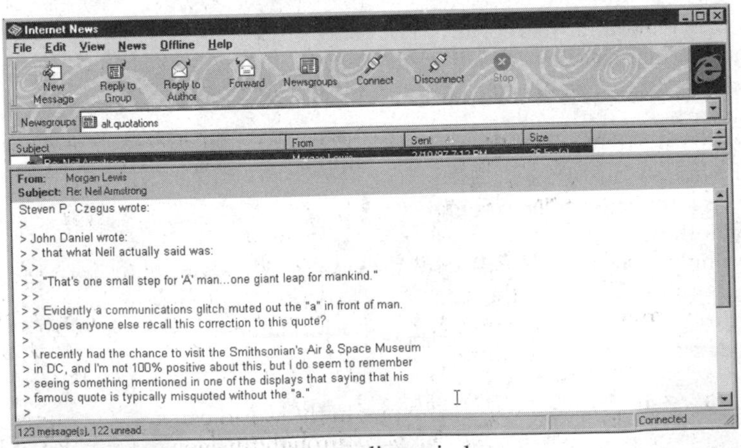

Figure 3 Typical newsgroup reading window

> **Beep! Beep!**
> You can control the degree to which your newsreader displays threads. By default, the threads are shown in a collapsed format. To expand the threads in Microsoft Mail, click **View, Expand** or **View, Collapse** as desired. In Outlook Express, click the **plus sign** or click **View, Expand** to see more and then click the **minus sign** to collapse a thread.

Subscribing and unsubscribing

Since the full list of newsgroups is so long, you'll appreciate the subscribe feature because it limits your view to only those newsgroups you choose. We subscribed to one in the previous exercise, but we want to show you how to go back and subscribe (or unsubscribe) to others. We'll show both processes in the next exercise.

Step-By-Step

GOAL: Learn to subscribe or unsubscribe to newsgroups

✔ Click **News, Newsgroups** or press **CTRL+W**.

✔ Click the **Subscribed** tab to see your subscribed groups.

✔ Click **All** to see all available newsgroups.

✔ Highlight the newsgroups to which you want to subscribe.

> You can use the **SHIFT** key or the **CTRL** key to select multiple groups.

✔ Click **Subscribe** to add the group(s) to the **Subscribed** tab.

> Be sure to check at least one that you don't want to keep so that later we can show you how to unsubscribe, or you can unsubscribe to alt.quotations.

✔ Click **OK** when you're finished.

✔ Select any group from the drop list **Newsgroups**.

✔ Click any message to read it.

> Sometimes, after seeing a few days worth of messages within a group, you'll decide to unsubscribe. Let's learn how to do that.

✔ Press **CTRL+W** to return to the groups listing.

✔ Click on a subscribe newsgroup that you wish to unsubscribe.

✔ Click **Unsubscribe**.

> Of course this newsgroup is still available to you at any time and you can restore it any time.

Replying

Often, reading an article will inspire you to jump in and share your views. If so, join the crowd, because we all get the same urge—newsgroups clearly show that natural human desire to have the last word. Replies are what keep the Usenet alive and humming. There are two ways to reply to an article:

❖ Post a follow-up article that everyone in the world can see. Of course, that's only if everyone in the world browses through this newsgroup, but at least it's there for anyone who wants to read it. Be careful what you post!

❖ Mail a reply directly to the author of the article you're reading and keep it between the two of you. This is a good choice either when you have a focused reply that would not interest general readers in the group or when you prefer to keep the reply private—well, as private as e-mail can be, anyway.

Beep! Beep!

You can view detailed information about any message by viewing the message and then with Microsoft Internet News, right-click the message, then select **Properties**. This will give you all kinds of details about the message's origin and the path it took across the Internet to your system. In Outlook Express you can click **File, Properties**.

The next exercise will show you how to reply to a newsgroup article. You should have an article on-screen from the last exercise. From there, we'll go to the reply function. The original message text will be included by default, but this is optional. Usually you can cut out most of it, leaving only enough so that your reply will make sense to other readers. Often, you can break up the article into chunks and insert immediately after each piece a reply that is tailored to that section of the original. Be sure to remove the original poster's signature file.

Step-By-Step

GOAL: Learn how to reply to an article

✔ Highlight an article.

✔ Click the **Reply to Group** button.

✔ Type your reply.

✔ Click **Send** to post the article to this newsgroup or click the **Close** button, then say **No** to return to the reader without posting.

   The **Send** button posts a public message to the entire newsgroup.

✔ Click **Reply to Author**.

✔ Type your reply.

✔ Click **Send** to post the article only to the original author or click the **Close** button, then say **No** to return to the reader without posting.

   This posts a private message to the original poster.

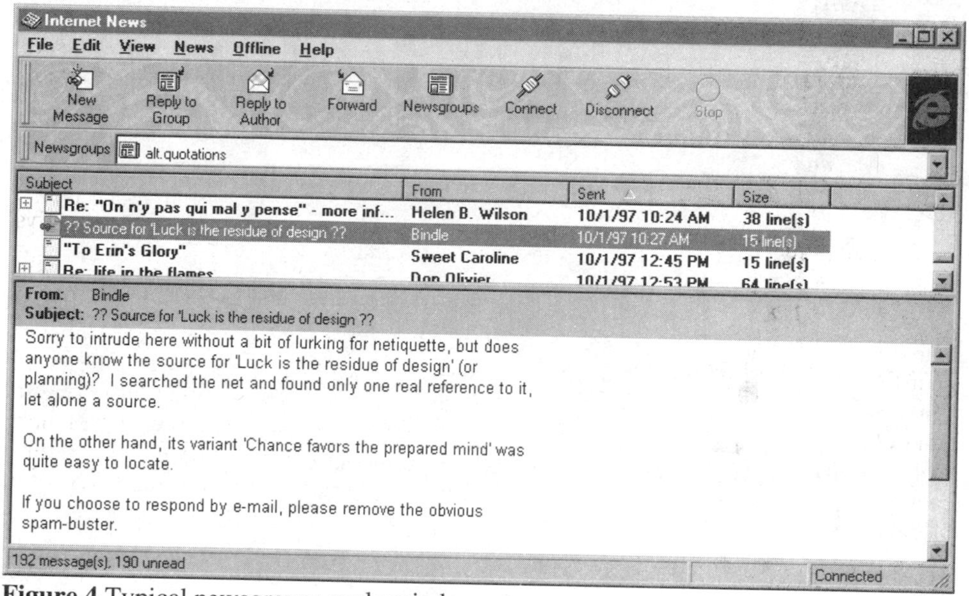

Figure 4 Typical newsgroups reply window

Posting an original newsgroup article

Sometimes you'll want to post an original idea to a newsgroup. Or, perhaps, you may have a question that you believe someone in the group might be able to answer. In either case, you'll want to create and post an original article for the newsgroup. It's basically the same as posting a follow-up, with one major exception: the subject line will be blank and you'll need to fill it in manually!

Step-By-Step

GOAL: Learn how to post an original newsgroup article

✔ Return to the list of articles in the **alt.quotations** groups.

✔ Click **New Message** to create a new message.

✔ Click in the **Subject** text entry box.

✔ Type *your own subject*.

   Leaving the subject line blank is a good way to get some of those flames you read about in the netiquette chapter!

✔ Press **TAB** to move the insertion point into the message body.

✔ Type the body of your message.

✔ Click **Send** to post the article to this newsgroup or click the **Close** button and say **No** to return to the reader.

✔ Click **File, Exit** or the **Close** button to close Microsoft Internet News.

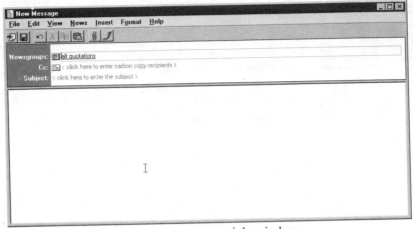

Figure 5 Typical new newsgroup new article window

Nine Keys to Newsgroup Success

There's much more to newsgroups than knowing the technical steps that you've learned. When you use newsgroups, you're jumping into a global realm that can literally reach anyone in the world. They are powerful communication tools that deserve a lot of respect, courtesy, discretion and common sense. These nine keys will help you to improve our global cyberspace community and to boost their potential value to you and your organization.

1) Get the FAQs
Almost every newsgroup has a FAQs (Frequently Asked Questions) file. Look for it or ask for it. Many questions you'll ask as a newbie to a group will already have been asked repeatedly. The established users of the newsgroup are tired of browsing through posts that ask the same old questions. Get the FAQs and *read* the FAQs before you get flamed for asking the group a "dumb newbie" question.

2) Lurk around first
Newsgroups can get quite personal and develop a timbre of their own. Each is slightly different. Until you've sampled that timbre, you don't know what might be considered offensive, rude or inappropriate. The proper term for sampling a newsgroup is "lurking." You know the kind of people who don't lurk: the same ones who butt into your verbal conversations. If you post to a newsgroup where you've never lurked, don't be surprised if you quickly get flamed.

3) Remember the global community
Lurking will help you abide by this principle. Newsgroups likely will have members from all over the world. Keep this in mind when you post. For example, if you live in the United States don't refer to the U.S. as "America." That's considered by people in other Americas to be arrogant. Also, ethnic and regional jokes will at best fall flat, could be misconstrued and might easily offend thousands of your fellow Interneters.

4) Forgive and forget

If you read something annoying, offensive, misplaced, misguided or just plain stupid, your best course of action is to forget it and move on. The Internet has enough band-width problems—it doesn't need electronic tennis matches of flames and counter-flames. Every group seems to have one or two people who never seem to have heard of netiquette and you'll come to know them quickly, so don't get upset with people who accidentally offend you. Save your flames for the really bad guys. Or, consider sending e-mail to a chronic repeater's ISP—you may get his account canceled, which you'll never do by getting involved in a flame war.

5) Follow the threads

Most interesting newsgroup articles evoke replies. And most up-to-date software links these posts together into "threads" that follow the same theme. Read the entire thread before posting a reply yourself. Several others may already have said the same thing. No one will appreciate reading your belated opinion that parrots what's already been said. Reading the whole thread also relates to the previous key—forgive and forget. If a post really has you steamed, you can count on it annoying others as well and they probably already have done plenty of flaming for you.

6) Short and sweet

Remember an ancient adage on writing that says, "I'm sorry this is so long... I didn't have time to make it short." We've got two tips for keeping your posts short.

First, keep them short. This actually takes longer than simply spewing forth every word on a topic that comes to mind. But the time you spend will be multiplied many times over by happy newsgroup members who in appreciation actually may read your post and actually may respond.

Second, don't make them long. You soon will get tired of wading through replies in newsgroups in which the respondent copied the entire text from the original post, which you just read. (These people often tack on only the clever reply, "I agree.") People can follow threads. You need not copy any more of a post than a brief con-textual reminder. Sure, it takes time to delete chunks of a post that don't need to be repeated, but the time you spend will be rewarded.

7) Put it where it belongs

Stick to the subject. Usually you can tell by the title, but make sure you're in the right place by lurking and reading the FAQs file. Post only when you're certain you're writing to the right audience. Posting to the wrong newsgroup wastes resources.

If you accidentally post to the wrong group, just forget about it. Similarly, if you see an accidental post, ignore it. One of the most annoying events in newsgroups often begins when someone accidentally posts to the wrong group, then six people post to say how silly this person is, then the person posts again to say to ignore the first post, which draws several more flames about brain size and family lineage, to which the original poster apologizes, then the apology draws a string of posts commenting on what a waste of resources this whole event has been. Twenty messages can cascade out of a single errant post. Post correctly and remember to forgive and forget when others slip—hopefully, they'll do the same for you.

8) Remember you're invisible

No one can see you smile on the Internet. No one can hear you chuckle. No one can see your tongue in your cheek. If you joke, don't assume that everyone understands that you're joking. Remember the global community. Jokes or twisted humor on newsgroups rarely come across as funny. If you must make a crack about something, at least use one of the emoticons we've listed in the netiquette chapter so that everyone will know that you *meant* it to be a joke. They still may not get the joke, but perhaps they'll understand you were *trying* to be funny and you won't get flamed.

9) Use e-mail when appropriate

Newsgroups are an excellent place to get answers to tricky or obscure questions. If you've read the FAQs file, lurked in the background for a while and followed all the threads, but still have a question—that's the time to post. But if the answer is not going to be of general use to the group, ask for replies by e-mail and make sure your e-mail address is included in your signature file at the end of your post. (It's supposed to be in the header, but a backup is a good idea.) Conversely, if you want to send a personal reply to a posted question, then use e-mail and spare everyone in the group the clutter of unnecessary, personal messages.

ORBITING IN CYBERSPACE

Dejanews
http://www.dejanews.com

DejaNews is a World Wide Web search engine for Usenet newsgroups. Even though it's a Web site, DejaNews has archived millions of Usenet postings. You can enter keywords and DejaNews will build a list for you of articles it pulls from its archives that contain those keywords. The basic searching service is powerful, but you're likely to find *too many* articles. You can narrow your search and increase your chances of finding exactly what you want by clicking on the *Power Search* icon. For even more control, click on the <u>Create a Query Filter</u> link so you can filter the search by newsgroup, by date range and by author.

Farcast
http://www.farcast.com

Farcast™ is an alternative to newsgroups. It's an agent-based, personal news and information service. Farcast lets you browse and search its collection of news, press releases, reference material and stock quotes. The service is available interactively 24-hours-a-day or you can contract with Farcast to automatically send you news articles from a wide range of topics. Farcast offers its service for a flat-rate fee, and they offer a free trial period.

Phase 3

Phase 3: Cyberspace

Now that you've learned how to use the basic tools, we want to show you some valuable things you can accomplish on the Web. We've included chapters that help you find specific information and do online research in major libraries all over the world. You'll also learn about how governments are getting into cyberspace and how you can interact with them. Then we'll close Phase 3 with business tips.

Consider these chapters to be just the start of your Web surfing. No book could contain it all! The Web is growing daily, but that's the beauty of the whole system. There's so much out there in cyberspace that everyone can have it his or her own way. And, if you don't find what you want today, just check back later.

As you use these chapters, keep in mind the Favorites Folders feature that you learned about in the Road Runner Browser chapter. Be sure to mark sites to which you plan to return. And a final reminder before you jump into all the Web sites in these chapters—remember that your Road Runner service also is a valuable resource for locating information. You're lucky because you're not limited to the standard Web services—in addition to everything that everyone else has, you have Road Runner!

❖ **Chapter 8** presents a starter-set of **cool Web sites** so you can do some fun surfing right away. After a while you'll have plenty of your own favorite Web sites, but until then, these ought to keep you busy.

❖ **Chapter 9** is about a Web feature called **search engines**. Search engines are Internet tools that search the World Wide Web for information you want to find—and it's a good thing they do. With all the information on the Web today, the proverbial *needle in a haystack* would be easy to find by comparison.

❖ **Chapter 10** uses a completely different approach to help you find information via the Web. It features online **bookstores, libraries, encyclopedias** and other reference sources. You can tap into some vast resources right from the computer in your own home. We think you'll be astounded at what you can find using the sites we present here.

❖ **Chapter 11** shows you how to access **government** services via the Web. Have you ever tried to track down a copy of your birth certificate? It just about took you forever, right? Well, now the Web can zip you directly to your hometown records. Only a few government agencies are truly set up to do business across the Web, but that's changing rapidly and you'll be ready when they are.

❖ **Chapter 12** presents an array of **business tips**. You'll see how to manage home finances and investments and you'll get tips on buying and selling businesses and on small business marketing. We even show you how to proceed if you'd like to buy or sell a home on the Web.

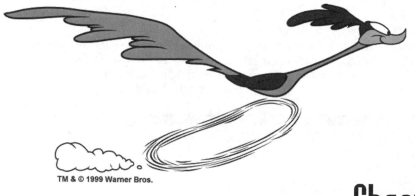

Chapter 8

What to See First: Cool Web Sites

Since you've subscribed to Road Runner, you've most likely heard about many amazing, exciting, interesting and enjoyable things that you can see and do on the Internet. Most of what you've heard about are things that you can see and do on the World Wide Web. As you learned in the Quick Tour chapter, there's more to the Internet than just the World Wide Web. Realistically, however, the Web is where you'll spend most of your time and find the best things to see and do.

But the Web is so vast that it's difficult to know where to begin. So we're going to give you some starting points. These aren't things that we endorse or support, they've just been selected to give you an overview of what's out there on the Web. The rest of the chapters in Phase 3 will present Web sites by category and will help you understand how to use some of them for your work or play.

Once you get started, you'll quickly develop your own set of favorites. Then, you'll find that browsing those favorites will lead to more, and to more, and to... well, let's just say that we give you our best wishes for an enjoyable cyberspace adventure.

Beep! Beep!
If you skipped the Road Runner Browser lesson, you'll benefit from reading it before you jump into this chapter. At least read about the Favorites Folders so you'll know how to record your favorite Web sites when you see things to which you want to return. And, there are plenty of other good tips in that chapter that will make your cyber-surfing more enjoyable and more productive.

Site Sampler

We'll begin by presenting a light and lively sampler of selected Web sites. We selected these sites because they'll be interesting to most people and because they show off what the Web can bring you, as well as the advanced features of the Road Runner Browser.

Smithsonian

The Smithsonian Institution has been around for more than 150 years and they've chronicled the world's technological progress. Now they're even using the latest in technology to report to you about technology—and much, much more (see Figure 1). Yes, the venerable Smithsonian Institution has taken the leap into cyberspace.

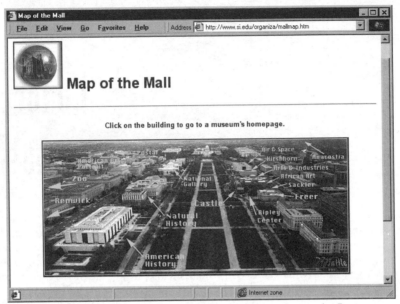

Figure 1 The Smithsonian - A great place to get to know the Internet

Since we've already given you the chapter on how to use your Road Runner Browser, we'll assume in this chapter that you know how to load a Web site. So, we'll just give you the URL of these sites and leave it to you to get there. This one is located at: *www.si.edu/organiza/mallmap.htm.*

This opening page is a user-friendly example of a clickable map graphic. You'll see that all of the major attractions on the Mall in Washington are labeled. When you decide what you want to see, you can click on the label or on the building to jump to the associated Web site.

If there were nothing else on the Web, you could almost justify having an Internet connection for this Mall map alone. It makes a terrific addition to your Favorites Folder. Once you've marked it you can come back for research projects, school reports, general curiosity or just for something to do on a rainy day.

NASA

NASA really has the space angle covered—real outer space and now cyberspace. They've got one of the most popular sites on the Internet. This, too, is a good example of a clickable map (see Figure 2). You can select a general topic and then surf off into a wealth of cascading sites that cover everything NASA does. To get started, jump to *www.nasa.gov* and then click on whatever looks like fun.

A really fun way to start is by clicking on the Human Space Flight link. After that you can click on the Space Flight link and find a vast store of information and images from space. Do you want to know about the next Shuttle flight? No problem, they're scheduled well in advance. So far in advance that you can even read about the Shuttle Atlantis' mission that's scheduled for launch on January 18, 2001! And you thought *2001: A Space Odyssey* was only a movie!

Figure 2 NASA - cyberspace is fun, but this is for real

If you have a color printer, you might enjoy downloading color images of the patches worn by the astronauts on each mission as well as loads and loads of images taken during the missions. They even have complete biographies of all the astronauts that you can print—in full color, of course.

Beep! Beep!

The Smithsonian and the NASA sites are easy to use because of their user-friendly, clickable graphic images. Most Web surfers, however, find these sites to be annoying - because the graphics require so long to load. But with your cable modem, you can use graphic-intensive interfaces such as these without dreading long download times. And, both sites are rich in images you can download. For example, NASA regularly presents spectacular, up-to-date images from its missions. These images are very large, however, which means that the download time is too long for many Web surfers, but you can download almost anything you want in a reasonable amount of time.

Star Trek Holodeck 3

Now that we've started down the space travel path, how about some fictional space exploration? Okay, let's beam over to the Star Trek Holodeck 3, which will bring you some impressive sights and sounds. The fun starts with the fanfare sound track on the home page (see Figure 3) and then takes off from there. You won't find a much better use of Web graphics anywhere in cyberspace.

We hope that your computer includes a sound card and speakers. The Internet is rapidly becoming a full multimedia experience and this site is a good demonstration of what's

Figure 3 Star Trek Holodeck 3

coming. In other words, if you think this is cool... things are only getting better. Even if you're not a Star Trek fan, visit *www.holodeck3.com* to at least get a glimpse of what a fun Web site can do and what your Road Runner Browser can do.

MapQuest

Space travel—whether fictional or real—is very exciting and a lot of fun, but it's time to get Scotty to beam us back down to Earth now. Where will you go once you land back here? Anywhere you like if you start with MapQuest (see Figure 4) at *www.mapquest.com*.

Figure 4 Map Quest - anywhere on Earth

This site gives you some insight into the problems that Web authors face in developing sites to look good on a wide variety of computers. For example, in Phase 4 of this book, you'll learn in the Web publishing chapter about the problems of writing for different screen resolutions in Windows. The MapQuest site solves this by letting you select a Web page tailored to your screen. If you don't know which choice to select when you see the menu of screen options, you can skip over to the chapter on Web publishing and read about Windows screen resolutions.

> ### Beep! Beep!
> Save this site in your Favorites Folder for the next time you take a cross-country road trip. Before you leave, visit this site, click on the <u>Trip Quest</u> link and enter the starting city and the destination city. Within seconds, you'll get a complete set of directions that you can print and take along. It can give you directions between more than 150,000 cities and towns in the U.S., Canada and Mexico!

This site gives you a demonstration of the ActiveX capabilities of your Road Runner Browser. ActiveX runs a program on your computer as if you had bought it and installed it on your system. It is a lot of fun—mostly because your high-speed cable modem service so easily handles the high graphic demands of this site.

Jargon Cutter

ActiveX - New technology that merges the power of your computer with the Internet. ActiveX takes the Internet beyond static text and picture documents to give you a new generation of active, exciting and useful experiences. ActiveX lets Web developers build applications that offer enhanced functionality and productivity beyond basic HTML document sharing.

Games and Programs

The Internet has launched a revolution in the software industry. Traditional retailing methods—such as stores with boxed products on a shelf—have not applied well to selling software. It's sort of the equivalent of selling apples in shrink-wrapped boxes; you've got to pay for it without seeing it and you know that it began to spoil the moment it was boxed.

The Internet has solved many of the software industry's distribution problems by making applications available instantly. The products now don't have to be sealed in shrink-wrapped boxes and shipped to stores to sit on shelves where they age. Instead, the Internet lets you go straight to the orchard, wander through the trees to see what you want and then grab the freshest version and use it immediately.

Another benefit to cyber-software is that you can obtain upgrades online as well. Instead of waiting for an upgrade to come to your store, you can have it almost instantly. And, software companies that use the Internet for distribution have incentives to upgrade more often than when the products went through stores because an upgrade doesn't create a warehouse of obsolete products.

Shareware

The Internet also has been a boon for the *shareware* industry. Shareware is software that you get to "try-before-you-buy." That means you can download it, install it and test it free. If you like the software and plan to use it, then you're expected to register with the author and pay a fee. It's a cool deal for you because you don't have to pay for software until you know that it works for you. And the shareware distribution system is so inexpensive that authors can offer software at very low prices.

Some shareware lets you download a full, working version right at the beginning. This means that they're trusting the honor system. We encourage you to take the time to register because it's in everybody's interest to keep a steady flow of top-flight shareware on the Internet. Many shareware products, however, automatically stop working after a trial period. Once it quits, you'll need to pay the registration fee and get a code that will bring the software back to life.

One of the best shareware sources anywhere is C/NET. Check them out at *www.shareware.com* (see Figure 5). They have hundreds of thousands of shareware titles and the supply grows steadily.

This site will let you casually browse the categories and titles and it lets you jump straight to an application by entering a keyword search. If

Figure 5 C/NET - Shareware for every need

you can't decide where to start, why not just select the "Title of the Day" and be surprised! This Web site is an excellent Favorites Folder candidate because it can bail you out at those times when you need some software *today*!

Shareware for Kids

Our previous selection certainly has enough shareware for everybody, but if you're looking for shareware for kids and don't want to tackle more than 200,000 titles, then try this site at *www.kidsdomain.com* (see Figure 6).

Figure 6 Kids' Domain - For kids of all ages

At this site, you'll start by selecting a major category, such as <u>Kids</u> or <u>Grownups</u>, or <u>Reviews</u>. If you select the <u>Download</u> link, you can choose between Windows or Mac versions of most software. The download (see Figure 7) is a good candidate for your Favorites Folder because you'll then be able to bypass the normal home page and jump straight to the software.

On the download page, you can get commercial demos by scrolling down to the bottom of the pages and clicking a <u>Demos</u> link. This a great resource for cyber-parents because they can evaluate software for their kids *before* they buy it at a store. It's not quite shareware, but it's better than a shrink-wrapped box on a store shelf. Cyber-parents will also find the reviews to be valuable.

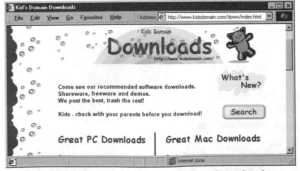

Figure 7 Windows and Mac software downloads

Family Sites

Okay, since we've started on the family idea, we won't stop now. Families are a major force on the Internet. There are Web sites for just about every aspect of families and family life that you can imagine.

In this section, you'll discover organizations that scour the Internet looking for safe, wholesome family fun. You'll learn about software companies that can help you monitor your family's Internet usage and restrict certain types of content. And you'll find sites that serve as centers for family-oriented material.

The Dove Organization

As you browse the Web looking at family sites, you might notice the seal of approval from The Dove Foundation (see Figure 8). They're a non-profit organization that encourages and promotes the creation, production and distribution of wholesome family entertainment. To learn what's behind that "Family Approved" seal, you can visit Dove's Web site at *www.dove.org*.

There's more here than just cyberspace help, too. Be sure to scroll down past this home page to the graphic image of their links. You then can click on any category that interests you.

In addition to helping you find wholesome Internet sites, the Dove Foundation has a rating list of more than 1,500 family-approved movies. This service is tied in with a video sales service they offer as well as a Children's Hospital movie channel. Their movie channel provides wholesome, uplifting movies to patients in every children's hospital in the U.S. and to their families staying in neighboring Ronald McDonald Houses. This entertainment is free to

Figure 8 Dove Foundation - Family Web sites

the patient and is shown on a dedicated channel on the TV in their rooms.

Family PC Fun

This is the Web site of a Sunday newspaper comic strip that each week features new family-oriented Web sites, Windows utilities, special Internet tips and a Web site created by a featured family. You can reach the site at *www.familypcfun.com*, (see Figure 9). In addition to new features each week, there's an archive of the sites featured in all past editions of the strip—just scroll through the listings in the "Archive" area on the home page.

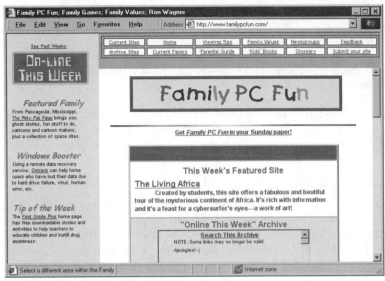

Figure 9 Family-friendly Web resources

Of course parents will find plenty of interesting things to see and do here along with the kids. There are links such as <u>Parental Guidance</u>, <u>Family Values</u>, and <u>Newsgroups</u> that connect you to family-related Internet information. And, if you have a family Web site of your own, you can click <u>Submit your site</u>, and maybe see yourself in the funny papers!

The CyberMom

The Internet not only has sites just for kids, but it also has sites just for parents. Almost any modern-day mom with Internet service will enjoy the activities, news, chat rooms and reading material at *www.thecybermom.com* (see Figure 10).

The Web site is organized as a house with virtual rooms. You can run all over the house jumping from room-to-room—pretty much the way the kids do when they're home. But in this house you'll never trip over toys on the stairs! For starters, you can visit the virtual bedroom and go to the virtual night stand where you'll find reviews of some non-virtual books—that means *real* books.

Figure 10 The CyberMom - Come on in and relax

The Play Room includes reviews of children's movies, books and software. In the Back Yard, you can share gardening tips. The Kitchen lets you exchange recipes and cooking tips. Throughout the house, you'll see coffee cup icons that link to related chat rooms in which you can discuss "mom" issues with other online women.

The CyberMom also is a good place for frequent visits because they have regular, on-going polls in which you can participate and share your own views. The site (at *www.thecybermom.com*) also features a selected Web site of the day that will give you an ever-expanding overview of other interesting information on the Web.

<u>Families in Yahoo!</u>

If you want to create a family Web site, Yahoo! will show you thousands of examples from other families. Of course, the Yahoo! list hasn't been screened as it has with the Family PC Fun Featured Family sites, so be prepared for just about anything!

Once you've launched your family into cyberspace orbit, be sure to submit it to Yahoo! so other families can find your site. Submitting your site is very easy. Once you've got your URL, just visit the Yahoo family page by jumping to *www.yahoo.com* and then going to Entertainment:People:Families. When you get to that page, click on the Submit button and follow the instructions.

Within a few weeks of submitting your family's Web site, anyone on the Internet will be able to go to Yahoo! and find you just by entering your name.

<u>Miscellaneous</u>

The Internet has opened a global communications channel that permits each of us to find something interesting, something valuable or something special. Any topic that can be imagined can now have a Web site and reach the world. A whole new frontier of information has opened up for highly-specialized and narrowly-focused topics. We'll close this chapter with a glimpse at a few examples, just to give you an idea of what's out there on the cutting edge of originality. Remember, though, this sampling is far, far smaller than the proverbial "tip of the iceberg."

Atomic Time

Personal computers are infamous for their lousy clocks. You'd think that for a couple thousand dollars, your computer's internal clock might do better than plus or minus a few minutes each month. Well, we're all stuck with lousy clocks, but the Internet now makes it simple and quick to reset our computer clocks to match the cesium atomic clock maintained by the atomic clock in Boulder, Colorado. Don't worry, you can't get a dose of radiation in cyberspace!

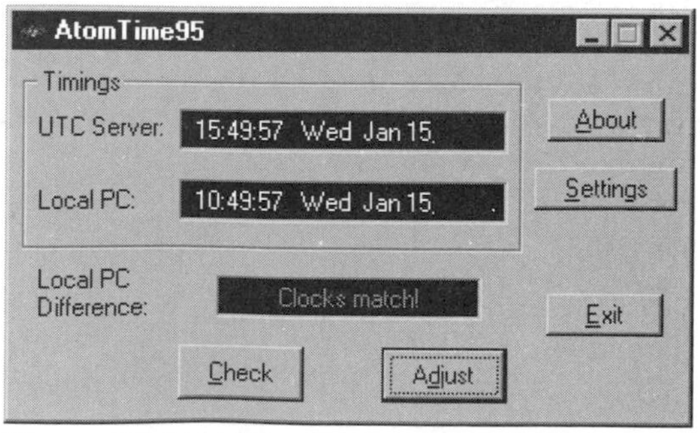

Figure 11 AtomTime updates your PC clock

The key is to download the Internet software client AtomTime (see Figure 11). You can find it by doing a Web search through most of the Internet search engines or you can go to *omni.cc.purdue.edu/~xniu/winsock/win3/utility.htm*, where you'll also find a fabulous collection of other valuable and interesting Internet tools. AtomTime is easy to install. Copy the downloaded zip file into a new directory and expand it. You'll get two files, atomtime.exe and atomtime.doc. The .doc file is the user manual and the other file is that program and can set your system's time.

> ### Beep! Beep!
> By adding a shortcut to this application in your Start folder and turning on all three checkboxes on the Settings/Execution page, AtomTime will automatically connect to the atomic clock and update your PC clock every time you start Windows 95. After updating the clock, the application will then exit. All of this will happen in the background. If you want AtomTime to update your clock automatically, but not every time you start Windows 95, you can install the Windows 95 Plus! package and use the System Agent application to schedule when to run AtomTime95.

Webopædia

The PC Webopædia is a top source for accurate, up-to-date information about personal computers. You can enter a search term or browse through its categories, and find a host of information that will help your PC run more smoothly and productively.

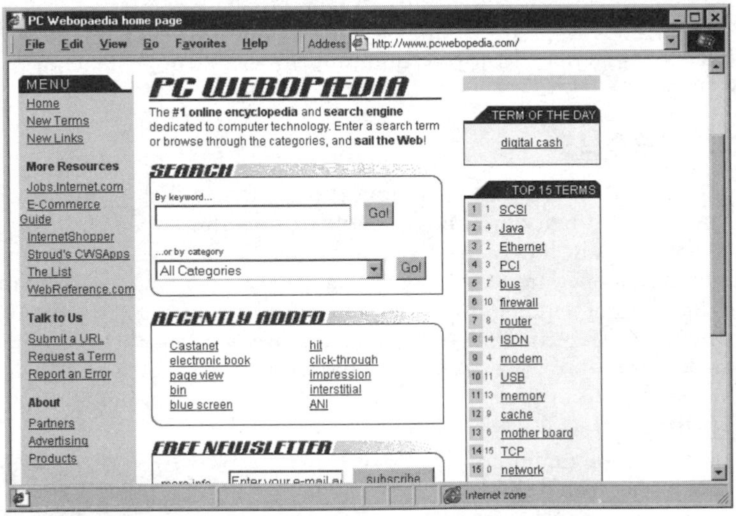

Figure 12 Webopædia - Help for PC users on all levels

It includes a rich glossary of terms that will help even an experienced user keep up with the speeding changes in the PC industry and the Internet. The Webopædia home page at *www.pcwebopedia.com* (see Figure 12) also includes a link to a library of shareware that will bring you some of the latest and greatest PC utilities, games and Internet software.

Summary

We hope you've enjoyed our brief overview of these examples of interesting Web sites. There's more out there than you can imagine, and we know you didn't get Road

Runner to see only Web sites that someone else selects for you. Fortunately, the Internet itself has tools that help you locate exactly what you want from the mass of over-information. At the end of this chapter, we've given you a few links that will help you find off-beat and interesting Web sites. Then move on with us to the next chapter and we'll show you how to find just about anything you want, when you want it.

ORBITING IN CYBERSPACE

The GamePen
http://www.gamepen.com

The GamePen offers games to download as well as online, real-time games that let you play directly in cyberspace. They also publish reviews of cyberspace games and present forums for gaming tips and news. This Web site supports not only Windows users, but Mac, Saturn and PlayStation. And, if you've been dreaming about writing your own computer game, but don't know how to get it in circulation, be sure to hit the JobPen link to discover job opportunities in the computer gaming world.

Seven Wonders of the Web
http://www.penncen.com/7wonders/7wonders.html

This site offers a revolving selection of fresh, leading-edge Web sites. If you add this site to your Favorites Folder and check it weekly, you'll see some amazing things over the years. There's something for everybody and even a few things for practically nobody! If a weekly menu of Web Wonders isn't enough, be sure to search through the archives listing for past selections. And, as you surf the Web looking for cool sites, keep in mind that you can submit your own selections to the folks at Seven Wonders. You might even submit a site that you created yourself!

Intermind
http://www.intermind.com

The Intermind Communicator™ makes it easy for everyone to get just the information they want from the Web, without repetitive searching, without bookmarking, and without sacrificing personal privacy. It also makes it possible for anyone to publish information on the Web that is delivered automatically to everyone else who wants to receive it, customized to each person's individual interests. It uses a new Internet tool, called a *Hyperconnector*™ that creates a tailored link between you, the subscriber, and a Web site that publishes information you want to receive. You can customize your Hyperconnector so that the Web site knows what you want it to send. This is a very new—and somewhat experimental—service right now, but it will evolve rapidly. It's the cutting edge of what's cool on the Web and you'll soon see it used by many of the Web sites you visit.

The Global Schoolhouse
http://www.gsn.org

The Global SchoolNet Foundation (GSN), a 501(c)(3) nonprofit corporation, is a major contributor to the philosophy, design, culture and content of Internet-based learning (see Figure 13). Their mission is to "harness the power of the Internet" to provide ongoing opportunities to support learners both in and outside of the school environment. GSN offers a variety of free support services to learners, but more importantly they provide the "training wheels" needed to get started! They collaborate with individuals, schools, businesses and community organizations to design, develop, and manage hundreds of collaborative learning projects each year.

Figure 13 The Global Schoolhouse

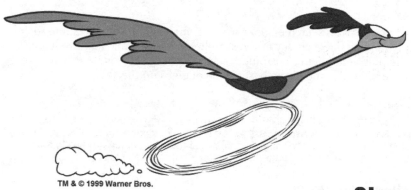

TM & © 1999 Warner Bros.

Chapter 9

Finding Your Way: Internet Searches

We wanted to start this chapter by telling you that the Web was growing like... but, what? We couldn't think of a metaphor to describe it because nothing has ever grown like the Web. Then we got it: the Web *is* the metaphor. Someday, we might say that something else is growing like the Web. But for now, *nothing* has ever grown like the Web since the Big Bang. Hey, that's it: "the Web is the Big Bang of cyberspace!"

Just as the Big Bang created too many stars to count, the Web has created too many documents to count. Fortunately, you're not going to need to count Web documents because a major part of the Web explosion has been Web searching services that can help you find the *stars* in cyberspace.

These Web searching services are called search engines and before long we might not even be able to count their number. Their phenomenal growth is no surprise because people are drawn to sites that deliver value and Web search engines are the most valuable sites on the Web.

Without search engines the Web would be like a phone system that had neither telephone books nor directory assistance—you would only be able to use a site if someone gave you its location. But with search engines you can locate Web documents based on keywords or topics that interest you. They're like a phone book, directory assistance, library card files and Sherlock Holmes all rolled into one.

Search Engine Principles

Web search engines are almost too powerful for their own good—or for your own good. You are unlikely to ever have a problem finding *something* on a given topic, but you may have a lot of trouble sifting through what you find to get *something you need*. There are tricks to using the search engines that will greatly enhance your success at locating targeted information.

We'll look first at how Web search engines work. Then we'll move on to some searching tricks that will hone the accuracy of the searches you perform. Next, we'll give you some tips on helping your clients, customers and prospects find your site. Then we'll close with an overview of some of the best search engines on the Web.

> ## Beep! Beep!
> Metasearch - Web sites that are made up of links to a wide variety of Web search engines. Some of them are no more than a collection of search engine links and some are actually interactive and will simultaneously submit your search request to several Web searching services. See page 109 for more on metasearch.

How search engines work

All search engines are based on computer-indexed information. Using a variety of methods, search engine developers gather information from around the Web and then store it and index it. Web search engines use two different, basic approaches that enable you to locate the information they have indexed.

One approach presents a list of categories. These categories are broken down first by major topic and then each major topic is broken down into an increasingly detailed hierarchy of subtopics. The search service lets you browse through its topical index to see the Web documents it has stored. Of course you have to guess the category under which your information might be located. Since there are no standards for dividing information into categories, you might have difficulty guessing the category under which the site's managers stored the information you want.

The second approach lets you perform a keyword search on the engine's indexed documents. This means that the search engine will give you a list of documents that contain a keyword, or keywords, that you specified. Since keyword searches don't rely on categories, they produce documents from a wide variety of topics—many of which may have nothing to do with the information you were seeking. Keyword searches are based on *boolean logic*.

> ## Boolean Logic
> Boolean logic is a mathematical system consisting of a set of elements and operators that specify relationships between the individual elements. The system was devised in 1854 by the Irish mathematician George Boole. Internet search engines use three important Boolean operators: AND, OR and NOT.
>
> These operators are important tools for you in using search engines because they can be used to widen searches or narrow searches to get the results you need. We'll illustrate their use with the three words, "hot air balloon."
>
> ### Using AND
> If you wanted to find hot air balloon sites on the Web, you actually need to search for documents that contain all three words "hot" and "air" and "balloon." Otherwise your search would produce a huge list of documents that contained any one of those words. The words could be entered as "hot AND air AND balloon" but most sites assume the AND operator if you don't specify anything between words. In other words, a space is an AND operator. Some search engines use a "+" symbol instead of the word AND.

Using OR

Since AND is the default for most sites, if you actually wanted to find pages that had any one of those words, you would have to enter "hot OR air OR balloon." But stand back if you do because the list might melt down your PC. You'd be getting every indexed document that contained the word "hot" or that contained the word "air" or that contained the word "balloon." Can you imagine the number?

Using NOT

The NOT operator can be used to eliminate pages that contain a certain word. For example, if you searched for "hot AND air NOT balloon" you would get just the "hot air" Congressional sites in Washington because all of the "hot air" sites that also contained the word "balloon" would be eliminated.

Read the directions

For the best search success, you need to know the default Boolean operator for the engine you're using. For example, if you enter *hot air balloon*, most sites use AND between the words, thus giving the highest priority to documents that contain all three words. But some will treat each word separately unless you use *hot AND air AND balloon*. And others might require you to enter the words in quotation marks, *"hot air balloon."* There's no substitute for reading the directions to be sure of the rules and the tricks. In fact, many of the engines, such as Excite, jump you to a user-friendly screen that can greatly increase your search accuracy with little extra effort.

Improving your search success

In addition to using Boolean logic in your searches, some search engines let you specify wildcards, similar to the wildcards you use in DOS filenames. For example, you could use "hot air balloon*" to find "hot air balloon," "hot air balloons," and "hot air ballooning." That's a very simple example, but wildcards can spell the difference between quick success and nagging frustration if you aren't sure how to spell a word.

 ## Jargon Cutter

Wildcards - Symbols that can substitute for other characters. The asterisk (*) usually represents zero or more characters and the question mark (?) usually represents a single character.

Wildcards can also be valuable in searching for someone by name. For example, if you were trying to find Peter A. Russell, the author of the book *The Global Brain*, you could search for "Pete* Russell" to find strings that begin with "Pete," have any number of characters in between (including zero) and that end with "Russell."

Another tool is the substring search. A substring is a portion of text that's contained within a longer string. Fortunately, most search engines automatically look for substrings. In the Peter Russell example, looking for "Pete Russell" would find pages with "Peter" and "Russell" because "Pete" is a substring of "Peter."

A few sites allow "natural language" searches. These are convenient and require the least thought, but then again, the results they produce may be less accurate. An example of a natural language search could be "I want to find all of the sites that talk about hot air balloons." The search engine would use a pre-programmed set of rules to eliminate the words it found to be extraneous and then search on the remaining words. You can't be sure, however, which words will be stripped and which will be included in the search.

Helping Others Find Your Page

If you create your own Web site, which we'll show you how to do in a later chapter, it's important to tailor your Web pages so that others can more easily find your site when they're using a search engine. You can find lots of examples of what *not* to do. One lousy example is making the title of your Web page "Welcome to Our Home Page!" But that's a perfect title if you want to attract visitors who've gone hunting for "Welcome" or "Home Page."

Create an accurate title

The title of your Web page doesn't have to be pretty. It's only going to show up in the title bar at the top of your browser's screen. The words in the title are going to be indexed into the search engines. But many Web sites waste the power of the title by using something nondescript. If you create a Web page, be sure to include a good selection of keywords that other people might use if they wanted to find something that you've included on your site. You've got only about a dozen words or so, so use them wisely.

SUBMITTING YOUR OWN SITE

There are two ways to submit your own URLs to search engines so other people can find your site. First, you can physically go around to every search engine with which you want to be listed and look for their submission link. Second, you can visit a comprehensive submission Web site that handles multiple submissions to most of the Web's best-known search engines.

Each method has its own edge. The advantage of using a submission service is obvious: you use a one-stop, time-saving site that minimizes your workload. The advantage to doing it yourself is more subtle: you get to be more careful that your site is indexed in the best category and that your listing is consistent with the pattern of other listings on that service.

We suggest that you try one or two manually to get the idea of how your listing looks after it's been indexed. You may be surprised by the keywords that are featured or by the title. You can't control the search engine, but you can control your pages. If you're not happy with the early results, delete the experimental listings, edit your Web pages, then resubmit and check the results after they have been indexed. After a few of these experiments you'll have a better idea of whether to do the rest of them yourself or use a consolidated service. In either case, you'll have refined the indexing ability of your pages.

Submit It!

This is a completely free submission service, supported by paid advertising, that handles all of the major search engines. You can visit it at *www.submit-it.com*. While you're there, you can test their metasearch engine.

> ### The PostMaster
>
> Try the PostMaster at *www.netcreations.com/postmaster*, another submission service. Before completing the lengthy submission form, be sure to read the FAQs file. This is intended to be a fee-based service, though they do allow some "Try Before You Buy" experimenting. But if you don't follow their terms when you post your free submission, they'll bill you for the full fee.

Keywords

Make sure that your Web site has some appropriate keywords near the top of the home page. Some search engines score documents by the location of the keywords, giving greater weight to keywords found high in your home page. And HTML has special codes that let you specify keywords for search engines.

Choose categories carefully

Finally, one important key to successfully being found can lie in going into each site individually to submit your page. By browsing the site thoroughly you can learn the most appropriate heading under which to place your site's URL. And you can learn if the engine allows you to submit multiple headings. Yahoo! is an excellent example. It allows you to list under multiple headings and it's got so many headings that you have to be careful to choose the ones you expect your visitors to try.

Web Search Engines

Web searching services are much like broadcast television networks. Most of them include paid advertising (like NBC or Fox) and some of them are public services (like PBS stations) that are funded by corporations or universities. And, as with broadcast television, you can ignore the ads and use only the search tools.

The Web's free search services come in two basic categories: search engines and metasearch services. The search engines are actual indexing computer systems that seek out data on the Web, index it, catalog it and serve it up to users as requested. A metasearch search service taps into multiple search engines so your query will check a broader range of sources. First we'll cover a few popular search engines and then profile one metasearch service. (NOTE: If you click on **Search** on your Road Runner Browser, you will automatically be launched to a search engine to which Road Runner provides direct access.)

Infoseek

Our first entry for general Web searching is Infoseek (*www.infoseek.com*). Its home page presents a format that you'll also see at several other search engines (see Figure 1). It has a list of categories that will help you browse through Web information that's related to topics that interest you. And, it has a text entry window into which you can enter keywords that it will use to search its internal database.

One of Infoseek's unique features is it's multilingual options. You can use Infoseek in either German, French, Spanish, Japanese and, naturally, English. Of course it's not magic. That means that no matter what language you use for the interface, by far most of the content on the World Wide Web is in English. So, you can read the commands in many languages, but you'll need to search for English terms to have the highest search success.

Figure 1 Infoseek - one of the Web's premier searching engines

One cautionary note, however. At the bottom of Infoseek's home page, you'll find an enticing link that offers to let you download a customized version of the Microsoft Internet Explorer that has Infoseek capabilities built directly into it. We don't recommend that you download this version because you already have a customized version that has Road Runner capabilities built into it. You'll get better results overall if you keep your Road Runner Browser and add Infoseek to your Favorites.

Excite

Another search engines that we recommend highly is Excite at *www.excite.com* (see Figure 2). Excite expands the original concept of a Web search engine and adds some "exciting" new features. In fact, some of these new features are so powerful that we've profiled them separately in later chapters. But here we'll cover Excite's basic search engine functions.

We suggest you start at a link that's located at the top of the page, called Excite Search. This link compares the Excite service to other Web searching services. After you read this, you'll see why we're excited about Excite. It's the most comprehensive and the most powerful of all the Web search engines.

Excite's keyword search engine accesses a database that includes more than 50 million fully-indexed Web pages. That's a lot of information! But Excite does more than just give you a lot of search hits. A huge index doesn't do you much good if it never returns relevant hits. Excite makes sure that your result list is packed with relevant documents, not just filled with junk. And, Excite's patent-pending technology for query acceleration makes the speed of many queries independent of the size of their database.

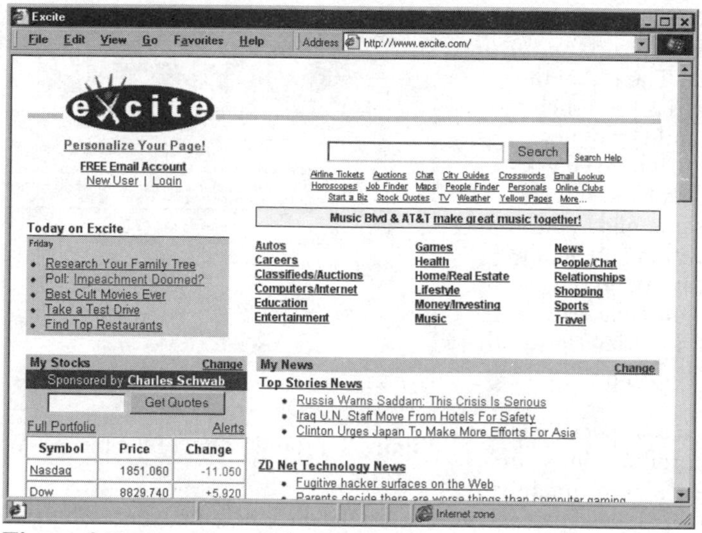

Figure 2 Excite - One of the Web's best search engines

Excite Live! gives you local weather, and top headlines, as well as a link that lets you personalize the service. We could hardly believe the power that this personalized service delivers. Configure your page to remind you of important birthdays, track a stock portfolio, give you the news you most want to read and even send you a tailored daily horoscope. This is definitely a page for your Favorites Folder!

The Excite home page even includes instructions on how to configure your Road Runner Browser so that Excite will be your default Web search engine. Click on the special link for Road Runner Browser users and follow the steps.

Before you leave Excite, check the bottom of their home page for links to some excellent reference sources. They bring you telephone directories, online maps, a dictionary and e-mail lookups. Though there's plenty here to keep you busy, there's even more. Let's move on now to another popular Web search engine, Yahoo!

Yahoo!

If you've read *Gulliver's Travels*, you might wonder why anyone would name themselves after the despicable Yahoos that Gulliver encountered, especially since this Yahoo! is so delightful (see Figure 3). Yahoo! offers two searching options on its home page. You can use a keyword search or you can browse through its listing by category.

Keyword searches are the best choice when you've got some sites in mind, such as "hot air balloon races." But those sites would be difficult to find if you browsed under headings. Under which heading would you expect to find hot air balloon races?

On the other hand, you might want to find pages that deal with a general topic, such as politics. If you performed a keyword search for "politics" you'd get every indexed page that contained that word. That would be gross overwhelm. But worse, it's possible for an important article about politics to *not* contain the word politics.

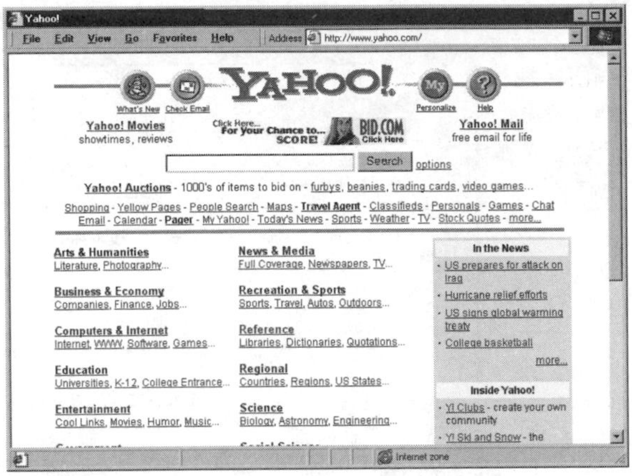

Fortunately, Yahoo! gives you both options right up front. But there's more. The top of the Yahoo! page has links such as New, Cool and Headlines. These links will help you skip past the old stuff. And if you're just bored some night and want to read something about anything, you can spend the evening sipping Jolt Cola, eating Twinkies and visiting sites in the Random link. Enjoy!

Yahoo! also has a special page that lets you refine your search (see Figure 4). Unfortunately, the path to this special page changes periodically, but somewhere on the home page, you're likely to find a link called Options or something similar. And, you can get to the options help screen by clicking on Search with the text entry box blank. Yahoo! will display a link entitled More... that leads to a screen with the Options link next to the Search button.

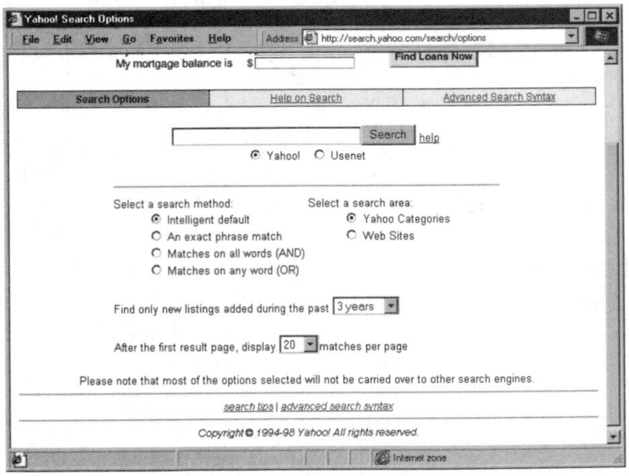

Figure 3 Yahoo! - One of the busiest Web sites

Figure 4 Yahoo! search options page

This page gives you the ability to choose between searching either the Web or newsgroups for your keywords. You also can specify to use the OR operator and force a search for whole words instead of substrings. The bottom of this page also has links to Web search tips and advanced techniques. Most search engines have similar services. It's important to checkout the tips pages for all of the search engines you use because each is slightly different.

DejaNews

DejaNews (*www.dejanews.com*) is a search engine for Usenet newsgroups. Even though it's a Web site, DejaNews has archived millions of Usenet postings. And it's even become a link within Yahoo! from which you can jump directly to DejaNews, or you can click on DejaNews after performing a normal Yahoo! search and apply your latest search criteria to a newsgroup search. DejaNews builds a list for you of articles it pulls from its archives.

Yahoo! Get Local

Yahoo! offers a feature that lets you find local links by entering your zip code. Of course you don't have to enter your *real* zip code, so the Local feature is perfect when you're planning a trip. The location of the Local link seems to vary between being at the top or the bottom of their home page. Once you find Yahoo! Local, just enter any zip code in the U.S. and get everything from history to weather to special events (see Figure 5). What you'll see varies from city to city because they use local links. So you may find a small city with an extensive collection of local information and history and then jump to a major city with skimpy listings. If your city isn't well represented, here's your opportunity to get published on the Web—create a local Web page and get Yahoo! Local to link to it.

Finally, don't overlook the "Add URL" button at the top of the Yahoo! main screen. You can use it to add your own Web site to Yahoo! so that other Web surfers can find you. The key to adding a URL is first to navigate to a category that is a logical choice for your own home page before you click on the link. When you're in the right place, clicking on it will start the Yahoo! procedure to add your page to that Yahoo! category.

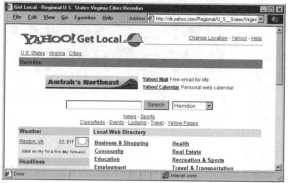

Figure 5 Yahoo! Get Local

All-In-One

All-In-One search is a metasearch service. It doesn't actually perform the search, but passes off your query to any one of a long list of actual search engines. This is a wonderful feature for checking the broadest possible set of resources. There are several on the Web, but we've chosen this one because it's highly-rated and the way they've broken down the categories gives it a user-friendly interface. It's located at *www.albany.net/allinone*.

As you can see in this screen shot (see Figure 6), All-In-One lists major search topics such as World Wide Web, General Interest and Specialized Interest. Beyond this page lie options to search these categories: Software, People, News/Weather, Publications/Literature, Technical Reports, Documentation, Desk Reference and Other Interesting Searches/Services.

And, if you have your own Web site and want to help other people find it via Web search engines, All-In-One has an extensive set of services that will list your site with other search engines, help you modify your site to attain the highest ranking on the results lists, plus it can monitor your site's ranking and alert you when other similar sites have moved ahead of yours in priority.

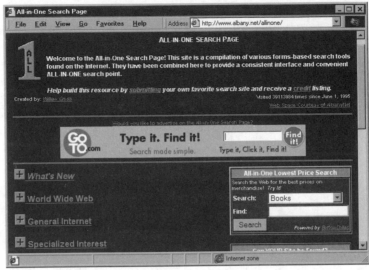

Figure 6 Try an Internet metasearch engine

All-In-One's ease of use lies in the "plus" signs that precede each heading. When you click on a plus sign, the heading's category expands and all of the related searching services under it are displayed. For example, the World Wide Web plus sign would expand to list a menu of Web search engines. Then you would fill in your query and click the Search button. All-In-One will submit your search to the selected service. Clicking on a minus sign collapses an expanded category back to its heading.

We'll close this section on free search services with a reminder to browse through the Orbiting in Cyberspace section at the end of this chapter. It can lead you to many more sites, including other metasearch sites such as C/Net's site at *www.search.com*, which is a large collection of Web searching services.

My Yahoo!
http://my.yahoo.com

Yahoo! offers a free, personalized service that lets you create a tailored information page. First you access a set up page that records your preferences for information, and the order in which you want it displayed. After that, every time you return to My Yahoo!, you'll get your tailored page. You can include stock quotes, weather in various cities, and news headlines from a long list of categories. All of the information is itself in the form of links that lead to more in-depth information on that same topic.

C/Net Search
http://www.search.com

This is one of the nicest search sites on the Web. It's a blend of a free service and a commercial service. Search.com blends its own commercial service in with other search engines. On the home page, for example, you'll see a link to search for software (see Figure 7) that looks like all the other links. That link, however, is owned by C/Net, the creators and sponsors of this site. It links you to a comprehensive download library of shareware and freeware.

Figure 7 C/Net - One of the Web's best scarch services

Snap Online
http://www.snap.com

Snap came on the Web search scene late, but quickly became the fastest-growing search engine on the Web (see Figure 8). It reflects the new direction in search engine philosophy by giving you much more than simple information searches. It also includes news and weather, plus links to online shopping and "Free Stuff" for downloading. The "Free Stuff" includes a Top Ten list of the latest and best free offers. As with other

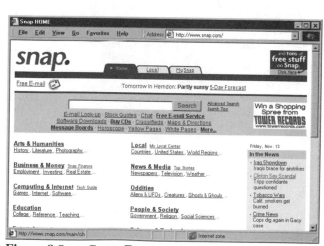

Figure 8 Snap.Com - Fast-growing information service

engines, you'll find a Local page and a personalization option, called "My Snap," that lets you set up your own, customized Snap home page.

NOTES

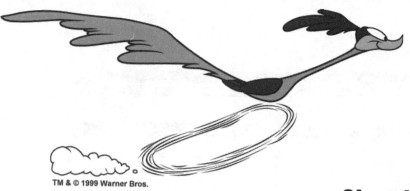

TM & © 1999 Warner Bros.

Chapter 10

Cyber•Info: Research Resources

Get comfortable with a snack nearby because you'll be in for a shock at how rapidly the world is making the transition to cyberspace. If you can't find what you want through the search engines we illustrated in the last chapter, here are some sites that will help you with more traditional research—the main difference is that you can do it all at home and you can use resources all over the world.

We'll first show you some online bookstores, then present some online libraries and finish with a collection of electronic reference sources that will either help you find information or find links to other reference sources. The Orbiting in Cyberspace section will point you to additional resources, including general reference sources.

Bookstores

Online bookstores come in two basic categories. Some are an electronic version of traditional bookstores—this means that when you enter them you can browse through conventional printed books by author, title or subject. Some of them improve upon the storefront bookstore by letting you search for books by keywords. But their main business is selling you printed books. The second category is a truly cyberspace bookstore that lets you directly download entire books. Of course some of these may also sell printed books, but their main business is electronically-published material.

Amazon

The Amazon site wins the prize for the most online titles: more than one million! That's a book a day for about 3,000 years. Their Web address is: *www.amazon.com* (see Figure 1). Visit them today for a real literary treat.

This site's value extends well beyond being a convenient book source. They've got in-depth studies of various authors that includes cross-referencing authors with their titles. They also let authors attach personal comments to their books, which may help you decide on a book when you're browsing. They also have a provision for online interviews of authors that includes insights into how they got started as a writer, how they write, what type of equipment they use and even fun stuff like their hobbies and favorite books.

Figure 1 Amazon has indexed millions of titles

You will also find special promotions, new developments and a special section for new titles. And in case you don't find what you need here, they've got an e-mail notification feature. You can input some criteria for books that interest you and they'll send you a message if a book on that topic arrives in stock.

And they've created a powerful search engine that will locate books for you by title, author, ISBN number, publisher or topic (see Figure 2).

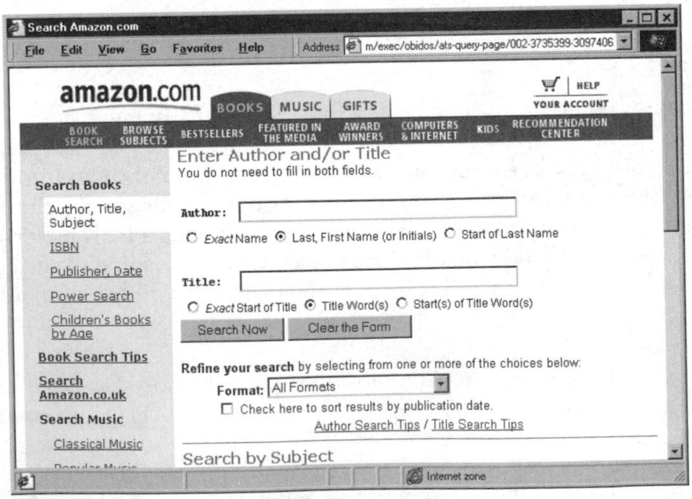

Figure 2 Amazon book search

While this is a commercial service, it's still worthy of your Favorites Folder because it offers so many value-adding features. You will probably find it useful for locating information on a variety of topics—it *isn't* limited to selling books.

BookWire

Since Amazon may overwhelm your senses, we've included a smaller bookstore. Of course, these days small still means extensive. One user-friendly example is Book-Wire, at *www.bookwire.com*, where you'll find an information-rich home page filled with links to book categories (see Figure 3).

From the home page, you can start with the <u>BookWire Navigator</u> link that brings up all of their links by category on one easy-to-browse page. Starting from this page, you should be able to satisfy all of your book needs.

Figure 3 Complete online book information

And, just in case there aren't enough books here, the folks at BookWire even include a link to help you learn how to get your own book published. It's an open-ended Web discussion board that links together messages by general topic, such as "What steps are you taking to get your book published?" You'll be able to post messages about your own books and to read messages from agents and publishers. We found this publishing section as a link near the top of the home page, but it moves occasionally, so look around if you don't see it right away.

How To Get Published

Does seeing all of these books stir up your own urge to get published? But you have no idea about how to begin? You won't be surprised that the Web can help you get your own book added to the lists you see here.

You can visit a cyber-literary agency in Washington, D.C., Adler & Robin Books, where you'll deal with Bill Adler, Jr. and Lisa Swayne. The agency's claim to fame is being "Number 1 in New York Times Bestsellers." They are also the second largest computer book agency in the world. If you want to know how they achieved such success, visit their Web site at *www.adlerbooks.com*. Bill and Lisa know the publishing industry inside out and share online some of their knowledge. Your best bet is to jump to the link on how to get published.

Their client list reads like a Who's Who directory: Dan Rather, Dick Clark, Ed McMahon, Fran Tarkenton, Geraldo Rivera, Helen Hayes, Howard Cosell, Jeff Smith (The Frugal Gourmet), Joan Lunden, Charles Osgood, Larry King, Margaret Truman, Mickey Mantle, Mike Wallace, Nolan Ryan, Pelé, Tom Shales, Ronald Reagan, Nancy Reagan, Sally Jessy Raphael, Senator Gary Hart, Senator George Mitchell, Senator William Cohen, Steve Allen, Tom Seaver, Willard Scott, Phil Donahue, Robert MacNeil and Ronald L. Wagner.

The Adler Books Web site includes postings of book ideas for which they are seeking writers, so check it out to see if you fit in? Already got a hot book idea? Then post a note and tell them about it.

Virtual Libraries

First we'll present the newest form of library in the world: the virtual library. These are not usually affiliated with a traditional, physical library, but exist only in cyberspace. They can point you to vast collections of information. Some actually store information on-site, but most are a collection of links to other Web resources. After showing you a few virtual libraries, we'll give you pointers to the Web sites of some real-world libraries that have gone online. You'll find something in these libraries for the whole family—and many of them will warrant saving in your Favorites Folder.

The Library Network

The Library Network presents a well-done, user-friendly front end that will speed your online information quests. Visit the home page, *tln.lib.mi.us*, which links you to online library resources from all over the world (see Figure 4). The main screen has a lot of buttons that will jump you to its various sources of information.

The Dialin Access Numbers link displays a list of many libraries around the country that will permit you to connect online. You can scroll through this window to find the dial-in phone number of a library near you.

Check out the home page link called Homepages to see a constantly-updated list of links to libraries that have Web sites. Most of the sites listed are in Michigan, but there are links to nationwide library sites, such as the WWW Virtual Library that we'll profile next.

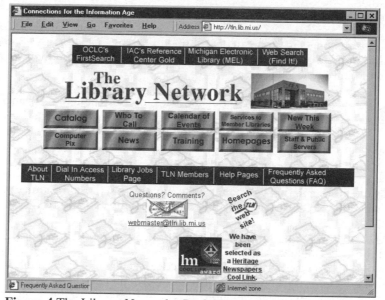

Figure 4 The Library Network - Perfect for your Favorites Folder

WWW Virtual Library

The Virtual Library uses a distributed subject catalog for topic organization. The home page, therefore, is a long list of major topics for which they have references. The Web address is *www.w3.org/vl*, (see Figure 5). We've included it because it's a

Figure 5 WWW Virtual Library - keeping it simple

nice contrast to the World Library featured earlier. This service uses the simplest possible Web page interface and you might want to recommend it to friends who aren't fortunate enough to be enjoying the speed of cable modem Internet access. And it's also a good choice for anyone using a slow computer. The pages here won't tax your computer's resources, which is quite a switch from some of the other virtual book sources.

The links at the top of the page give you a variety of display options for the topic listing. The <u>Catalog Subtree</u> link expands the listings shown here into subtrees that go as deep as three levels (two levels under the major topics). The Library of Congress Classification redisplays the screen with a much shorter list of standard topics. There is also a link that lists resources by Subject, which is so comprehensive we've included it in the Orbiting in Cyberspace section. Don't let its plain appearance distract you from the wealth of knowledge that you can tap through this site—the appearance is a resource-friendly gesture.

Real Libraries

The sites featured here are online outlets of traditional, physical libraries. Some have provisions for borrowing material via mail, but many only let you use their service to search their archives and catalogs.

You'll find the whole spectrum, from the massive Library of Congress, to small Presidential libraries, university libraries and all the way down to small, community libraries. This is a rapidly-growing area on the Internet and it's hard to predict what's online and what's not.

There are countless libraries in cyberspace, so we'll begin with a representative overview and some resources that will point you to more. From those resources you'll find links you can follow to find everything that's available online in libraries.

Library of Congress

LOCIS (Library of Congress On Line) is the Library of Congress' mainframe-based collection of databases that includes a public access catalog of bibliographic information, federal legislation, copyright registered works, braille and audio materials, guides, organization descriptions and foreign law abstracts. From the home page, which is located at *www.loc.gov* (see Figure 6), you can find links to connect to LOCIS through a variety of Internet methods.

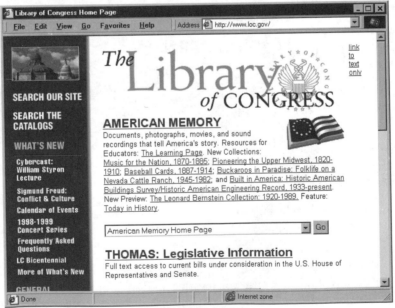

Figure 6 Library of Congress - a national treasure

You'll be able to get Web pages that offer Web and Gopher searches of the databases, as well as links that let you connect via Telnet or Telnet 3270, a Z39.50 Gateway, or through the FTP.

Jargon Cutter

Telnet - An Internet function that lets you remotely control a computer system. These days the most common use of Telnet is with libraries that permit users from anywhere in the world connect to their main computer. Telnet software doesn't do any more than connect you to the system, then you'll use the host computer's operating system commands.

Even the U.S. Government is joining us mainstream folks out here in cyberspace because they offer links here to other Internet search services such as The Awesome List, Whole Internet Guide and Catalog, Clearinghouse for Subject-Oriented Internet Resource Guides (University of Michigan) and the Categorical Catapult.

University libraries

Jump into Yahoo! and click on the home page link <u>Reference Libraries</u>, then click on <u>University Libraries</u>. They have a list of hundreds of choices! Think that will be enough? If not, keep checking because the list grows constantly and they display the newest links at the top of the list, marked with a <u>New</u> link.

The Yahoo! page has a <u>Special Collections</u> link at the top of the list that only had eight selections—at least something here is manageable. The <u>Special Collections</u> link is a good list to remember if you're having difficulty finding obscure information or rare books or images. These links truly have some unique research materials that could give students an edge when they prepare reports for school.

When you start clicking on the university library links you need to be ready for anything. Most of them use hypertext Web pages, but sometimes you'll find Gopher and Telnet links. These shouldn't be any problem for you because Gopher is built into the Road Runner Browser and you can download a Telnet application. Gopher pages will hardly look much different from Web pages, except for appearing very plain.

Local libraries

There's no pattern to the libraries that have established Web sites. This is partly because there's a dilemma for large information systems: vast information resources come up against budget considerations. Putting a huge collection online in today's tight budget environment isn't easy. Thus, many small communities have an active online library presence while some major communities are not yet fully developed.

Clearwater Public Library

We browsed through a few local libraries and selected one that we found to be an excellent model of what can be done by community libraries. The Clearwater, Florida Public Library (see Figure 7) has done an outstanding job of presenting their online research and resource services as well as giving local patrons a comprehensive source of information on hours, locations, library policies and special events. See for yourself at *public.lib.ci.clearwater.fl.us/cpl*.

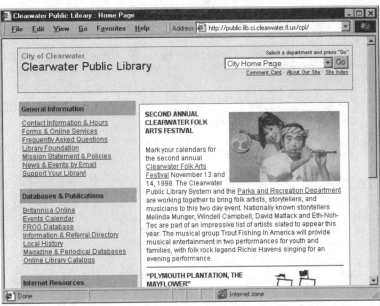

Figure 7 Clearwater is setting standards for local libraries

Some of the valuable features available in this cyber-library are: the <u>Card Catalog</u> (Telnet to access their catalog file); the <u>Reading Room</u> (divided into Bibliographies, Literature, Nonfiction and Periodicals); the <u>Reference Desk</u>; the <u>Youth Room</u>; and <u>FROG</u> (Florida Resource and Opportunity Guide). FROG is a wonderful resource that area residents can use to track activities, organizations, events, and programs that meet the daily information needs of citizens, businesses, and community organizations in the Tampa Bay Area. While you probably won't use this directly, you can use it to lobby your local library system for better service—it's a well-done site for a local organization.

And, this site could be a Favorite just for its <u>Reference Department</u> link alone—thank goodness there's so much more. The <u>Reference Department</u> has everything from an e-mail link to <u>Ask the Ready Reference Staff a Question</u>, to international currency rates, to Bartlett's Quotations, to nationwide Lottery Numbers. And you can even find the Vital Records offices in every state, which means that you actually can locate the right address to order a copy of your birth certificate! If you've ever tried to do that before the Internet, you know what a wonderful service this is.

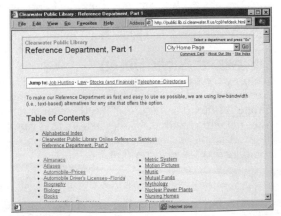

Figure 8 Ready Reference Department

New York Public Library

You can access the New York Public Library (NYPL) online. It's a valuable resource for many research projects—or just for fun! Their URL is *www.nypl.org* (see Figure 9). Many of their online features are accessed through the link at the top of the home page called NYPL Online.

If you click on the Catalogs link, you'll get the Telnet address to tie directly into the NYPL computer system. And, we also recommend the Research Centers link because it takes you to On-Lion for kids, a special section for families with Leo the Lion as your tour guide. This page also includes a guide for parents on using the Internet, prepared by the Office of Chil-

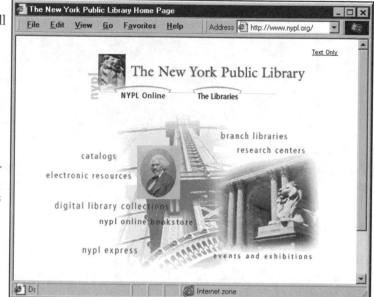

Figure 9 NYPL - cyberspace research access

dren's Services and the Office of Young Adult Services. It offers advice and guidelines for parents who are concerned about their family's use of electronic resources.

Electronic Reference Sources

Online reference material is growing too rapidly to pin down. Some experts estimate that more information is added to the Web every week than one person could read in a lifetime. There's so much information that often the search engines deliver more than you could ever use. If that happens to you, there are alternatives. First, you can return to your Road Runner home page and look at the information we make available to you. For example, see our Bookshelf reference source.

Bookshelf

Just think, any time you're logged in to Road Runner, you're only a couple of mouse clicks away from an amazing array of online information. You can use our Bookshelf to access the Merriam-Webster dictionary, Time Life Medical Encyclopedia and Roget's Thesaurus (see Figure 10). To access these online resources, click on the Home button in your Road Runner Browser. Your path to our "Bookshelf" service will vary, depending on your location, but you shouldn't have trouble finding it.

Figure 10 Bookshelf - may be all the resources you need

Many users have found all they ever need right at home here on the Road Runner system. But if you still need more, there are many other new electronic reference sources. Here's one great example and others follow at the end of the chapter.

Think Quest

The *Library of Entries* serves educational web sites created by students for the ThinkQuest and ThinkQuest Junior contests (see Figure 11). You'll find that the link Search the Complete Library of Entries makes navigation easy and helps you track down the information you need. The home page is *library.advanced.org*.

From the home page, you'll have several choices of reference sources, including current and past year entries, keyword search and the Lesson Plan Area. The Think Quest Winners offer a fabulous resource with a wide selection of categories that take you to information all over the world. The sites were created by students and the vast array of represented countries will certainly convince you that the Web truly is World Wide!

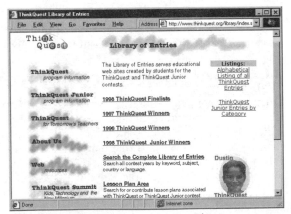

Figure 11 Think Quest student entries

The students have covered an amazing range of topics: genetics, earthquakes, volcanoes, cloning, African wildlife, sports, art and literature. Mark this site and return often. There's enough here to entertain and amaze you for a long time—and it's always growing. Each year there will be new entries. This site is becoming an excellent online research resource.

ORBITING IN CYBERSPACE

BookWire library index
http://www.bookwire.com/links/libraries/librarymenu.html

Here's a rich listing of Web-accessible libraries from around the globe. This is an excellent model of what the Internet does best. In fact, this site may make you run screaming from your computer. You could literally spend the rest of your life exploring just the links on this site and still tap into but a fraction of all that it offers. You can use this site to locate almost any information you want from libraries in these basic groups: Asian, Australian, Canadian, European, United States and Others. For example, the European option on this page can lead you to hundreds of world-wide resources through the Bodleian Library at the University of Oxford.

Reference Shelf
http://alabanza.com/kabacoff/Inter-Links/reference.html

The Reference Shelf is a potpourri of reference sources collected from around the Web. It's just one page, but it's a top candidate for your Favorites Folder because you could stay busy for days exploring its links. A few valuable examples are City/Zip Code Lookup (with geography info), plus facts and maps for nearly every country in the world. The Perpetual Calendar link alone is worth saving the URL—where else can you instantly find a suitable-for printing calendar for any month of any year?

Web Museum
http://sunsite.unc.edu/wm

This is a remarkable collection of Internet resources. It's a free art museum created by Nicolas Pioch, a student studying economics at the École Nationale Supérieure des Télécommunications in Paris. It's a personal creation that has no support, no funding, and practically no personnel. In fact, they'd like your help because the WebMuseum is a collaborative work that encourages visitors to contribute to the site and improve the WebMuseum. This site is a past winner of a "Best of the Web Award."

Internet Public Library
http://ipl.sils.umich.edu

Don't let the name mislead you—this is a *must see* source on the Web for all kinds of information (see Figure 12). It's more like a library-museum combination with special sections for younger surfers who will enjoy the Teen and Youth links. Other features include the Reference Center, Computers & Internet and the interactive Ask a Question. The Exhibits section is a rich resource of constantly-updated online information.

Figure 12 Internet Public Library

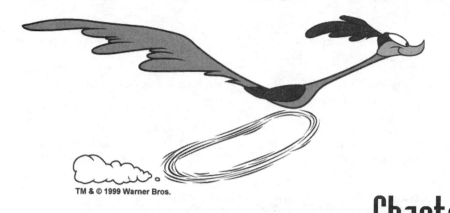

TM & © 1999 Warner Bros.

Chapter II

For the People: Government Online

This chapter may boost your faith in government because you'll see some remarkable ways in which your tax dollars have been at work in cyberspace. It's truly heartening to see how the Internet can be used to make our governments more accessible and responsive. All kinds of previously obscure government information can now be tapped quickly and accurately right from your home. Just think, you might never need to stand in line again at a government office if governments continue to jump onto the Internet bandwagon.

It's amazing, actually, that the U.S. Government isn't the main focus of the Internet. We're lucky. Somebody back in the early 1960s was wise enough to realize that the Internet would be more robust if government stayed out of it. They were right, and fortunately, the government still doesn't control the Internet, although they have tried to impose some new restrictions.

But now that 30 years of freedom for the Internet has created a powerful, universal Web, government is slipping back into the party—but mostly as an equal guest. Instead of controlling the Internet, the government sites you'll see here are very much like their civilian counterparts: they try to bring value to Web visitors.

The Web is an excellent resource for government information because we all need it and it's always hard to find. Before the Web, a search for government information was often a frustrating game of passing the buck. Perhaps when President Truman said, "The buck stops here," a lot of government agencies took that to heart and have tried to pass everything on up to the Oval Office. With the Internet, finally, the buck stops wherever you want it to stop.

You can find on the Web just about everything you'd want to know about the U.S. Government as well as your state and local governments:

❖ Congressional records, laws, regulations, Supreme Court rulings, Executive decisions;

❖ Indexes to agencies with phone numbers and addresses, current information online; business hours, and directions;

❖ Copies of birth certificates, marriage licenses, business licenses, applications for forms, sources for forms.

In each Road Runner locality you can access links to city and county government by clicking one of the government buttons that you can reach from your home page (see Figure 1). You can find more government sites in the Index, which can be reached by clicking the Road Runner character.

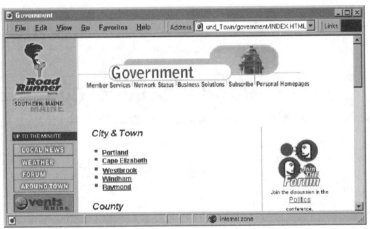

Figure 1 Typical link to a Road Runner government page

We'll give you some samples of sites from all levels of government: Federal, State and local. Of course you'll only see a few here, but they'll help you know what you can expect to find. Finally, the Orbiting in Cyberspace section will give you some good resources to track down Web sites from which you can obtain the government information you want.

Federal Government

The last chapter included a taste of government Web sites through its descriptions of libraries. Even though we've already covered the Library of Congress, we'll mention it here because it is an excellent resource for a large amount of Federal government information. The Library of Congress includes information on:

❖ Federal Government: General Resources, Executive Branch and Independent Agencies, Legislative Branch (includes Congress), Judicial Branch, and the Military, FOIA (Freedom of Information Act);

❖ State and Local Government: Indexes for state and local information, state maps, Council of State Governments, and the National Center for State Courts;

❖ <u>Foreign and International Government</u>: General information by country, CIA Factbook, State Department information, world constitutions, foreign relations, NAFTA, GATT, the United Nations and much, much more.

The Internet is rapidly removing many of the traditional geographical barriers to business that kept many businesses working close to home. But through these resources, you may be able to find opportunities to do business with faraway governments. Or, you might use these services to obtain information about doing business in other cities other states or even other countries—not other planets, though, not yet anyway. Before the Internet, setting up an out-of-town business and getting all the required business licenses was a chore. But now, even a small, home-based business can expand to just about anywhere in the world.

InfoSpace Federal Government Resources

An excellent first stop for government information is InfoSpace (see Figure 2). InfoSpace enables users to easily and instantly locate listings of people, businesses, government offices, toll-free numbers, fax numbers, e-mail addresses, maps and URLs, all integrated into one Web site with nearly 100 percent accuracy. InfoSpace has developed a patent pending technology that fully integrates all of its services, giving you one comprehensive reference source.

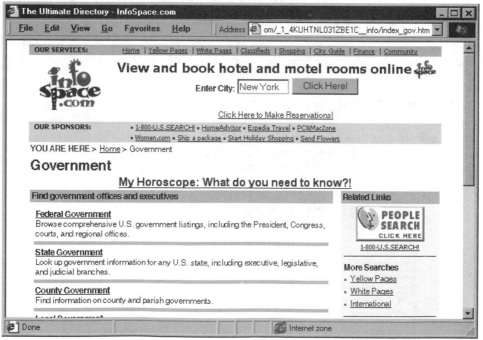

Figure 2 - An excellent resource for government listings, and so much more!

Once you visit InfoSpace, you'll quickly discover it's got much more than just government information. For government resources, click on the <u>Government</u> link on the home page. From there you can follow a series of links to find the resources you want. It's a very handy, one-stop reference source. It even includes embassies!

You can access government services via most search engines. One example is the Web site: *www.yahoo.com*. We've profiled Yahoo! in other areas of this book, so it's a good all-around resource. For government information, go to the home page and click on the <u>Government</u> link. It's organized quite differently from InfoSpace. Instead of succinct, direct links to government categories, it's organized by topic (see Figure 3).

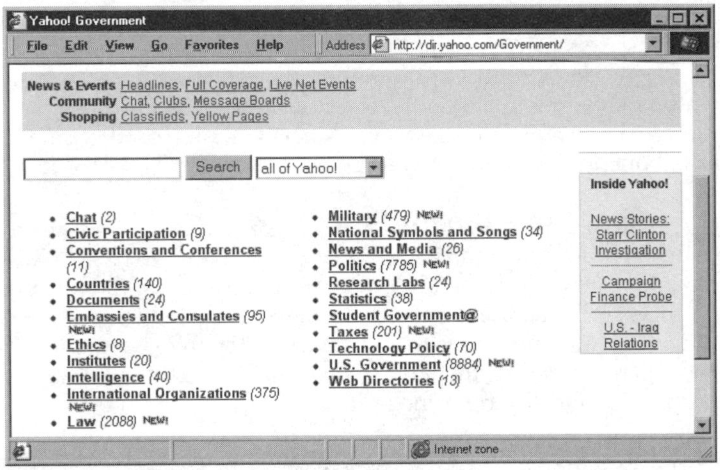

Figure 3 - Yahoo! Government, an alternative approach

Next, we'll profile a few services that almost everyone can use. First, some Federal sites and then a sample of state and local government sites that will get you on-track in your own community.

United States Postal Service

If you have a mailing address but no zip code, you can use the USPS Web page at *www.usps.gov/ncsc* (see Figure 4). The <u>Zip Code Lookup</u> link on this site can deliver a complete, 9-digit, USPS-regulation address. Or, you can use it to check an address or find out the city that goes with a zip code.

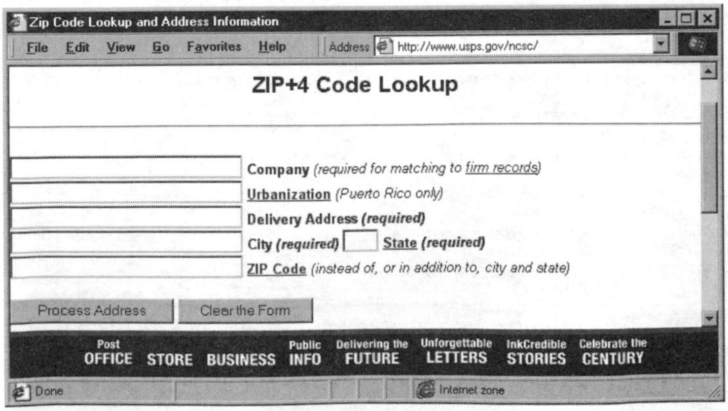

Figure 4 Locate or verify any zip code in the U.S.

Here's a Step-By-Step exercise that shows how to use the USPS Zip Code Lookup.

Step-By-Step

GOAL: Learn to correct an address with the USPS Web site.

✔ Start the Road Runner Browser.

✔ Press **CTRL+L**, type *www.usps.gov/ncsc* and press **ENTER**.

✔ Click **Zip Code Lookup**.

✔ Click in **Mailing Address**.

✔ Type *3000 timberwood* and press **TAB**.

✔ Type *herndon, va.*

✔ Click on **Process Address**.

> Note that the address has been corrected (it's actually three words now) and the full 9-digit Zip Code has been added.

✔ Press **ALT+LEFT ARROW** to return to the previous screen.

✔ Click **Clear the Form**.

> Enter your own address, but make a couple of errors. For example, if your address ends with "Drive" then reverse the abbreviation and use "rd." Leave off your zip code or reverse a digit when you type it. If you make too many errors, the database can't figure out what you meant, but it will handle quite a few problems.

✔ Press **ALT+LEFT ARROW** until you return to the first USPS page.

The USPS Web site can give you much more than this, including complete, current postal rate tables for every form of mail. You can even find out how to buy mail-order stamps. This Web site has made a lot of Bookmark lists.

Census Bureau

You pay for the Federal census, but how could you have used the collected census information before the Web? It hasn't been easy, but the Web changes that. Maybe a better question is, now that you can get it, what do you do with it? There is such a rich source of information available at the Census Bureau's site at *www.census.gov* (see Figure 5) that almost anyone in business can find something here to use. For example, before planning an expansion, a new product or moving your family across the country, you can check the Census Bureau's Internet demographic information to help you make the decision.

Try the <u>Market Place</u> link to learn how to order Census Bureau information in hard copy or on CD-ROM, or you can try <u>Data Access Tools</u> to get a lot of the information online. The <u>Economy and Geography</u> links are fabulous resources for developing business plans and proposals. And, if you're not sure how or where to find what you want, click on <u>Ask The Experts</u> to send an e-mail question. This is a wonderful site that makes public a lot of valuable, yet previously obscure, information.

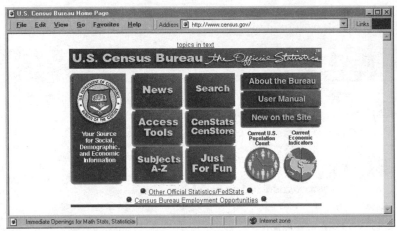

Figure 5 You've answered their questions—now see the answers

Small Business Administration

The Internet has revolutionized almost every existing business, but it also has spawned countless new business ideas. A massive wave of corporate and government cutbacks, downsizing and layoffs have pushed a lot of displaced workers to form small or home-based businesses. If you have your own business or if you work for a small business, then the Small Business Administration (SBA) Web site at *www.sba.gov* (see Figure 6) should be in your Favorites Folder.

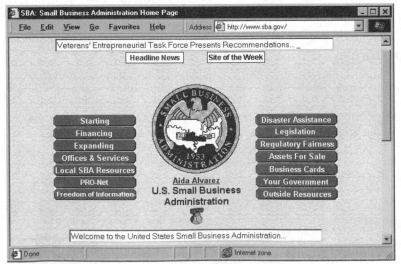

Figure 6 A good resource for small- or home-based businesses

You'll find links to the SBA's <u>Program Offices</u>, <u>Special Interests</u> and <u>Great Business Hot-Links</u>. They also have an extensive shareware collection of more than 538 titles for applications that can help you run a small business. The shareware listing can be arranged either by an index, in one long listing or by searching.

The new business links are <u>Starting Your Business</u>, <u>Financing Your Business</u> and <u>Expanding Your Business</u>. They lead to pages with compiled information, gathered from the Web and other government agencies, that offer information or assistance.

Congressional E-Mail Directory

There was a time when you could take pride in just finding out the phone number or address of your Congressional Representative and Senators. Now, thanks to the Web site at *www.webslingerz.com/jhoffman/congress-email.html*, you can get complete contact information on them (phone, fax, snail mail, e-mail) and jump to their Web sites. The Congressional E-Mail Directory is a sure-fire hit for your Favorites Folder (see Figure 7). When you get to your state page, click on a link to the Web page and click on another to e-mail directly from the Web site.

This site is an excellent example of Web publishing because it has a high-quality look and a user-friendly interface, but hasn't resorted to bandwidth-hogging graphics. So, note this site for two reasons: an outstanding information source and a model for good Web site design.

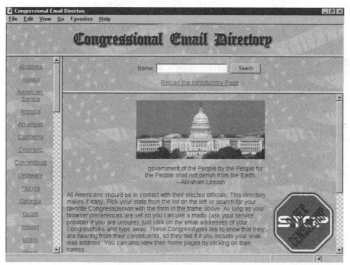

Figure 7 Tell 'em exactly what you think

State Governments

Your first stop for state government information can be one of the major search engines. In Yahoo!, for example, go to *www.yahoo.com/government*. Then click the <u>U.S. Government</u> link, then <u>State Government</u>. These links aren't the state Web sites, but it will give you a list of links related to any selected state.

Figure 8 Government On Line - A state government resource

State Technologies, Inc., which has run conferences and seminars on how government can use technology, now runs an Internet database of sound government practices (see Figure 8). The service is called Government Online (*www.gol.org*).

Beep! Beep!
Remember to check the Library of Congress for state and local government information. The Web page at *lcweb.loc.gov/global/state/stategov.html* gives you a meta-index of state and local information, state maps, links to state home pages and some organizations that pertain to state and local government issues.

Local Governments

There are too many local governments online to even begin to profile, but a good search engine will help you find the ones that represent your local area. County governments have reported that their Web sites have attracted new businesses to relocate or open branch offices. And, they've helped many companies learn how to do business with both the government as well as other companies within the area. You'll find them very useful for looking up hard-to-find records or, perhaps while researching the family tree.

The challenge, as always on the Internet, is finding the site you want. Of course, you can turn to Excite or Yahoo! and search the state name. But if you're looking for a good Favorites Folder site that can be a ready reference for information pertaining to local governments, try visiting *www.civic.net/lgnet* (see Figure 9). This site is maintained by the Local Government Network (LGNet), a service of The Innovation Groups and The Center for Civic Networking.

Information available here includes training, workshops, conferences, online help, publications and an online resource directory. If you do business with local governments, be sure to list your products and services with the "Vendor Directory and Information." This is a central location for state vendors to publicize contacts, online catalogs, purchase

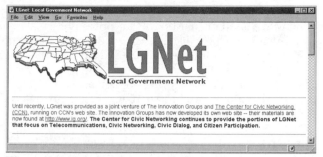

Figure 9 LGNet includes detailed information on most major U.S. cities

schedules, and special offers. This link leads to a forms-based database that will accept your information directly from this page.

Cities

There are too many cities to count, right? Well, not too many for the Internet. There is one Web site that lists online information on more than 5,000 cities! City.Net, at *www.city.net*, is the Internet's most comprehensive guide to communities around the world (see Figure 10). City.Net is updated every day to provide easy and timely access to information on travel, entertainment and local business, plus government and community services. There's a world map at the bottom of the page to help you zero-in on the region you want, or you can perform a direct search.

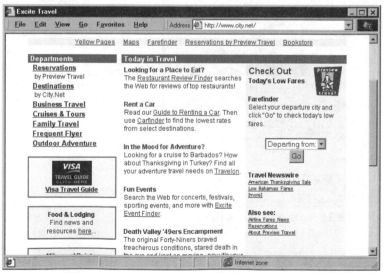

Figure 10 City Net - You'll know more than the mayor's office

Once you locate the city you want, you'll learn things about the city that even the mayor doesn't know. Radio stations, television stations, newspapers, city directory, transportation, maps, sports teams, universities, magazines and zines (electronic magazines), virtual tours, schedules of events, parks and tourism information. If you travel a lot, this is another "must have" Favorites Folder site because if you check here before you go, you'll feel like a native when you arrive. Naturally not every city is represented, but the most popular travel destinations have extensive coverage.

If your ties to your hometown have fallen victim to our high-tech, high-mobility society, use this site to savor a taste of home. No, no, only kidding—your Road Runner Browser doesn't have a taste plug-in—yet.

Airports

Picture this. You're late catching a flight. You've jammed your clothes into your suitcase, rushed out the door without eating and driven like a NASCAR racer to make it on time. You burst through the doors, knock down three people getting to a scheduling monitor to check your gate. Then you see it: it's delayed an hour, or worse, CANCELED. What would you have given to have seen that monitor at home?

Commercial airline information is a valuable commodity and it's perfectly suited to the Internet. And now you can get it in real-time, complete with the exact location, altitude and speed of any airline flight. There are many different resources that provide such information, so you probably will need a comprehensive site that includes a lot of aviation links. Aviation Internet Resources (*www.air-online.com*) is an excellent collection of all sorts of airline information (see Figure 11).

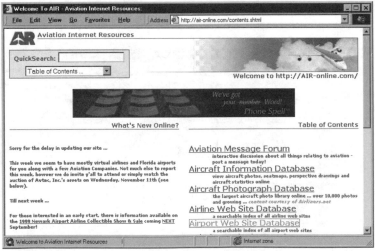

Figure 11 Aviation Internet Resource

To demonstrate the incredible, real-time, inflight information visit *www.thetrip.com* and click on their FlightTracker link. It might be hidden under another link, but it's there. You can enter the airline code and flight number of a specific flight, or just test the system with their random flight demonstration button.

Next time you're picking up someone at the airport, hit this page with their flight info a few minutes before you need to leave and see *exactly* where their plane is!

As we browsed airports, we saw a graphic illustration of the one-world, global community that cyberspace is becoming: the Web site of the Russian airline Aeroflot (*www.aeroflot.org*). From there, you can see the Sheremetyevo-2 Air Gateway in Moscow (see Figure 12). When the Internet was first conceived in the early 1960s, can you imagine what the founders would have thought if they had known that one day

Figure 12 We all are one!

anyone in the U.S. could pull up a map of the gates at the Moscow airport? To old Cold Warriors, that would have been a terrifying thought. Now, it's just another interesting Web site—we accept it and wonder when they'll offer real-time flight schedules.

Shortcomings aside, current airport Web sites illustrate how the Internet is changing our lives by conveniently bringing us valuable, hard-to-find information—no matter where in the world it's located. If you think about it in absolute terms, it's almost barbaric that we've had to go to airports without seeing the schedule monitors until *after* we're there. It's too late then! But the Internet is growing rapidly to bring airport screens—and countless other such timely information services—into our homes in real time.

Federal Government
http://www.fedworld.gov

FedWorld is a hypertext menu of various Federal Government computer resources. The National Technical Information Service (NTIS) maintains FedWorld to help with the challenge of accessing U.S. Government information online (see Figure 13). Most of the links are to other Web sites, but this site also includes Telnet links to several Federal computer systems. You'll find most links under the <u>Index of Subject Categories</u>, but you will find direct links to some popular sites, including Web, FTP, Gopher and Telnet sites.

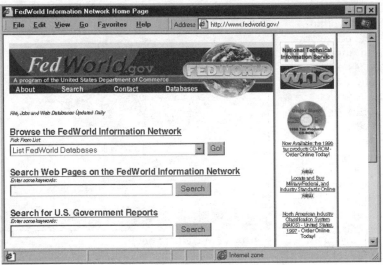

Figure 13 FedWorld - A good Federal information resource

Federal Government Web Locator
http://www.law.vill.edu/Fed-Agency/fedwebloc.html

Sponsored by Villanova University Law School, this site lists more than 200 Federal Government Web sites. This site has a search engine that is an excellent tool if you've got a question about a topic but don't know which agency could handle your request. For example, what agency would you contact if you wanted to know about the progress on cleaning up the Exxon Alaska oil spill? A search on the words "oil spill" produced a link to the Oil Spill Public Information Center.

USA CityLink
http://citylink.neosoft.com/citylink

You can use this site to find information on cities around the U.S. and you can submit links to your own city. The USA CityLink Project lists cities, states and freenets. Here's what they say on their home page, "The USA CityLink Project is a city's interface to the world. It is the Internet's most comprehensive listing of World Wide Web pages featuring U.S. states and cities."

U.S. Government Web site
http://sunsite.unc.edu/govdocs.html

This site enables you to search for U.S. Government documents on the Web, such as press releases, speeches (including some audio and video clips) and the National Trade Data Bank. Take careful notes because many of the references you find here may be good value-added links for which you can provide links on your own Web site.

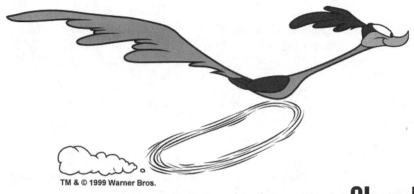

TM & © 1999 Warner Bros.

Chapter 12

Making It Pay: News, Business and Finance

This chapter focuses on several types of news and business information sources available on the Web. Many, like Time, Money and Sports Illustrated magazines, are built into Road Runner as part of the basic service. In addition, your cable company has made sure that the best local news sources are integrated into your Road Runner service along with these national news services.

There is probably more news than you can ever use within the combined resources of Road Runner and Pathfinder but there are many more out on the Web, some of which filter out everything you don't care to know and serve up only the categories of news you specify. (In Pathfinder, this service is called Personal Edition.)

We'll also give you some financial news links that can deliver stock quotes as well as track news that will affect corporate stock prices. These services can be used to track a personal portfolio, a major corporate investment plan or even to track the ups and downs of your competitors. You'll also get some good resources for marketing tips, general business information and consulting services.

General News

The nation's newspapers and magazines are scrambling to go online and it would seem that before long every major publication will have a presence on the Web. Most Time Warner publications have been online since the early days of the Web—all the way back to 1994!—and by the time you read this it will be likely that only those publications with very small circulations (and smaller financial resources) will *not* be on the Web.

Pathfinder

Time Warner, the parent company of Road Runner, maintains Pathfinder, a "mega site" of news, information and entertainment from the company's various magazines, book publishers, record labels and television and movie studios. Some of this same information is built into the Road Runner service (such as the daily online editions of

Time, Money and People magazines as well as CNN). You will enjoy faster service than regular Internet surfers because each Road Runner system has a direct link to the Pathfinder content that is distributed from New York City using special broadband conduits.

Pathfinder offers information from more than 70 information providers and can be reached from a number of different points in the Road Runner service.

Online newspapers

Chances are that your local newspaper has joined forces with Road Runner to provide you with the best source of local news. Local news outlets can be found through your Road Runner home page. These links keep local readers up to date on news and events that are often omitted by major news organizations. And, these local online newspapers are a great way to stay abreast of events back home while you travel.

What about newspapers outside of your Road Runner cable service area? Or, would you like to see your former hometown paper? The leading newspaper chains in the country are linked together in the Newspapers Online site (*www.newspapers.com*), which collects the best from various newspapers in one convenient Web site. There are also links to a variety of other publications, such as trade journals, college and university papers, as well as online news sources (see Figure 1).

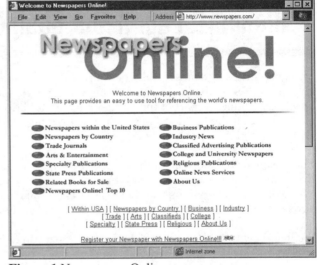

Figure 1 Newspapers Online

Beep! Beep!

The Washington Post (*www.washingtonpost.com*) and The New York Times (*www.nytimes.com*) are excellent selections for your Favorites Folders because they carry so much news that is of national and international interest. Use New Century Network to find other newspapers or use an Internet search engine to check for newspapers in any city in the U.S., or in the world!

Tailored news services

In cyberspace, you no longer have to seek the news. Lucky you! With Internet news services, the news will seek you through a tailored news service. Tailored news services have many different forms, but they all have one principle: they spare you the burden of being smothered by a crush of over-information that you don't need.

As helpful as tailored news services are, there is a disheartening number of these services available and the list is growing all the time. Worse, there is no more a "right" service to choose than there is a "right" pillow to choose. The good news is that these services are either free or inexpensive, they are easy to find, and subscribing and un-subscribing is simple. Hence, the best strategy for choosing the right Internet news service for your needs is to sample a lot of them and then decide.

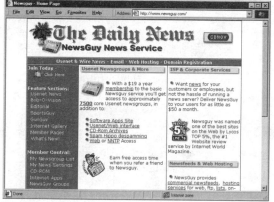

Figure 2 The NewsGuys Web service

An obvious way to begin searching for online news services is to check out Yahoo and Lycos. Nearly all search engines have a news link. They point to a mixture of news services, but you can look through them to find some tailored services that will filter the news for you.

You can get tailored news services from *www.newsguy.com*. This site is a collection of Usenet groups, tailored news feeds, newsletters and other electronic news sources (see Figure 2). So, if you want to hook up directly to your own news

source, this type of service is the answer to your needs.

CRAYON

With so many services from which to choose, we needed some very scientific criteria to select one tailored news service to feature here. So, after much browsing and careful consideration, we used the highly scientific method of picking one because it's got a cute name: CRAYON (CReAte Your Own Newspaper). The CRAYON news service is at *crayon.net* (see Figure 3). Though it made the cut because of its name, CRAYON turned out to be a marvel of Internet technology.

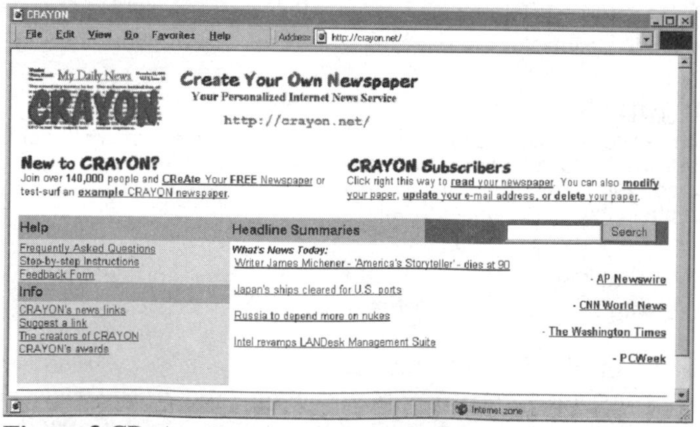

Figure 3 CReAte Your Own Newspaper

Creating your own newspaper with CRAYON is simple. Imagine going to your local paper's office and telling them exactly what you want and do not want to read, the order in which you want the sections printed and then the next day they deliver to your door a tailored version of their newspaper! That's how CRAYON works. You can even specify your own title so you can really feel like a publisher.

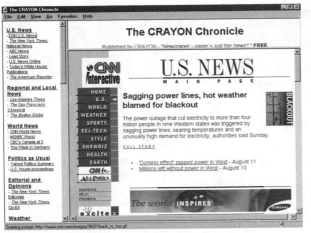

Figure 4 Sample Crayon tailored news page

You can include multiple selections from any of the major headings: U.S. News, Regional and Local News, World News, Politics as Usual, Weather Conditions and Forecasts, Information and Technology Report, Arts and Entertainment, Sports Day, The Funny Pages, The Tabloid Page, and Cool Web Sites. When you finish, CRAYON generates a Web page with links to the news features you select (see Figure 4). This generated page can be delivered one-section-at-a-time or in one big page. The one big page averages about 60K in size—which won't be a problem for you as a Road Runner customer—and it presents your selections in one continuous page.

Beep! Beep!

After CRAYON generates your paper, you'll need to save the file. You then can open the page and add it to your Road Runner Browser's Favorites Folders. Then you'll be able to get to this page quickly anytime you want to see it.

If you notice that today's CRAYON paper has yesterday's images or text, you need to remember that the Road Runner Browser has a cache for Web pages and images that it's previously downloaded. If the information on a page is stale, click the refresh button, or press **F5**, or right-click the screen and click **Refresh**. This forces your Road Runner Browser to download the page and images to update your screen display.

Jargon Cutter

Cache - Web browsers store the pages you load into a memory buffer called a cache. This reduces Internet traffic because if you return to a page you've seen, the browser gets it from the cache instead of downloading it again. We'll cover caching in-depth in the Road Runner Browser chapter in Phase 2.

Also, remember that you can return to CRAYON anytime and generate a new Web page, changing your links, the title, or the order of the sections.

It hardly could be simpler and definitely can't be cheaper. Just watching this service work is an interesting experience. A word of caution, though: the page you generate with this service could be addictive. Starting from here, you could spend an entire day surfing through the ever-increasing cascade of links that your selected pages unveil. This is a "must get" service.

Investment Management

You'll find that the Internet offers just about as many financial services as it does news services. You'll be able to track stock portfolios, get real-time stock ticker tape, receive special alarm notices via e-mail if certain maximum or minimum stock prices are triggered, track financial headlines and order tailored financial news reports.

You can access an incredible wealth of information on every company that trades stock publicly. This can be a boon when you're considering making an investment, or even if you're just curious about how your biggest competitor is faring.

Beep! Beep!

Remember, you don't have to own a stock to track it. You can use a stock service simply to track the players in your field of interest or to practice dealing with stocks or to test your market theories. You can set up a portfolio with 100 shares of your targeted stocks so you can easily decipher the impact of stock price swings.

NYU EDGAR

New York University maintains a terrific site for investors or anyone who needs to research company histories or statistics at *edgar.stern.nyu.edu*. The EDGAR (Electronic Data Gathering and Retrieval) site was developed by the NYU Stern School of Business Information Systems Department. Perhaps one of its most valuable features is the Profile Search that lets you search and view corporate profiles by entering keywords.

If you're investigating companies, you'll find plenty of uses for the links to the <u>Donnelley Library of SEC Materials</u> and <u>Corporate SEC Filings</u>. One of its richest resources is the link called <u>Reciprocal Links</u> that will point you to a whole world of financial Web links. Be sure to check out their <u>Interesting Links</u> jump for such tidbits as the <u>Economics of Networks</u>.

Tracking investment stocks

Road Runner is a good choice because it offers one-stop shopping for all types of stock services and allows you to tailor your service to your needs. Your starting point is the business section of the Road Runner National news page (see Figure 5).

You can get quotes by entering a stock symbol. If you don't know a symbol, you can look it up by company name. And, this service offers far more than just stock quotes—we deliver a wealth of the latest, in-depth investment information.

Figure 5 Sample online stock quotes

To track news about companies whose stocks you have picked, or to gather intelligence about companies in which you might want to invest, use the Road Runner link to the Reuters Business News that is built into our system. This on-the-fly news wire is updated continuously.

With all of the Internet resources for business and financial news, perhaps you'll soon retire to a tropical island with nothing but a beach and Road Runner. But there are more ways to earn money than just through investing. Let's move to the next step: using the Internet to sell your professional skills—or just to sell the hand-made wind chimes you make as a hobby.

Marketing Sites

Internet marketing sites provide the full spectrum of marketing information. You can get help with selling products and services you produce in a home-based business and even get help for selling the business itself. You can find online advertising agencies, marketing consultants, marketing software, and advertising forums. The Internet has brought us all a whole new world of marketing possibilities and channels. Fortunately, it also has brought us the tools to explore these new possibilities.

Beep! Beep!

The next time you need to buy or sell a car, or even your home, be sure to check your Road Runner service. This is a rapidly changing field and new sites come online constantly. A search with Yahoo! or Lycos will be a good start, too. And check out newspapers and magazines that run online classified advertising.

Often the key to finding the services or contacts you need will be to use the Web search engines. To get you started, however, we've included some helpful sites here. As with most sites, you'll find links here to other, related Web sites.

Marketing consultants

Marketing in cyberspace is a paradox: on the one hand it's completely different from any other marketing and on the other hand it's the same as it's been for thousands of years. It's different because it's interactive and buyers can tailor their own presentation. But then it's the same as always because even the coolest, high-tech Web site won't sell much if it doesn't focus on delivering value. Many people have sought professional advice to help them learn to merge the new with the traditional.

Figure 6 Internet marketing pioneers

Fortunately, expert help is available online. Let's begin with one of the best, Poppe Tyson (pronounced "poppy tyson"), a venerable, well-established agency that has been at the forefront of the move into cyberspace (see Figure 6).

Poppe Tyson

Poppe Tyson is an international advertising agency owned by Bozell, Jacobs, Kenyon & Eckhardt, the world's fourth largest marketing communications company. But there's more to them than size: they were selected as an "Agency of the Year" by *Marketing Computers* magazine. Visit them at *www.poppe.com*. Some of Poppe Tyson's clients prove its ability to handle cyberspace marketing. For example, you may have seen one of their most visible projects: bringing major auto races into cyberspace.

Each year, over the Memorial Day weekend, the Web site for the world's most famous race is a very busy place in cyberspace. It's maintained by Valvoline Motor Oil, one of Poppe Tyson's clients. They coordinate both the marketing content and the technical expertise required to bring the Indy 500 Web site to life (see Figure 7). Now the Valvoline site includes many of the major Indy-car and NASCAR races.

Figure 7 Valvoline brought auto racing into cyberspace

Beep! Beep!

Poppe Tyson's Web site offers good cyberspace value. They provide a treasure trove of in-depth marketing expertise. They've got links that give you a behind-the-scenes view of the people and the equipment that helped put the Indy 500 online. Of course they hope to attract your business while you're surfing their site, but that's what well-done Web sites are all about.

GoSite

If you need a service that can develop hypertext versions of existing materials and transform logos, graphics and photos into Web formats that are ready to go online world-wide, check out the GoSite service at *www.gosite.com* for details. Costs for using a company such as GoSite will be lower than with a full-service agency such as Poppe Tyson, but then that doesn't include paying for the development of an advertising program. GoSite can create Web graphics that fit an existing, traditional marketing program and help format existing material into a valuable, user-friendly Web site. They also can create a complete Web server, register a domain name, upload the completed Web files and maintain the entire site.

GoSite is a nice compromise between a full-service agency and a total do-it-yourself Web service provider. One tool they use to bridge the gap between the two is the GoGadget Administrator, an Internet site manager that makes simple work of some otherwise complicated tasks. GoGadget makes maintaining a Web Site as simple as clicking a mouse. It will automatically consolidate the files between a company's computer and its GoSite Server by clicking a button. Even Internet novices will be able to set-up and control e-mail accounts, forward files and create auto-responding e-mail.

So if you want to market your handmade wind chimes but you've got a limited budget, then this is a good place to start. But beware—we discovered one fellow who had run a quiet little business selling parts for classic Ford Mustangs from his garage. He put it on the Internet and was so successful that he actually had to remove it for a while and then rent commercial space and hire help before he could go back online!

Consumer Information

Your Road Runner home page presents a wealth of financial and consumer information. You'll find a menu of cyberspace connections to such topics as financial markets, business headlines, software and books, corporate reports, and lots of links to other, related Web sites.

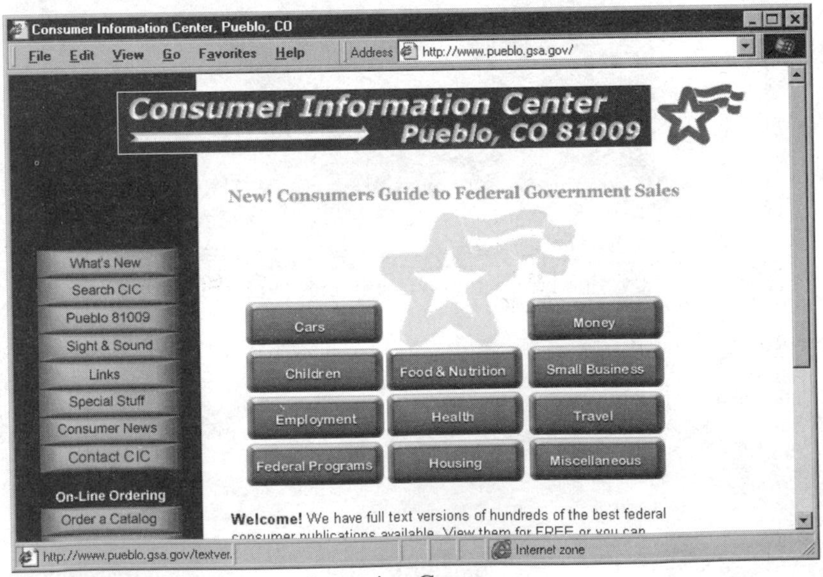

Figure 8 The Consumer Information Center

For example, you could find the Consumer Information Center (see Figure 8). This page (*www.pueblo.gsa.gov*) offers hundreds of the best federal consumer publications available. All are *free*! Pick a category from their navigation grid to see what's in their latest catalog. Check out Special Stuff to see other great information. And, they offer a

Search feature with which you can zero in on precisely what you need. Take time to look around. We expect that you'll find it to be helpful and valuable.

Beep! Beep!

Remember, any time you see any of our content that you expect to become one of your frequently-visited sites, click on **Favorites, Add to Favorites** in the Road Runner Browser, then select a folder in which you want to store the address. From then on, you'll be able to quickly return without navigating through a menu system.

Selected Economics Resources on the Web

The University of Michigan has a service that offers up-to-date worldwide economic information (*www.lib.umich.edu/libhome/rrs/classes/econ.html*) on everything from copyright issues to international currency exchange rates. It's actually a list of many other Internet resources . You'll see a comprehensive list of links that contain documents on various business topics. Many of the pages include other links, so most likely you'll find what you want here.

Another good resource for economic data is the "Shortcut to All Resources" page (*wueconb.wustl.edu/EconFAQ/node1.html*) that's maintained by University of Mississippi professor Bill Goffe. You probably can't imagine an economic topic that's not covered here. It's got everything from universities, the White House, Congress, the Federal Reserve, Department of Commerce, Bureau of Labor Statistics, the World Bank, global economic links, corporate financial information, consulting and forecasting services, published papers, online journals and databases, online newspapers, and economics software.

Better Business Bureau

The Better Business Bureau (BBB) is a traditional source for lots of business information. Its URL is *www.bbbonline.com* (see Figure 9). It's also available through your local Road Runner home page.

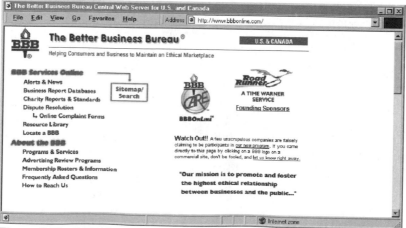

Figure 9 The BBB Online

Beep! Beep!
Road Runner is one of the founding members of the BBB Online. We also provide ongoing support to the BBB to help sustain this important and valuable online resource, so naturally we are proud to help you access their consumer information.

Like the rest of us, this venerable institution has moved into cyberspace to keep up with the times. For example, every year the Council of Better Business Bureau announces online 15 companies as finalists for their annual "Better Business Bureau Torch Award for Marketplace Ethics." The award finalists are selected for demonstrating a commitment to exceptionally high standards of ethical business practices. Surely there's some inspiration for your own excellence lurking in the stories about such select companies.

The <u>Better Business Bureau Code Of Advertising</u> page as an excellent information source to use in reviewing a marketing plan. For example, with all of the "free" things floating around on the Internet, you might want to read the "Free" topic in these guidelines before you apply that often-misleading word to your products or services. Another company-saving topic is their <u>Scam Alert</u> link that can keep you up-to-date on the latest con schemes. A good example is an exposé entitled "Don't Get Scammed By Office Con Artists," that reveals the explosion of fake offices that are being established to hide con artist activities. We hope that these same principles don't become a problem on the Internet.

Beep! Beep!
Newsgroups aren't a part of the Web, but they're an integrated part of your system and they're easy to use. Start your newsgroup reader, then browse through the list of newsgroup headings until you see a folder named: **biz.*** Open this folder to reveal the topics inside, then click on any sub-heading that interests you.

Selling Your House

Increasingly, the Web is becoming an alternate real estate marketing tool. New real estate sites are springing up weekly and existing ones are expanding. None of them are fully developed and none of them are fully national in scope—yet. We suggest you use the Web search engines to find local real estate sites. Yahoo has extensive resources dedicated to real estate listings, news, classified ads, interest rates, and mortgage information.

The Web's real estate content is not restricted to online companies—there are lots of individual listings, many of which are put up by private individuals who hope that someone on the Internet will find their listing and buy their home. To find listings for your area, go to Lycos or Yahoo! and perform a search on the keywords: "real estate listings XXXX." (Substitute the target state or city for the XXXX).

Listing your own house on the Web can be a snap. Many of the sites have simple forms for sellers to complete that will automatically place your listing on their site. Others let you mail them the information, including photos, and they'll publish your listing for you. Expect to pay a fee if the service does the work.

One good resource for real estate information is the Internet Real Estate Directory (IRED) at *www.ired.com* (see Figure 10). IRED has links to many real estate topics.

And, naturally, those links will lead to more links and more links, etc. Before long you won't even remember you started out just looking for real estate information—but that's why the Web is so popular, isn't it?

Figure 10 IRED - Internet Real Estate Directory

SearchAmerica, Inc.
http://www.searchamerica.com

SearchAmerica is your online link to approximately 220 million surnames, businesses and telephone numbers (see Figure 11). It covers 95 percent of the households and businesses in the United States. Their primary searching software accesses multiple databases and regional Bell Companies to locate individuals or businesses. All residential and business records are continually updated and verified against current phone numbers to maintain accuracy. This Web site offers maximum coverage and the most accurate information available today. Commercial applications are available for companies that need additional coverage, Social Security number searches and address information.

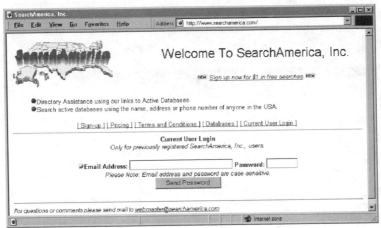

Figure 11 More than 220 million listings

BizQuest
http://www.bizquest.com

BizQuest is a business service that maintains an database of international business transfer information. They list both "general" businesses (up to $2,000,000 in sales) and "mid-market" businesses ($2,000,000-$50,000,000) in sales. You may perform free searches for business buyers, sellers, brokers, appraisers, lenders and other services, but you'll have to complete a registration form before each search. For an annual fee, they'll give you a password that allows you to search without having to register each time you return to the site.

Certified business brokers
http://www.certifiedbb.com

Certified Business Brokers is a professional firm with a broad range of business skills and experience available to assist you in the sale or acquisition of a privately owned business. With over 60 years combined experience in business sales and acquisitions and a track record of over 1,000 businesses sold, Certified Business Brokers can be an essential element in buying a business or selling your current business.

Business Exchange Network
http://www.biz-exchange.com

The Business Exchange Network is a clearinghouse of information for the buying and selling of small-sized to mid-sized businesses. Sales are handled through their Web site, as well as through several traditional avenues. They publish a monthly newspaper, "Businesses for Sale," and two weekly publications, "Business Buyers Weekly Report," and the "Business Brokers, Agents, and Intermediaries Report." They offer another non-cyberspace option for the information on their Web site through a fax-on-demand system. If you're considering using such a service, you might want to read their articles dealing with all aspects of buying and selling businesses.

M&A Marketplace
http://www.mergernetwork.com

The M&A Marketplace Web site is designed for buyers and sellers of companies and for financial intermediaries who are involved in mergers and acquisitions (M&A), divestitures, and corporate finance. They've got links that let you explore companies for sale, buyers seeking sellers, joint ventures, financial sources and a host of other related topics. Full searching and browsing capabilities are reserved for visitors with paid memberships. They even provide an area on the site for members to network directly with other members.

IOMA
http://www.ioma.com

This site is home to the Institute of Management and Administration (IOMA) and Information Services for Professionals (see Figure 12). It's an excellent guide to business resources on the Internet. IOMA, a leading publisher of management and business information, offers sample articles from a variety of newsletters, as well as 90-day trial subscriptions. Whether managing a law or accounting office, a defined contribution investment plan, or a computer network, professionals from virtually every industry can find invaluable, career-enhancing information in these IOMA newsletters.

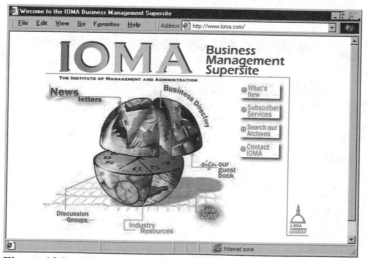

Figure 12 Institute of Management and Administration

Socially responsible business mailing list archive
http://www.envirolink.org/archives/srb

To quote from the site's home page, "At last, a place for the enlightened discussion of Socially Responsible Business and Investing. This is THE forum for discussion and information exchange focused around aspects and topics of socially responsible business (SRB) and investing (SRI)." The SRB and SRI topics are combined to create a more accessible and popular conference area by combining the two inter-related subjects. You can click on the Subscribe link to join the mailing list or you can browse through this archive and view documents sorted by author, subject or date.

Small and Home-Based Business Links
http://www.ro.com/small_business/homebased.html

Here's a wealth of information for small and home-based businesses. It includes coverage of small and home-based franchises, business opportunities, small business reference material, information to help you run and market your small or home-based business, small and home-based newsgroups, searching tools and services for small business. Just about anything related to small and home-based businesses can be found in these links.

Business@Home
http://www.gohome.com

There is a "workquake" under way in our society that will forever change the way we do business. This site exists to help you thrive in this time of structural change with news-to-use and how-to information that helps you and your family survive in today's fast-changing business world. Business@Home (see Figure 13) provides more than valuable business information. Because the desire to balance our work life with our personal life is a major force driving this "sea-change" toward working from home, this site has extensive resources that help you navigate the waves for smoother sailing into your professional future. We offer (and encourage) thoughtful, engaging comment on how to make a life while making a living.

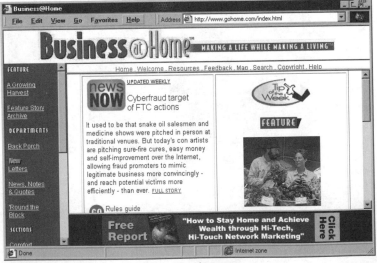

Figure 13 Help for home-based businesses

Phase 4

Phase 4: Web Publishing

Now that you've seen what other people have put out there on the Web, it's your turn. What do you have to say or to show to the world? Whatever it is, you can make it instantly available to anyone, anywhere in the world.

Perhaps you've just bought a new home and you'd like all of your online relatives to see some photos. Is there some other exciting announcement you'd like to share with friends and relatives? Perhaps there's a new baby in your life—you can have "bragging" photos online within hours.

These chapters will just get you started and show you the basics of creating a Web site of your own. Please understand that most of the world-class Web sites you've been surfing to were created by full-time professionals who do nothing else but design, build and publish Web content—and most are highly-paid for their work. So, don't worry about creating a stunning, world-class Web site—after all, your friends and family just want to see those photos and they want to see them today!

❖   <u>**Chapter 13**</u> is an introduction to **Web publishing**. You'll learn about the options available to you for creating your own Web pages. You may be surprised how easy it is to present basic information on the Web.

❖   <u>**Chapter 14**</u> introduces **Web graphics**. It helps you understand the different computer formats for Web graphics and what software tools you can use to create and edit graphic images. We even give you a Web site that offers a wealth of tips on scanning existing documents, drawings and photos into your Web documents.

❖   <u>**Chapter 15**</u> closes the book with a light-hearted look at **copyright issues** in the electronic age of cyberspace. You'll encounter a lot of text and graphics on the Web that you'll be able to quickly download, save and reuse. Usually, that information will be protected by copyrights. But the good news is that securing permission for reuse usually is a snap. We'll help you understand what you can and cannot reuse without permission and give you tips on getting the permission you need.

❖   <u>**Chapter 16**</u> is a **Windows primer**. Naturally, this is an excellent resource if you're a new Windows user, but the tips that we include also surprise many experienced Windows users who haven't yet picked up some of these time-saving hints.

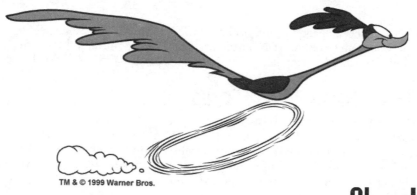

TM & © 1999 Warner Bros.

Chapter 13

Your Cyber•Spacestation: Web Publishing

When the Web first appeared, writing hypertext, HTML-language pages required high levels of computer expertise, diligence and patience. But today, creating HTML can actually be enjoyable and as simple as using a word processor.

Road Runner Home Page Hosting

As a benefit of your Road Runner service, you can have an area in which to create and store your own Personal Home Page free of charge. You can e-mail your friends its unique URL and they will be able to see your handiwork from anywhere on the World Wide Web.

There are limits to the amount of information (in terms of bytes of data) and the kind of information (it must not be a commercial site selling goods or services and its contents must fall within generally accepted community standards regarding decency and good taste) that can be on your Personal Home Page. Also, there are certain technical guidelines regarding the use of third-party plug-ins and server scripting routines that are permissible. Information about how to create your Personal Home Page on Road Runner can be found in the User Services area on the Welcome page.

Producing World Wide Web documents has become so common that you can create them with WordPerfect for Windows and Microsoft Word for Windows. Both of them greatly simplify the once arduous challenge of creating simple hypertext documents. So, now you can use an old friend as you become part of the Web. We'll highlight the strengths and weaknesses of word processors, and then we'll discuss more advanced, dedicated Web editors.

But there's more to writing for the World Wide Web than the technical side of producing hypertext documents. Knowing how to use tools doesn't make you a skilled craftsman. Since your Web site will instantly broadcast your image world-wide, you'll want to do your best to get your information out to the rest of us.

We've included some home page tips that will help you know what you can expect to do yourself and when you might need a consultant. When you've finished this chapter, you'll be fully prepared to become a player in the electronic world of the Web.

Tools, Tools, and More Tools

There are more tools available for publishing Web hypertext documents than anyone can count. New ones are released almost daily. Before the recent dramatic expansion of Web tools, only programmers and computer specialists had the skills to create Web pages. But the Web's popularity explosion has prompted major software developers to create tools that enable mainstream users to create Web pages.

It's become so easy, in fact, that you may already have created Web pages without knowing it. That's because you can convert existing documents—including graphics and tables—into perfectly-formatted Web documents.

Creating *world class* Web pages requires a technical expert because the leading edge of technology always stays ahead of the mainstream user. Someone is always pushing existing technical limits and if you want to play on the frontier, you'll need the skills of a full-time professional. But today, most users can create attractive, professional Web pages. We'll cover basic Web-development tools in several categories:

❖ Word processors;
❖ Conversion programs;
❖ Stand-alone HTML editors;
❖ Graphics software;
❖ CGI tools;
❖ Java.

Word Processors

Corel WordPerfect 7 and 8 include built-in Web publishing features, as well as automatic conversion of files to and from HTML, .GIF and .JPEG (see Figure 1). The latest version of Microsoft Word also has built-in HTML features. If you're converting documents for the Web, WordPerfect and Word are good choices because of their popularity.

Convert File Format	? ☐ ☒
File: D:\HOTDOG\Family\main.htm	OK
Convert file format from:	Cancel
HTML	Help

Figure 1 Windows word processors will convert HTML documents automatically

You also can use them to open existing Web pages. For example, let's say you've seen a Web page that you want to study to learn techniques for your own pages. You can save the page with your Web browser, then open it in your word processor. If you want to save the entire HTML source code you can click **File, Save As File...** and use the dialog box with the **Save File as Type** set to **HTML (*.htm, *.html)**.

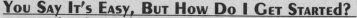

You Say It's Easy, But How Do I Get Started?

Programmers long have learned their craft by analyzing the source code of existing programs. It's much easier to learn to program by example than it is to start from scratch. Often, programmers modify an existing program to fit their own needs. Using the same technique will help you learn to write HTML-encoded Web pages by studying and modifying existing Web pages.

When you encounter a Web page that has a feature you would like to learn, click **View, Source** to see its HTML source code. The default viewer is the Windows Notepad and you can use it for basic editing or to save the file on your system for later editing with a more sophisticated application. And it's certainly adequate if you just want to highlight a section of the page, copy it to your clipboard and paste it into another HTML document.

Even if you're content with Notepad's limited abilities, some Web pages are too large for it, so you may need to designate another editor as your viewer. But the Notepad is a good choice for most users.

HTML conversion applications

HTML conversion applications will convert existing documents, databases and other file types to HTML format. They often do a better conversion job than a word processor. Conversion applications can be especially valuable for productivity if you need to Web-publish a large number of existing documents. We'll introduce you to two popular applications from SkiSoft.

SkiSoft Web Publisher

This application can be a major efficiency tool for organizations converting reams of documents. One of its biggest selling points is its batch conversion mode that can convert hundreds of documents in a single pass. It's not perfect, but it's better at mass production than using Word and manually working through each document.

The SkiSoft Web Publisher automatically converts files from Word, WordPerfect, AmiPro and Excel, but it doesn't convert the native format of any of these applications. Instead, it accepts documents in the Rich Text Format (.RTF). All four of these applications can save files in the .RTF format. So, the SkiSoft Web Publisher won't directly convert your archives of ancient WordPerfect 5.1 text without first converting all of them into .RTF. But even that process can be automated.

Tables in your word processing documents are converted directly into HTML tables. And the Web Publisher converts normal word processor images into .GIF files. Plus, it builds a cross-linked table of contents and an index of key terms with each item in the index linked to the appropriate text in your documents.

If you've spruced up your word processing documents with numbered lists, bullets and style headings, you'll be thrilled to know that the Web Publisher will convert all of these into HTML. It even converts bullets nested within numbered lists. Your styles can be converted into standard HTML heading codes.

Web Presentation Service

SkiSoft also offers the *Web Presentation Service* that publishes your Microsoft Power-Point presentations on the World Wide Web. Web Presentation Service converts a presentation of up to 20 slides into a linked collection of HTML text files and .GIF graphics files that are ready to post on your Web Server. Each presentation slide becomes a full-color Web page. It automatically creates buttons beneath each slide that lets site visitors jump forward or backward as they view your presentation. It also creates an Outline page that has a hyper-linked heading to its related slide.

Downloading the SkiSoft Conversion Tools

Go to *www.SkiSoft.com* (see Figure 2) and you'll find links to both of the products reviewed here: Web Publisher and Web Presentation Service. Before you download, read their FAQs file that may answer any questions you have about the products. The free usage license for the downloaded applications is only for 30 days, then you'll need to register them to comply with copyright requirements. This site includes samples of documents and images that have been converted using SkiSoft products.

So, SkiSoft gives you several user-friendly methods to create great-looking Web pages without needing to become a techno-wizard. Actually, you will soon find that even the stand-alone HTML editors don't require a technical genius. Let's graduate now to the next step up the HTML development ladder.

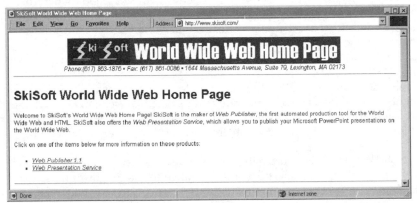

Figure 2 SkiSoft - converts existing documents into Web pages

Beep! Beep!

Have you ever wondered how HTML originated? HTML is based on SGML (Standard Generalized Markup Language), which was developed in the 1980s and became a formal standard in 1988. HTML used part of the SGML, added URLs (Uniform Resource Locators) plus the HTTP (Hypertext Transfer Protocol) and created the Web. This is making a long story very short, but you can find a wealth of additional resources by conducting a Web search for HTML and SGML. For more advanced information, you can search for DHTML (Dynamic HTML), which adds lots of embellishments that make Web pages more interactive and interesting. DHTML is in the HTML 4 specification which is supported by Version 4 of both the Internet Explorer and Netscape.

Stand-Alone HTML Editors

Stand-alone HTML editors are dedicated Windows applications designed specifically for creating HTML files. They offer more hypertext features, better control and more flexibility than word processors and conversion applications. As a trade-off, however, they require a greater learning curve and they lack some of the advanced features you've come to expect in Windows word processing applications.

To get started, you first could create some Web pages in WordPerfect or Word, and then open them in a stand-alone HTML editor. Most likely you'll fine-tune some things that didn't convert as you expected, which will give you the opportunity to ease into using a dedicated HTML editor. You probably will quickly pick up HTML using this method and soon be creating Web pages directly in an HTML editor.

We'll profile both HotDog Pro and Microsoft Front Page here because they each have distinctively different features, strengths and weaknesses.

HotDog Pro

HotDog Pro (see Figure 3) is a loyal puppy for many Web authors, so you, too, may choose it as your own HTML editor. HotDog comes in two versions: HotDog Professional and Hot-Dog Express. The Professional version has additional features that make it a must for professional use, yet its intuitive interface enables novices to get started quickly. For example, it has a complete HTML reference source that

Figure 3 HotDog - the Web editor from "Downunder"

lets you drag an HTML code from a menu directly into your Web page. The Express version is for people who need to create Web pages but don't want to learn HTML.

HotDog lets you use your Web browser to preview your pages, or you can use its built-in preview mode (called "Rover") to check your work. Though HotDog may not offer the "what you see is what you get" benefits that you have when developing Web pages with a word processor, you get total control over every aspect of HTML.

The Professional version employs all of the latest features of HTML, including Dynamic HTML (DHTML), JavaScript and Cascading Style Sheets (CSS). The Express version employs only the more basic HTML features. You can download a free, trial copy of either version of HotDog so you can test it before you buy it. HotDog is a product of Sausage Software, located at *www.sausage.com*.

Microsoft FrontPage

FrontPage is among the most user-friendly Web site development applications available. Its strength is that novices can get an attractive and powerful Web site up and running very quickly without ever having to learn HTML, graphics details, programming code or advanced computer skills. With FrontPage, practically anyone can add sound and animation to a Web site. And it will create an index for you—without requiring any programming skills—that lets your visitors zero in on the information they want from your site by searching your site for keywords.

> **Beep! Beep!**
> Certain software, called extensions, must be installed on a Web server for it to take advantage of all of FrontPage's features. (Road Runner's Personal Home Page hosting service is compatible with FrontPage.)

If your main objective is to get *something* on the Web quickly and easily, then FrontPage is the best. It lays out your entire site so that you can easily see the relationship of all the various pages on your site (see Figure 4).

If your main objective, however, is to create a very specific look and feel, then you'll need something like HotDog. FrontPage achieves its user-friendly status by applying some constraints to your development options. Breaking out of those constraints may require the use of a stand-alone editor. Of course you could start the basic development with FrontPage, then tweak the HTML manually in HotDog.

FrontPage is relatively expensive, compared to some other Web development applications. You'll have to balance the expense against other factors, such as how much time you can afford to spend on Web site development and your overall computer budget. In any case, be sure to shop around because FrontPage is discounted at many retailers.

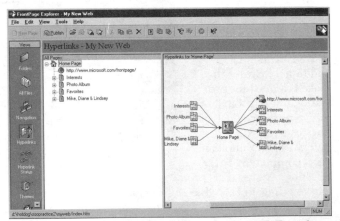

Figure 4 With Front Page you don't see the HTML codes

> **Beep! Beep!**
> Your Internet Explorer Web browser includes a free copy of Front Page Express, a reduced feature version of the stand-alone Front Page suite. For very basic Web editing, or just to get your first home page online *today*, use Front Page Express. It also lets you edit any Web page that you load into your browser—simply click **Edit, Page**.

Whenever you are deciding which Web editing application to use, be sure to check Web sites of the top applications (*www.sausage.com* and *www.microsoft.com*) so you can keep up with this rapidly-changing field. Whatever application you choose, you'll see there's lots of room for improvement—but improvement is coming quickly!

Graphics Software

Once you begin writing HTML pages, you won't get far without wanting to add some graphics. The popularity of color printers and the color graphics that now adorn millions of Web pages has encouraged development of a slew of advanced graphics programs. "Corel Draw" and "Adobe Photoshop" are popular commercial products, while "PaintShop Pro" and "LView Pro" are popular shareware products for graphic image manipulation. The next chapter goes into Web graphics in detail.

Graphics tools let you make Web pages attractive and interesting. And with these tools you can create image maps. Image maps are graphic images that are hypertext links on which users can click to jump to other Web information.

HTML extensions now include support for "client side" image maps that can be implemented without programming skills. Before the client side function was added, image maps could only be created through computer programming that was beyond the level of the average Web author. But clickable image maps are so simple now that HotDog even has a snaglet that automatically creates the HTML codes required to configure a clickable map on your Web site.

Common Gateway Interface Tools

Common Gateway Interface (CGI) is a programming specification for Web servers that makes it possible to have HTML pages tell the Web server to run programs that make your Web pages interactive.

CGI is called "server side" because it uses the server's processor to run the program. Input for the program is transmitted from the client to the server-based program. After the program runs, its results are transmitted back to the client.

User-friendly CGI tools include a wealth of valuable "pre-canned" programming scripts that can be referenced—called by the Web server—in existing hypertext documents. In other words, you won't have to start from scratch for every specialized function you want your Web site to perform. Advanced tools such as "Front Page" enable Web authors to create sophisticated database applications without doing any actual programming.

Beep! Beep!

Until recently Web authors needed programmers to achieve special effects such as form mail, site searches and clickable image maps. If this discussion of CGI sounds like too much work, then forget about it and use "Front Page" or some other sophisticated Web development tool. CGI isn't necessary now to create these effects.

Two of the most common uses on the Web for CGI programs have been clickable image maps and e-mail forms. The use of CGI for clickable image maps is certain to drop now that HTML includes "client side" image maps that do not rely on the server's processor. But, for now at least, CGI formmail routines can interface with HTML forms on your Web page to create a user-friendly feedback form.

Jargon Cutter

Formmail - a program used on many Web servers that enables users to send e-mail to the host organization by completing a form in a Web browser. The advantage of formmail is that Web authors can design forms that ask for specific information, rather than letting each visitor ask questions in free form. Sophisticated mail forms include error-checking to verify that zip codes and phone numbers are entered in proper format and that no essential fields have been left blank.

Java and JavaScript

Java and competitive variants enable a Web browser to download programming code from a Web server. The downloaded code extends the functionality of a browser so that it can perform elaborate tricks that are not built-in. Leading Web sites may use Java to nearly eliminate all Web browser limitations. The programming language required to implement Java applications is not yet for mainstream users, but you can hire a Java programmer to write some code if you've got an application in mind.

As opposed to CGI, Java is a "client-side" program. Because Java code runs on the client computer after being downloaded by your Web browser, it transfers the computing demands from the Web server to client computers. This permits a server to handle more traffic because Java is transferred to the client computer, and uses the client's processor.

Many users have computers that will not perform well while running Java applets. So, until your average Web visitor has a Pentium, consider the computing limitations your visitors might face before you implement an elaborate Java application.

While we're on the subject of considering the computing limitations of your Web visitors, we'd like to present some pointers for testing your Web site.

Testing Your Web Site

If you are involved in authoring Web pages and creating a Web site, you will most likely also be involved in the testing process. To create a truly user-friendly Web site, you'll need to consider four basic factors:

- ❖ Modem speed;
- ❖ Web browser;
- ❖ Windows screen resolution;
- ❖ PC processing power.

Even if you're not involved with the testing, be sure that you find out if the tests included consideration of these factors.

Test with a slow modem

Most likely your Web site's tests will be conducted on a hard drive in your own PC or on a network. No doubt you'll be quite satisfied with its performance, as you will when you test it using your Road Runner connection. But you'll have no idea how it will look to a visitor with a 28.8kbps modem and a slow Internet service provider. Not everyone is lucky enough to have the speed you enjoy right now, so your site needs to offer something incredible if it makes users wait. Of course you may not be concerned about appealing to visitors with slow modems—the use of those modems is fading rapidly.

As a minimum, you can offer a text-only option at the top of your home page so that visitors with slower computers can bypass any fancy graphics your site might include. On the other hand, ask yourself why you've chosen to include fancy graphics. These days, it's pretty tough to create a graphic that will earn a "Wow, that's cool" response. But it's real easy to create one that will earn, "Forget it, I'm not waiting that long."

Test with different browsers

The differences have narrowed between the appearance of the displays in the top Web browsers. At first, every browser seemed to have its own unique interpretation of HTML and you could hardly recognize the same page on two different browsers. But now the field has been narrowed to two dominant browsers that are reasonably similar in their displays. Whether you design your pages for Internet Explorer or for Netscape Navigator, be sure to test your site with the other browser. The Internet Explorer is now the most widely used browser, though the Netscape Navigator remains quite common.

What about all the other browsers on the market? The dominance of the top two browsers has nearly eliminated the need to consider other browsers. Anyone these days who uses something other than Internet Explorer or Netscape Navigator is someone who wants to be different. You're probably safe creating your site for the majority of users and offering a note that says "Designed for Internet Explorer, click here to download your copy now," along with a link to get the browser they need.

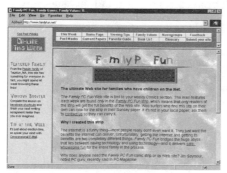
Figure 5 800 X 600 resolution

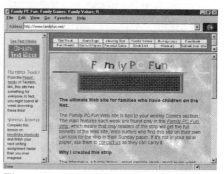
Figure 6 640 X 480 resolution

Test with different screen resolutions

Here's a tricky factor to consider. What are the implications of different screen resolutions? You can create a Web site that looks great on your own monitor at 800 X 600 (see Figure 5), but that falls apart at 640 X 480 (see Figure 6). For example, a heading that fits neatly across a page in the higher resolution may wrap into two lines at the lower resolution. People who view your page at higher resolutions won't experience such problematic differences (see sidebar on page 168).

Changing screen resolutions in Windows is not a quick procedure because you may need to restart Windows after every resolution change. However, most new video cards now permit "on-the-fly" resolution changes without restarting Windows after each adjustment. With the right system, Windows 95 lets you quickly switch back and forth between different resolutions, which is highly recommended during Web site development.

HTML Width Percentage Commands

Did you wonder how the buttons in the box at the top of the example site fit into that box even at different resolutions? According to the theory we're giving you here, they should have been jammed up at the 640 X 480 resolution. So, what gives?

HTML lets Web authors specify the width of graphic images, normally in pixels. (Pixels are the dots that make up a computer screen.) But a fixed number of pixels doesn't work because if the buttons fit at 800 X 600, they'd take up three rows at 640 X 480. And if they fit at 640 X 480, there would be a lot of blank, wasted space on 800 X 600 screens.

Fortunately, HTML includes a percent option on width specifications that can help your Web site accommodate visitors with varying screen resolutions. The buttons above all use the command **WIDTH=16%**. That means these six buttons occupy 96 percent of the width of the box no matter what the current screen resolution.

Visitor PC processing power

Eventually we'll see Web standards that are as universally implemented as those on television. But until that time, consider the potential computer limitations that your visitors might face.

First, remember some visitors may still be using 486 PCs that will be strained to run a complex Java application. This is changing rapidly because now even Pentium computers are quite inexpensive. Before long you can create your site to work best on a Pentium or better. And, if you expect your audience to be mostly upscale computer users, then it's safe to assume they'll all have Pentium computers or equivalent.

Decisions, Decisions... So Many Choices

Are you feeling stressed over all of this information? It is *a lot* to absorb. And there are more products appearing every week to handle a constantly increasing array of Web features—trying to keep up is futile. To simplify your decision-making, we'll present a couple of situations that might apply to your needs for Web publishing.

Home-based businesses, small business Web

Small companies (1 to 20 people) and large will be able to take advantage of their cable company's infrastructure to provide high-speed Internet access and connectivity to their company's mainframes, provided the company is within the cable service area. These businesses will be able to access all the consumer information that Road Runner customers get at home, too. To get more information about Road Runner Business Solutions, call your local Road Runner business office.

> ## BUSINESS WEB RESTRICTIONS
> Trying to run a business off of a cable modem installed in the home will not be satisfactory because business users place different demands on a network that has been configured for home use. It is also a violation of the service contract the user has signed with the cable company. Cable customers wishing to run a small business from home should contact the Road Runner Business office for details.

A business might need the services of a Web site developer or design consultant to enhance their information to take advantage of the latest graphic techniques and HTML technologies. Most communities have a growing list of these entrepreneurs who are springing up to fill the demand for new media services. While it is always a mark of good citizenship to do business locally, the nature of the Web allows you to contract these services to organizations in a different state. Keep in mind that no one who uses your Web site will know its geographic location, so it can be maintained anywhere in the country—so you're free to find a deal on Web server space a thousand miles away.

Tools

Families and small organizations often begin their Web site with a word processor. Nearly anyone who is skilled in a Windows word processor can put basic information on a Web page. They'll use either WordPerfect or Microsoft Word as we discussed earlier. They are also likely to use one or more of the SkiSoft programs to quickly convert some existing material to the required Web format.

Beep! Beep!
Would you like to see examples of well-done family Web sites to help you get started on yours? Check out Family PC Fun at *www.FamilyPCfun.com*, the Web site of a newspaper Sunday comic strip. The Web site includes lots of great family links but you'll really like the weekly "Featured Family" that showcases the best of family Web sites. Check the Archive section to see lots of family sites. Once you get yours up and running be sure to submit it and maybe we'll see you in the funnies!

If you own a small or home-based business you may want to contract with a local Web-page designer to fill in your weak points after you create the basics. College campuses are a good place to find HTML authors. You will probably find a suitable HTML author with a notice on a student union bulletin board or through an ad in the school paper. But then again, HotDog Pro has enough features so that many average computer users learn it fast enough so that their businesses don't suffer.

A small business also may need an ad copywriter to help with the writing and an advertising consultant and an artist to help with graphics and design. If you've used such marketing professionals before, you will probably find that they have expanded their services to include Web technology. In fact, students in most college marketing courses are developing Web pages in class exercises. So, perhaps a college student would be satisfactory in this aspect of your Web site development, too.

If information on your Web site needs frequent changes, you can update your Web site quickly if you use a Web service provider that permits you to load your updates directly into your site's home directory with FTP. You don't want the accuracy of your information to depend on someone else's schedule for loading your updates. Web services are often staffed by people who may not understand the importance of responding to your schedule. But direct FTP capability will ensure that you have control over your Web site's content.

Summary

Well, that's a solid introduction to Web publishing. Internet technology changes too rapidly for us to put any more details in a book. You can probably see by now that Web site development can be fairly simple or it can be a never-ending story that becomes a full-time job. Don't get discouraged early. People who are able to create top-notch Web sites can earn more than $100 per hour for HTML development work. You can't expect to match the impressive technical level of the best sites on the Web without devoting a lot of time to it.

The important thing to remember in Web site development is to get started and become a participant instead of merely a spectator. You can improve your site as you learn more, and that will enrich the Web for us all. See you in cyberspace!

HTML specification
http://www.w3.org/MarkUp

Here's a link to the table of contents for the complete specifications of the latest version of HTML. This is not a user-friendly guide to HTML, but it is a highly detailed reference source about all aspects of HTML, its development and its specifications. The definition and usage of all legal HTML codes are contained here. It includes complete coverage not only of HTML but also of the use of Cascading Style Sheets. Many of the resources elements on this site have been created in special versions that can be downloaded directly to your system so you can access them in your Web browser without depending on your Internet connection.

Self-taught Web publishing
http://www.lne.com/Web

This is the home page for the books *Teach Yourself Web Publishing with HTML in a Week* and *Teach Yourself More Web Publishing with HTML in a Week*, both by Laura Lemay. These books describe how to write, design and publish information on the World Wide Web. In addition to describing the HTML language itself, they provide extensive information on using images, sounds, video, interactivity, gateway programs (CGI), forms and imagemaps. Through the use of dozens of real-life examples and actual HTML source code, the books help you not only to learn the technical details of writing Web pages, but also teach you how to communicate information effectively through the Web.

Elite Servers
http://www.eliteservers.net

Check out Elite Servers as a host for your Web site if you need a commercial home page that includes secure credit card ordering (a commerce server), automated e-mail forwarding, list servers or a RealAudio server. Elite offers sites for as little as $7.95 per month. A comprehensive business site could cost more—but not much more, even for complete service. Elite provides technical support only for an hourly-rate charge, so you'll need to know how to upload pages yourself via an FTP client and you'll be on your own if your HTML pages, Front Page extensions or CGI scripts need trouble-shooting. Nonetheless, it's a good service to use if you need features not available with your Road Runner service contract.

O'Reilly Associates
http://website.ora.com

O'Reilly Associates has emerged as a powerhouse of technology on the Internet. They've published a library of more than 80 excellent technical reference guides that delve into details far more deeply than we have in this book. Actually, mainstream users may find the topics covered in this site to be too technical, but if you are performing or managing the hands-on work involved in publishing your organization's Web site, then you absolutely *must* place O'Reilly's URL in your Favorites Folder.

Web Page Background Color Chart
http://www.familypcfun.com/ColorTxt.htm

Here's a valuable tool when you're using background colors or font colors on your Web site. It's an HTML color chart that shows exactly how the colors will look on your monitor. It gives the colors right inside each color box using standard color names that are recognized by Internet Explorer and Netscape Navigator. There's also a chart available (ColorHex.htm) that uses HTML hex format. Be sure to grab these pages and save them on your system for future use.

The World Wide Web Handbook
http://www.ucc.ie/~pflynn/books/wwwbook.html

This is a Web site for the book, *The World Wide Web Handbook An HTML Guide for Users, Authors and Publishers* by Peter Flynn, published by International Thomson Computer Press. It profiles the book, including its Table of Contents and includes a downloadable version of the "HTML Reference Card" that is included with the printed edition of the book.

Fill-out forms overview
http://www.ncsa.uiuc.edu/SDG/Software/Mosaic/Docs/fill-out-forms/overview.html

This site focuses on creating fill-out forms for your Web pages. One of its most valuable features is a listing of 13 forms done in HTML (at last count) that you can use as examples. They range in complexity from "ludicrously simple" to extremely advanced. It's a good place to download sample pages that will help you develop your Web publishing skills.

Random tips and hints on constructing Web pages
http://www.nd.edu/PageCreation/TipsAndHints.html

Here's a Notre Dame University site that gives tips and hints on constructing HTML documents (see Figure 7). Be sure to check out the "Clickable Graphics" tutorial that gives you a clickable graphic map demonstration-tutorial. This site is not an encyclopedic presentation on creating HTML documents—and it admits to being "Mac-centric" on some points—but it does address a number of issues that are encountered frequently. Mark this URL because this Web site is also a good place to track HTML changes as well as other changes in Web technology.

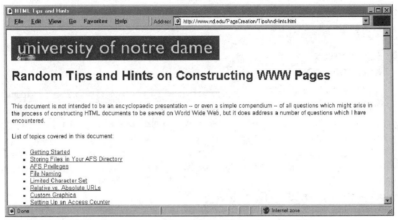

Figure 7 HTML tips - everything from the basics to video

Jeff Mallett's Web Authoring Page
http://www.lyricist.com/Jeff/html.html

Here's an online guide to publishing on the Web by Internet guru Jeff Mallet. Click on any one of these headings to jump to fact-filled text that can help you get started with your Web publishing: Authoring HTML, Web Authoring, Java and Authorization.

 ## Jargon Cutter
WYSIWYG (pronounced "whizzy-wig") - Stands for What You See Is What You Get. Windows word processors are WYSIWYG because what you see on-screen is pretty much what you get when you print. DOS programs weren't WYSIWYG because they displayed text as plain characters, and you had to print to see how your document looked. Windows HTML editors are not WYSIWYG—yet. So far, they display only text, so you must use your Web browser to see how they'll look on the Web.

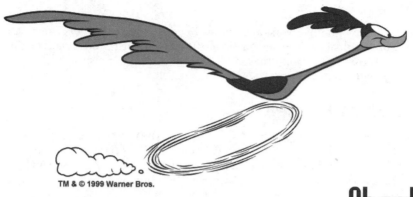

TM & © 1999 Warner Bros.

Chapter 14

Pictures in Cyber•Space: Web Graphics

A picture is worth—how much is it? A thousand words? Ten thousand? Whatever the number, the Web is a perfect illustration of that ancient adage. Remember that for nearly thirty years the Internet existed in text-only format, distributing technical and academic information between large institutions. And in its text-only format, the Internet remained the realm of scientists and academics. But the creation of the Web permitted the Internet to go graphic and the graphics are what made it go public.

Well-done graphics can lend an appealing look to static, boring technical information. Graphics can also create simple explanations for difficult concepts and convey messages quickly and efficiently. And, graphics can bypass language barriers by creating universal, pictorial labels and instructions—perfect for the World Wide Web.

Unfortunately, Web graphics have been a double-edged sword. While cutting easily through difficult concepts and making the Internet interesting to us everyday folks, graphics have also cut severely into Internet bandwidth. The result is that the Internet—designed to carry efficient, text-only documents—is now clogged with millions of graphic images. But that's a price we're willing to pay because without the graphics few people would ever venture into cyberspace.

There will be a happy ending to this, however, because technological advancements will soon alleviate Internet bandwidth problems. Road Runner cable modem service will greatly decrease your personal bandwidth limitations. Web sites located on the local Road Runner servers can contain rich graphics that will easily and quickly be reviewed by Road Runner customers. Nonetheless, most of the rest of the Internet is shackled with more limited technology, which will hold you back—until they catch up with the high-speed access that we deliver.

Until most of the Internet has a bandwidth capacity that matches Road Runner, we suggest you go easy on the graphics for Web sites you design and create. If the audience for your site is largely within the Road Runner service area, you could break this rule. Or, if you have a dual audience, you might consider designing a site that has a low-bandwidth limited graphics version that non-Road Runner customers can reach by jumping to from a link at the top of your Road Runner site. Still, you should begin now to master Web graphics because they are here to stay and your visitors will expect you to use graphics to improve your site's value.

Web Graphics Primer

You'll see two file formats in common use on the Web: .GIF (Graphics Interchange Format) and .JPEG (Joint Photographics Expert Group). .GIF is the more common of the two, but .JPEG is catching on fast. There are pros and cons to both, so you'll have to decide for yourself which to use on your own Web site.

We'll present an overview of both major formats, tips on choosing the right one for a given application, overviews of graphics drawing, editing and conversion software, plus tips on graphics saving and editing. You'll find many excellent graphics resources from around the Web, including links to other Internet books that deal specifically with graphics and scanning.

.GIF graphic files

The .GIF format (Graphic Interchange Format) is good for all types of images and is compatible with a wide variety of graphics applications. .GIF was developed in 1987 by CompuServe to be a device-independent method of storing pictures. .GIF allows high-quality, high-resolution graphics to be displayed on a variety of graphics hardware and is intended as a common exchange and display mechanism for graphic images. A .GIF picture file has an extension .GIF.

The 1987 .GIF format was upgraded and released again in 1989, but used the same .GIF extension. Some graphic applications distinguish the two .GIF formats as GIF87 and GIF89. Even though the .GIF 8 bits/pixel format only supports 256 colors and has relatively large file sizes, .GIF remains one of the most popular choices for storing images. .GIF format is best when used with images containing flat areas of color that have little or no shading. .GIF is well-matched to inexpensive computer displays because it can store only 8 bits/pixel (256 or fewer colors) and most PCs can't display more than 256 distinct colors at once.

Sizing Web Graphics

The graphic images used on the Internet are sized by pixels. Pixels are dots on your screen. A typical Windows screen is made up of 640 pixels horizontally and 480 pixels vertically. For short, this is called a 640 X 480 screen resolution. But Windows has other resolutions. Another common Windows resolution is 800 X 600. Thus an image that is 240 pixels high would run 50 percent of the height of a 640 X 480 screen, but would occupy only 40 percent of the height of a 800 X 600 screen.

If your graphic image displays in different sizes on different screens, you'll have difficulty planning the text so that it will fit around the graphic. Fortunately, HTML gives you two important—but little-used—tools to help control the relationship between text and graphics on your Web pages.

The clear break command

HTML has a code, <BR>, that causes a line break. You could use a series of consecutive <BR> commands to push your text down below the bottom of a graphic image. But if you put in just enough of them to push the text down past the graphic on a 640 x 480 screen, then the page will look different on an 800 x 600 screen. The solution is not to use multiple <BR> commands, but to use an option with the code that forces the next line break to occur *after* it clears the current graphic image. Use the HTML tag code <BR CLEAR=LEFT> or <BR CLEAR=RIGHT> depending on which side of the screen the image lies.

The percentage width command

HTML lets you control the width of graphic images with the WIDTH command that normally is expressed in pixels. But instead of using pixels, you can use a percent so that the size will be uniform across all screen resolutions. For example, if you used <IMG SRC="image.gif" WIDTH=25%>, the image would be 160 pixels wide at 640 x 480 and 200 pixels wide at 800 x 600 resolution.

Beep! Beep!

.GIF Internet images are downloaded in 8 X 8-pixel blocks. Knowing this can help you increase your site's download efficiency. For example, if you size a graphic to be exactly 64 X 24 pixels it will download in 8 blocks by 3 blocks, or 24 blocks. But if you sized the same image at 65 X 25 it would require 9 blocks by 4 blocks, or 36 blocks, a fifty percent increase! This would increase the download time, yet the on-screen size difference would barely be noticeable—a real waste of bandwidth.

.JPEG and .JPG graphic files

JPEG (pronounced "jay-peg") is a standardized image compression mechanism. The name .JPEG is derived from the original name of the committee that wrote the standard, the Joint Photographic Experts Group.

.JPEG is designed for compressing either full-color or gray-scale images of natural, real-world scenes. It works well on photographs, naturalistic artwork and similar material, but not well on lettering, simple cartoons, black-and-white or line drawings. A .JPEG picture file has an extension .JPEG or .JPG.

.JPEG stores full color information: 24 bits/pixel (up to 16.7 million colors). Therefore, with full-color hardware, .JPEG images can look far better than .GIF files. And, .JPEG files can be much smaller than GIFs so they are *usually* superior to .GIF in terms of disk space and transmission time.

We say "usually" because applications that save images in .JPEG files or convert images to .JPEG files permit adjustments to the image that alter the image quality and file size. Both the compression method and the percentage of compression are user-controllable and directly correspond to the quality of the compressed image.

It is possible to save a .JPEG image in a file that is larger than its .GIF counterpart. Of course it also can be smaller. The trick is to learn to adjust the quality optimally because there is a point of diminishing returns with every image. In other words, eventually you'll reach the point where increasing the quality adjustment doesn't improve quality, but does continue to increase the file size. That's why .GIF can be a nice trade-off because it creates a reasonable middle-of-the-road file in terms of balancing quality versus file size—and requires no tweaking skills.

.JPEG files often use a file extension of .JPG because of file naming limitations in MS-DOS and Windows 3.x. For example, if you use a Windows 3.x application to save a .JPEG graphic file, your system will convert the extension to .JPG. There will be no difference between the two files and you can rename it with a .JPEG extension if you transfer it back to a Unix, a Windows 95 or a Windows NT system.

Capturing images from Web sites you visit

You'll see a vast array of graphics as you surf the Internet, and your Road Runner Browser makes it easy to save them to your hard drive. Of course you'll have to keep in mind that almost all Internet graphics are protected by normal copyrights, but you can easily e-mail the source site for reuse permission. If you want to include a graphic on your site because you're cross-linking to the source site, they will probably be happy to grant permission to increase their site's exposure.

Beep! Beep!

If you're seeking permission to reprint or reuse a graphic image from a Web site, where do you start? First, go to the bottom of the home page of the Web site and look for a link to e-mail to the "Webmaster." Since Webmasters are responsible for the design and maintenance of Web sites, they'll know the source of the graphics. Often, you'll be told that the graphic is "public domain" and you're free to use it. But even if it's not public domain, most places will be glad to grant you permission to use their graphics if you'll link to their site and give them credit. See our copyright chapter for more information.

Once the copyright considerations are handled, you can have a field day collecting graphics all over cyberspace. Here's a quick Step-By-Step exercise that shows you how to capture a graphic to your hard drive.

Step-By-Step

GOAL: Learn to save an Internet graphic image

✔ Start the Road Runner Browser.

✔ Press **CTRL+L**.

✔ Type *www.fedworld.gov*, then press **ENTER**.

✔ Place the mouse over the logo image at the top of the screen.

✔ Click the right button.

✔ Click **Save Image As...**

Select an appropriate directory in which to save this image before you complete the next step.

✔ Click **Save.**

You can open a saved graphic image in the Road Runner Browser at any time, or you can reference it in one of your own HTML pages.

That was easy, but what about capturing the background image? That, too, is easy with the Road Runner Browser. The next exercise will show you how to save any Web site graphic background on your own system. Of course if you plan to use the saved image on your own Web site, be sure to ask the original Webmaster if the image is copyrighted and get permission to use it if it is.

 ## Jargon Cutter

Background image - A .GIF or .JPG image file that is used as a background behind the text on a Web page. Usually the image is small so it downloads quickly. Then the Web browser repeats the image on the screen, like a wallpaper pattern. Many Web pages have no background image—they're plain white or they just use a color—so there's no background image to capture.

Step-By-Step

GOAL: Learn to save an Internet background graphic

✔ Start with the same page used in the previous exercise.

✔ Click the right mouse button on any blank area of the page.

✔ Click **Save Background As...**

✔ Click **Save** to save the image on your hard drive.

   Select a directory and change the name as desired.

Windows 95 also lets you save a Web page background image to your clipboard so you can paste it into your favorite graphics application. And, the Road Runner Browser lets you designate a Web page background image as your desktop wallpaper.

Tips On Selecting an Image Format

The best graphic format to use depends on the application and the desired effect. So, to make some sense out of your choices, we'll share these Internet graphics tips that are provided courtesy of Kody Kline of *Extreme D.T.P.* in Tulsa (see Figure 1). Kody is a master computer graphics artist. See for yourself at: *www.ionet.net/~kkline*.

Transparent background

All graphic images are rectangular in shape, even if they store pictures of irregularly-shaped objects. If you want an irregularly-shaped object not to have a rectangular outside shape, you'll need to use the GIF89a format because only GIF89a lets you make a transparent background for your image. A transparent background creates the illusion of an irregularly-shaped picture because the transparent background allows the colors behind the picture to show through the transparent color, even though the actual image outline remains rectangular.

File efficiency

If you want to reduce the download time of your large graphic images, you'll find that a moderately-compressed .JPEG image can cut the file size and download time by approximately 70 percent with only minor loss of quality. Much greater detail can be obtained in full-color photographic quality in a low compression .JPEG versus .GIF because of the .GIF color limitations.

Interlacing

Although the flashy 16.7-million color .JPEG images may look excellent on your computer, remember that many people who access your Web site will not have adequate video hardware or the higher speed modems to handle these images efficiently. .GIF format supports an "interlaced" option that quickly displays a blurred full-size image of the .GIF, then, during repeated passes, fills in and sharpens the image. This doesn't reduce overall download time, but at least it gives visitors a quick taste of the image that may entice them to wait.

Whichever format you select, a compromise between a high-quality photographic image and concerns for long transmission times can result in a usable graphic that can deliver pizzaz without visitors needing a nap during download.

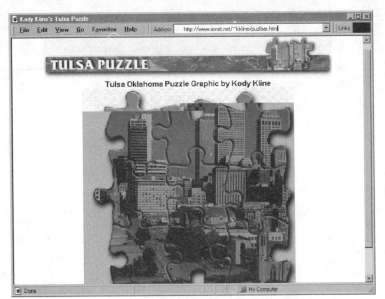

Figure 1 DTP Extreme - a top-notch Web graphics designer

Original graphics art

Creating a world-class site requires world-class graphics. Very few part-time graphics users can create the level of the very best graphics that you'll see today on the Web. And even if they could, they probably lack the expertise to optimize the balance between image quality and file size. Creating world-class Web graphics is truly a professional job.

For a home-based or small business, or for your family's Web site, you don't need world-class, eye-popping graphics. A simple, colorful graphic image will spruce up your site and you won't have to quit your job to create it. So, perhaps your creative juices are stirring and you want to try your own hand at Internet graphics. If so, then we'll give you do-it-yourselfers a quick introduction to creating Internet graphics.

Graphic Drawing Packages

A review of all the good graphics programs would be a book in itself, so we'll trim the list and show you some of the most popular—in other words, some of the most inexpensive—applications. In fact, some of them are *extremely* inexpensive—for example, free! These won't create the top-of-the-line world-class graphics, but you'll save money. Everything involves trade-offs. Besides, if you're a novice, you most likely wouldn't be able to justify the time it would take to learn to use those highly-specialized tools.

Client-side Clickable Maps

Until recently, Web authors needed to use CGI programs—running on the Web server—to enable users to navigate via clickable image maps. The need for CGI programming skills put clickable maps out of reach for most Web authors. But a new HTML standard—called "client-side" clickable maps—is simple enough so that most Web authors will be able to create clickable image maps.

Client-side clickable maps means that the action occurs on the client computer. Once the Web page is downloaded, the server won't need to be involved with handling the site's clickable maps. This helps alleviate some of the Internet bandwidth problems, lessens the strain on Web servers and simplifies the work of Web authors.

In the last chapter, we outlined the HotDog and FrontPage HTML editors. Both of these automate the tedious job of mapping coordinates on an image map. With either one, you won't have to write, test, compile and upload a CGI script to handle the jumps. Instead, the editor will generate the HTML code and correctly place it into the HTML page that you're editing.

Paint Shop Pro

Paint Shop Pro is a shareware graphics application. You can download and test it before you pay (see Figure 2). Paint Shop Pro is a user-friendly, image viewing, editing and converting program. With support for more than 30 image formats, and several drawing and painting tools, this may be the only graphics program you will ever need.

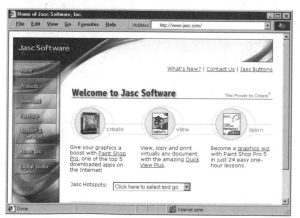

Figure 2 Paint Shop Pro - a great way to start

Paint Shop Pro is an excellent graphics tool for beginning Web authors. It handles all required formats to get you started. The home page is at *www.jasc.com* where you can read about it, check its lengthy feature list and download a free, trial copy. The Jasc Software Web site has a rich resource of graphics tutorials, tips and step-by-step instructions on how to create specific graphic effects.

Even though Paint Shop Pro is not the most powerful graphics application, it has plenty of professional-level features and can create some terrific graphics. For the money, this is the best value for Web graphics. But if you're not on a tight budget and you're ready to tackle the intricacies of some truly world-class graphics features, check out the next topic.

World-Class Graphics

Adobe Photoshop graphics software enables designers and photographers to create original artwork, correct color, retouch and composite scanned images and prepare professional separations and output with complete flexibility. With such a wealth of powerful painting and selection tools, plus multiple layers, special effects filters, and lighting effects, Adobe Photoshop is a professional's dream application. You can learn more at *www.adobe.com* (see Figure 3).

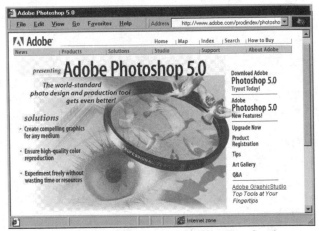

Figure 3 Adobe - world-class Web graphics for the most demanding artist

Photoshop includes more than 40 standard filters, including multiple choices for image sharpening, softening, stylizing, distortion, video, and removal of noise, dust and scratches. Its powerful lighting effects lets users apply multiple light sources to an image and choose from a range of colors, intensities, and angles.

With Photoshop, you can create an original image or start with a scanned image. It lets you create effects in separate layers—like transparent sheets of acetate—upon which you can combine graphic elements plus paint and edit without changing the original background image. Photoshop's user-friendly interface lets you drag-and-drop selections from different files or from different layers. And you can save the finished image in a wide variety of different file formats, including .GIF and .JPEG. Its .GIF support extends to the GIF89 format that lets you create transparency and interlacing.

LView Pro

Somewhere in between the full-featured graphic applications and the beginner's applications, you might find that you lose some graphics conversion abilities. Via the Web you can download an excellent, shareware graphics conversion application, called LView Pro, that was authored by Leonardo Haddad Loureiro of MMedia Research. You'll be free to distribute LView Pro to others for trial and leisure utilization. If you decide to use it in business, however, you'll need to register your copy with MMedia to comply with copyright regulations.

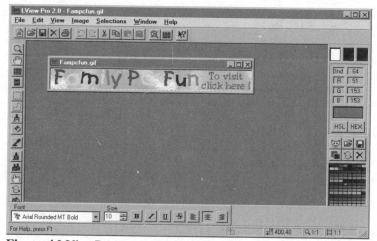

Figure 4 LViewPro - a must for conversion

You'll find an vast array of features considering that you can try out this application free via the Internet. It lets you flip, rotate, resize and crop images, and it gives you a full-range of powerful image enhancement tools. LView Pro (see Figure 4) can import .BMP, GIF87, GIF89, .JPEG, .PCX, .TIF, .TGA, .PPM, .PGM, .PBM and .DIB formats. Its .GIF features include a transparency that uses a simple "dropper" that lets you touch a background color that you want made transparent. A simple menu option tells LView Pro to automatically save all of your .GIF files in interlaced format—an excellent choice if you expect your visitors to be using dial-up modems to browse your site. And it has complete facilities for creating animated GIF images.

To get a trial copy of LView Pro, visit the LView home page at *www.lview.com*. The registration fee for commercial use is relatively inexpensive, compared to some of the professional graphics software. While you're there to download the application, check out the link entitled, <u>Transparent color</u> and save it or print it so you can create transparent backgrounds for your .GIF images.

<u>Oh, No, There's More!</u>

Just when you nailed down the facts on Internet graphics, things changed. A new graphics format is emerging. It's all about law suits and patents, but the result to you is a new format. After .GIF had become a standard on the Web, some lawsuits were filed over alleged patent infringements. Someone thought they'd suddenly be able to collect royalties from everyone who uses .GIF.

The real result? .GIF had been showing its age in a number of ways even before the lawsuit, so the announcement only hurried the development of a new and much-improved replacement. Now we all have a new graphics format with an extension of PNG (pronounced "ping"). The PNG format (Portable Network Graphics) was developed as free software and CompuServe intends it to be free of patent infringements.

For more information on PNG, check out its home page, which is maintained by Greg Roelofs at *quest.jpl.nasa.gov/PNG*.

Image Scanning

Scanning is a computer function that transforms existing photos, graphic images, drawings, sketches, maps, illustrations or even your child's museum piece. Once stored digitally, the captured image can be manipulated with computer graphics software. Scanned images can be retouched in the computer to optimize their on-screen appearance or they can be printed or included in a word processing document. Your primary use of a scanner will probably be to capture images and save them in either .GIF or .JPEG formats that you can use in your Web documents.

Since some quality is always lost during the scanning process, make sure that your original image is the best quality you can get. For best results the images should have high contrast and be perfectly sharp. As with photocopiers, you may need to adjust the brightness and contrast to capture an acceptable image. You will quickly discover that there's a bit of an art to optimally scanning images, but we've included some excellent scanning resources in this chapter and in the Orbiting in Cyberspace section at the end of this chapter.

Scanner basics

For professional results you should consider only flatbed scanners that are used on a desktop. A flatbed scanner is a scanning device that accepts flat art (photographs, drawings, clippings, illustrations). Most flatbed scanners are designed to handle 8.5 x 11 inch originals in *reflective media*—images that reflect light. Some flatbed scanners will handle transparent media (such as Ektachrome transparencies and 35mm slides), but you may have to add a special transparency adapter to activate this function.

For increased flexibility in paper handling, you can find scanners that accept legal-size documents. If you need to scan a large number of existing documents, be sure you select a scanner that includes a document feeder option because flatbed scanners normally accept only one document at a time.

Scanners will include scanning software, but the quality and features vary greatly. You're not likely to find a full-featured application bundled with any scanner, though all are adequate. If possible, stick to applications that give you the ability to scan and save in all the common file formats that you will want to use (especially .GIF and .JPEG). Good scanning software should also allow you to crop and rotate before or during saving. It's an absolute must that your scanner have a TWAIN (Technology Without An Interesting Name) module. TWAIN is a crucial feature because it's supported by all major applications and allows you to scan directly into applications such as WordPerfect, Word, Paint Shop Pro and LView Pro. It's fun to watch WordPerfect ingest a color photo directly into a document (see Figure 5). What a way to spruce up a report, newsletter or family announcement!

Figure 5 TWAIN - scan images directly into a word processor

If you're interested in going beyond the basics of scanning, the next sidebar will take you about as far as you could want to go. A note of caution, though: this could become a full-time job.

Advanced Scanning and Graphics

Below, we'll show you where to access online graphics lessons that will teach you advanced scanning and other graphics techniques. You can learn everything from how to produce transparent backgrounds (a must for irregularly-shaped images) to optimizing your graphics for size and download speed.

Advanced scanning

For some productivity-enhancing scanning tips, check out Michael J. Sullivan's Web site at *www.hsdesign.com/scanning* (see Figure 6). This is a fabulous scanning resource, but it's only the tip of the iceberg. For in-depth lessons and tips you can buy Michael's book, *Make Your Scanner a Great Design and Production Tool*, North Light Books, 1995.

Michael is partner and artistic director of Haywood & Sullivan in Quincy, Massachusetts, an award-winning full-range design firm that excels at communication design using various media. He also is founding partner of Pilgrim New Media in Cambridge, Massachusetts, a multimedia titles publisher.

Advanced graphics

Jump to *www.warwick.ac.uk/~cudbh/I3course/graphics.html* where you'll find a set of graphics lessons from Bronwen Reid at the University of Hull, in the U.K. Lessons here include backgrounds, transparencies and interlacing. Also, you can use this site to jump to other sites with graphics tips.

Figure 6 Michael Sullivan - scanning tips and resources

Yahoo! .GIF files
http://www.yahoo.com/

Computers_and_Internet/Software/Data_Formats/GIF

Yahoo! has an entire category for .GIF graphics. This is the direct URL for the page. From within Yahoo!, you can step manually through the categories: Computers and Internet, Software, Data Formats, .GIF. This page probably includes more on .GIF than you'll ever need to know. .GIF licensing has been a mess for years, but if you're a .GIF graphics developer you can check here to make sure you're up to speed on the latest word on licensing of the .GIF technology.

Web graphics sources
http://redtape.uchicago.edu/users/mdmendoz/art.html

From clipart to fonts to graphics, these links will connect you to a wealth of art and graphics resources. Have fun! This page is a perfect Favorites Folder candidate for anyone who needs to locate graphic images for Web sites. At least start here, because many of the pages listed here will have other links.

Scanning FAQs
http://www.infomedia.net/scan

This page contains a wealth of scanning FAQs, presented by Jeff Bone, formerly Electronic Media Coordinator, University of Alabama at Birmingham, School of Medicine; and more recently founder and president of Infomedia, Inc., a top-flight, information systems integration and development company, serving the southeast. To give you easy access, the topics on scanning artwork and photographs have been broken down into four primary categories: line art, halftones, grayscale and color. In addition to these tips, you also can read about tricky, yet very important, resolution issues and copyright issues.

Cool Graphics on the Web
http://www.fishnet.net/~gini/cool

This is your one-stop resource for clip art and Web page graphics—thousands of free and low cost images (see Figure 7). If you are searching for high quality graphics for your Web page, this site can save you a lot of work and time. When using regular search engines to locate textures, you'll come up with more "misses" than hits. Frequently, the sites that come up using the keyword "textures" are totally unrelated to actual textures, backgrounds or Web page graphics—wasting a lot of time, but this site is a collection of the best sites carrying free or low-cost Web page backgrounds, textures, icons, GIFs, sound files, fonts, and related graphics. You will find lots of treasure here.

Figure 7 Thousands of graphics files for downloading

Crystal Graphics
http://www.crystalgraphics.com

This site specializes in graphic enhancements for PowerPoint presentations (see Figure 8). They can energize your Power-Point presentations with TV-style 3-D effects. Try the free demo! They also have an extensive library of 3-D graphics and tools for creating your own graphics and even for enhancing video productions.

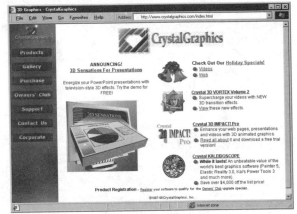

Figure 8 3-D graphics enhancements

Free Graphics by Syruss
http://www.syruss.com

Just look at all the categories on the home page of this site (see Figure 9). Each category is organized by similar-type graphics that include the actual images so that you can easily decide what you want. If you're creating Web pages, you'll want to bookmark this site as a permanent resource for your graphics needs. The really cool part is that it's all free!

Figure 9 Lots of free graphics and Web graphics tips

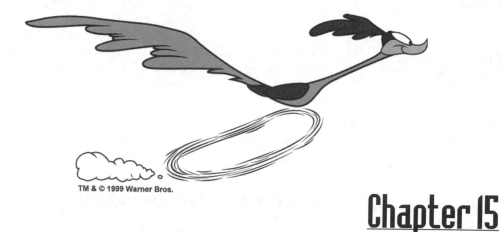

Chapter 15

Cyberspace Copyrights: Top 10 Myths

While you're working in cyberspace, you're going to encounter more written material than you've ever before been able to access. After all, that's the exciting part about the Internet—it brings into our homes and offices just about any information we want, instantly. In this book you'll learn how to access information instantly and you'll see that it's easy to copy and paste Internet information into reports, e-mail, news-group postings and your own Web site. But instant access doesn't give anyone instant rights to copyrighted material.

There are a lot of myths in cyberspace about the status of copyrighted material. There is a tendency to think that anything you can bring up on your monitor belongs to you. Usually, this is not true. Electronic material is protected by copyright law just as well as traditional, printed material. We want to give you some food for thought about electronic copyrights so you don't put yourself or your organization in a bind over some material that you've copied and pasted from the Internet.

This is one of those proverbial "good news—bad news" situations. The bad news is that violating copyright laws is easy to do and it can get you into trouble even if you do it accidentally. The good news is that it is easy to stay out of trouble.

So, we've compiled answers to ten common myths about copyrights as applied to the Internet. This information is based on work done by Brad Templeton, who in 1989, founded the ClariNet Communications Corporation's news service. ClariNet was the Internet's first electronic newspaper. Brad was a pioneer in understanding what types of online content can and cannot be freely reused.

Please note that while most of the principles covered here are international in scope, some are derived from Canadian and U.S. law. This chapter is intended to clear up some common intellectual property law misconceptions that are often seen on the Internet. It is not intended to be a complete treatise on all the nuances of the subject, but it lays the groundwork of understanding.

Beep! Beep!
Note: Please do not run an Internet search to find Brad Templeton's e-mail address so that you can e-mail him to ask for legal advice—use other resources or consult a property-rights attorney.

Copyright Myths

Here are Brad's Top 10 Copyright Myths, followed by a summary of the main points. Be sure to check out the Orbiting in Cyberspace section at the end of the chapter in which we point you to some other Internet sources on copyright issues.

1) If it doesn't have a copyright notice, it's not copyrighted

Not true. This was true in the past, but today almost all major nations follow the Berne copyright convention. For example, in the U.S., almost everything created privately and originally after April 1, 1989 is copyrighted and protected whether it has a notice or not. The default you should assume for other people's works is that they are copyrighted and may not be copied unless you *know* otherwise. There are some old works that lost protection without notice, but frankly you should not risk it unless you know for sure.

It is true that a notice strengthens the protection, by warning people, and by allowing one to get more and different damages, but it is not necessary. If it looks copyrighted, you should assume it is.

This applies to pictures, too. You may not scan pictures from magazines and post them to the Internet, and if you come upon something unknown, you shouldn't post that either.

The correct form for a copyright notice is:

> "Copyright (dates) by (copyright holder)."

You can use the copyright symbol © instead of the word "Copyright" but "(C)" has never been given legal force. The phrase "All Rights Reserved" used to be required in some nations but is not now needed.

2) If I don't charge for it, it's not a violation

Absolutely false. Whether you charge can affect the damages awarded in court, but that's essentially the only difference. It's still a violation if you give it away—and there can still be heavy damages if you hurt the commercial value of a protected property.

This is an important consideration for business Internet users because your Web site may offer summaries of key information within your industry. A natural source for this information is the Web sites of other companies. If you need to offer the material verbatim, then provide a link on your site to the information that you are referencing. If you need to excerpt portions of it, be sure to ask the owners of the source Web site for permission to reuse their material. If they know that you're not charging for the material and if you give them credit and include a link back to their site, many companies will let you use portions of their content.

3) If it's posted to Usenet it's in the public domain

False. Nothing is in the public domain anymore unless the owner explicitly puts it in the public domain. Explicitly, as in you have a note from the copyright holder stating, "I grant this to the public domain." If you don't use those exact words, then words very much like them.

Some argue that posting to the Usenet newsgroups implicitly grants permission to everybody to copy the posting within fairly wide bounds, and others feel that Usenet is an automatic store and forward network where all the thousands of copies made are done at the command (rather than the consent) of the poster. This is a matter of some debate, but even if the former is true (and in this writer's opinion we should all pray it isn't true) it simply would suggest that newsgroup posters are implicitly granting permissions "for the sort of copying one might expect when one posts to Usenet" and in no case is this a placement of material into the public domain. Furthermore it is very difficult for an implicit license to supersede an explicitly stated license of which the copier was aware.

Note that all this assumes that the poster had the right to post the item in the first place. If the poster didn't, then all of the copies are pirate, and no implied license or theoretical reduction of the copyright can take place.

Copyrights can expire after a long time, putting something into the public domain, and there are some fine points on this issue regarding older copyright law versions. However, none of this applies to an original article posted to Usenet.

Note that granting something to the public domain (PD) is a complete abandonment of all rights. You can't make something "PD for non-commercial use." If your work is PD, other people can even modify one byte and put their name on it.

4) My posting was just fair use!

The "fair use" exemption to copyright law was created to allow things such as commentary, parody, news reporting, research and education about copyrighted works without the permission of the author. Intent and damage to the commercial value of the work are important considerations. Are you reproducing an article from the New York Times because you needed to in order to criticize the quality of the New York Times, or because you couldn't find time to write your own story, or didn't want your readers to have to pay to log onto the online services with the story or buy a copy of the paper? The first is probably fair use, the others are not.

Fair use is almost always a short excerpt and almost always attributed. (One should not use more of the work than is necessary to make the commentary.) It should not harm the commercial value of the work—in the sense of people no longer needing to buy it (which is another reason why reproduction of the entire work generally is forbidden.)

Note that most inclusion of text in Usenet follow-ups is for commentary and reply, and it doesn't damage the commercial value of the original posting (if it has any) and as such it is fair use. Fair use isn't an exact doctrine, either. The court decides if the right to comment overrides the copyright on an individual basis in each case.

There have been cases that go beyond the bounds of what's been covered here, but in general they don't apply to the typical Internet misclaim of fair use. It's a risky defense to attempt.

Web-based material is, however, another matter. If you are providing commentary, the question might be asked, "Why do you need to provide the content at all?" If it's on the Web, then the page with your commentary can simply include a link to the material that you are referencing.

5) If you don't defend your copyright you lose it
False. Copyright is effectively never lost these days, unless explicitly given away. This is often confused with trademarks, which can be weakened or lost if not defended. A trademark is intended to protect the rights of an ongoing, active organization. If the organization ceases to use its trademark, then it only makes sense for another organization to be able to pick up the rights. Written material is quite different because it's hard to imagine how, after some period of time, it would make sense for another author to put his or her name on a written body of work and republish it as original.

6) Somebody has that name copyrighted
You can't copyright a name or anything short like a name. Titles usually don't qualify, but you could not write a song entitled: "Everybody's got something to hide except for me and my monkey." (J. Lennon/P. McCartney)

You can't copyright words, but you can trademark them, generally by using them to refer to your brand of a generic type of product or service. Like an "Apple" computer. Apple Computer "owns" that word applied to computers, even though it is also an ordinary word. Apple Records owns it when applied to music. Neither owns the word on its own, only in context, and owning a mark doesn't mean complete control—see a more detailed treatise on this law for details.

You can't use somebody else's trademark in a way that would unfairly hurt the value of the mark, or in a way that might make people confuse you with the real owner of the mark, or which might allow you to profit from the mark's good name. For example, if you were giving advice on music videos, you wouldn't want to label your works with a name like "MTV."

7) They can't get me, defendants in court have powerful rights!
Copyright law is mostly civil law. If you violate a copyright you usually would get sued, not charged with a crime. "Innocent until proven guilty," is a principle of criminal law, as is "proof beyond a reasonable doubt." In copyright suits, these don't apply the same way or at all. It's mostly which side and set of evidence the judge or jury accepts or believes more, though the rules vary based on the type of infringement. In civil cases you can even be made to testify against your own interests.

8) Copyright violation isn't a crime
Actually, recently in the U.S., commercial copyright violation involving more than 10 copies and value of more $2500 was made a felony. So use caution. (At least you get the protections of criminal law.) On the other hand, don't think you're going to get people thrown in jail for posting your e-mail. The courts have much better things to do than that. This is a fairly new, untested statute.

9) It doesn't hurt anybody—in fact it's free advertising

It's up to the owner to decide if he or she wants the free ads or not. If he or she wants them, you'll get a reply to your inquiry for permission. Don't rationalize whether it hurts the owner or not, ask them. Usually that's not too hard to do. Time past, Clari-Net published the very funny Dave Barry column to a large and appreciative Usenet audience for a fee, but some person didn't ask, and forwarded it to a mailing list, got caught, and the newspaper chain that employs Dave Barry pulled the column from the Internet. Even if you can't think of how the author or owner gets hurt, think about the fact that piracy on the Internet hurts everybody who wants a chance to use this wonderful new technology to do more than read other people's flamewars.

10) They e-mailed me a copy, so I can use it

To have a copy is not to have the copyright. All the e-mail you write is copyrighted. However, e-mail is not, unless previously agreed, secret. So you can certainly report on what e-mail you are sent, and reveal what it says. You can even quote parts of it to demonstrate. Frankly, somebody who sues over an ordinary message might well get no damages, because the message has no commercial value, but if you want to stay strictly in the law, you should seek permission.

On the other hand, don't go nuts if somebody posts your e-mail. If it was an ordinary non-secret personal letter of minimal commercial value with no copyright notice (like 99.9 percent of all e-mail), you probably won't get any damages if you sue.

Copyright Summary

Almost everything written today is copyrighted the moment it's written and no copyright notice is required.

A copyright violation does not depend on whether you charge money or not, though damages usually increase if you charge money.

Postings to the Internet are not granted to the public domain. And, they don't grant you any permission to do further copying except perhaps the sort of copying the poster might have expected in the ordinary flow of the Internet.

Fair use is a complex doctrine meant to allow certain valuable social purposes. Ask yourself why you are republishing what you are posting and why you didn't rewrite it in your own words. And consider just providing a link to the material.

Copyright is not lost because you don't defend it—that's a concept from trademark law. The ownership of names is also from trademark law, so don't say somebody has a name copyrighted.

Copyright law is mostly civil law where the special rights of criminal defendants you hear so much about don't apply. Watch out, however, as new laws are moving copyright violation into the criminal realm.

Don't rationalize that you are helping the copyright holder by increasing the exposure of his or her information. The Internet has made it easier than ever to secure permission, so be sure to ask first.

Posting someone else's message to a newsgroup is technically a copyright violation, but revealing facts from the message is okay. For almost all typical e-mail, nobody could wring any damages from you for posting it anyway. Nonetheless, why not e-mail the original author for permission?

Trademarks versus Internet domain names

One Web site listed in the "Orbiting in Cyberspace" section at the end of this chapter deals with the narrow—and highly volatile—aspect of trademark law that concerns the issue of trademark rights versus Internet domain names. This is a hotly-contested, highly-debated issue that could involve your organization if you build an online business presence. To track the latest news in this unsettled area, visit Georgetown University Web site (*www.law.georgetown.edu/lc/internic/domain1.html*).

This site is served by advisors Harold C. Wegner, Professor of Law, Director of the George Washington University Law School Intellectual Property Program, and Director of The Dean Dinwoody Center for Intellectual Property and Freedom of Expression and by David G. Post, who is a Visiting Professor of Law at Georgetown University Law Center and is Co-Director of The Cyberspace Law Institute.

The bottom line is that right now, there are no firm, legal guidelines and anything can happen. Possession of a trademark, or even your own legal name is no guarantee that you will retain the rights to use any domain name if you are sued.

For example, when the Web was emerging as a technology, many people registered their own last names as a domain name. Later, some companies with the same name have sued the individual owners who then lost the right in court to use the domain name that used their own last name. There are many disputed domain name cases open right now and discussions are going on to create policies for handling disputes.

Fortunately, the Web is a good medium to keep track of such open-ended material, so we've listed some resources to close this chapter. These sites will help you keep up with the rapidly-evolving world of cyberspace copyright issues.

Orbiting in Cyberspace

Copyright Clearance Center Online
http://www.copyright.com

This is the online version of the Copyright Clearance Center, a non-profit organization that provides collective copyright licensing services. It's an excellent resource for electronic copyright information. They help ease the permission burdens and consolidate payment rights for organizations of all sizes and types.

Electronic Freedom Frontier's intellectual property law primer
http://www.eff.org/pub/CAF/law/ip-primer

This is a primer written by J. Diane Brinson and Mark F. Radcliffe to help you understand intellectual property law issues as they apply to the development and distribution of multimedia works. The information was derived from the Multimedia Law Handbook (Ladera Press, 340 pages, 1-800-523-3721).

The United States Patent and Trademark Office (USPTO)
http://www.uspto.gov

The USPTO provides a link to the U.S. Copyright Office (see Figure 1), which you can access by clicking the Copyright link on the home page. It also includes topics on securing trademark rights, submitting applications, who may apply, how to search for conflicting, previously-registered trademarks and rules for using (TM), (SM) and "circled R" symbols. Some of the information here can help you sort out the relationship (or lack thereof) between Internet domain names and registered trademarks.

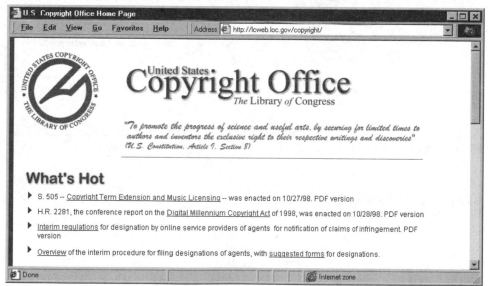

Figure 1 USPTO - U.S. copyright and trademark issues

Brad Cox on Electronic Property
http://www.virtualschool.edu/mon/TTEF.html

Brad Cox is a professor at George Mason University in Fairfax, Virginia. He's the author of *Superdistribution: Objects as Property on the Electronic Frontier*, an in-depth study of the problems of product distribution in the electronic age. On the Web home page listed here, Brad covers four different aspects of our cyberspace world: Electronic Commerce, Electronic Money, Electronic Goods and Electronic Property.

Intellectual Property Law
http://www.intelproplaw.com

The intellectual property law server (see Figure 2) provides information about intellectual property law including patent, trademark and copyright. Resources include comprehensive links, general information, space for professionals to publish articles and forums for discussing related issues.

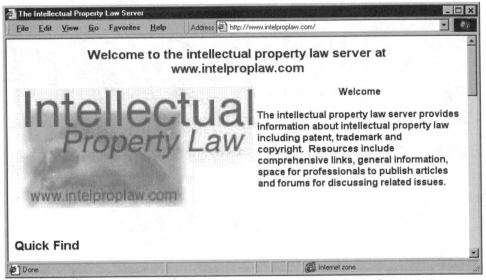

Figure 2 Comprehensive resource for all types of copyright information

Copyright Society of the U.S.A.
http://www.csusa.org

The Copyright Society of the U.S.A. is a nonprofit corporation that was organized in 1953 to foster interest in and advance the study of copyright law and the rights in literature, music, art, the theater, motion pictures and other forms of intellectual property. The Society's membership is comprised of individuals, business organizations, law firms and associations which are involved in or affected by copyright, including those based on new technologies for creating and using copyrightable works. The Society is governed by a Board of Trustees consisting of outstanding members of the copyright community in business, education, and the practice and teaching of law. **Note:** This is *not* the United States Copyright Office of the Library of Congress through which you register your copyrights.

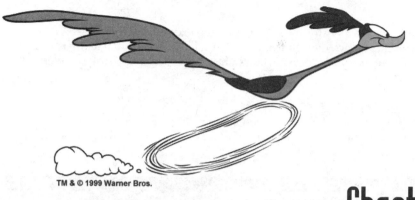

TM & © 1999 Warner Bros.

Chapter 16

Boosting Efficiency: Windows Primer

If you're new to Windows, some of the Step-By-Step exercises in this book might be confusing. So, we'd like to give you a brief Windows overview so you'll understand the basic terms. If you're already comfortable with Windows, however, you can skim this section. But note the tips we've included in this appendix so you can point it out to friends, family members and coworkers who need help getting started.

Common User Access

Everything that you do with Windows takes place within an object on the screen called a window—pretty clever name, isn't it? Every window you'll use has common characteristics, a fairly common set of menu commands, a common set of keystrokes, and a common set of controls for interacting with users. Put those factors together and you've got something called Common User Access (CUA).

When programmers write a Windows application, they don't start from scratch and make up their own rules, keystrokes and menus. Instead they abide by the CUA standard. This is terrific for you because all applications take on a similar look and feel so that learning new ones becomes simpler. And, when you switch back and forth between applications, you don't have to mentally shift gears each time and use a completely different set of standards.

Beep! Beep!

Nothing involving humans is truly standard, is it? Well, Windows is no exception. While we've just told you that Windows has common components throughout all applications, the creative human element shines through as well. That means that you'll see more than the basics because programmers have created some of their own tools and user-interaction devices. Still, even these original Windows creations will have similarities with the basics. Use Windows with an eye toward seeing as much commonality as you can, and don't be thrown off-balance by the differences.

You can buy whole books on Windows and take full-day Windows classes, so these few pages are by no means a complete Windows lesson. But we can give you the basics so you can at least perform the Step-By-Step exercises in this book. As you do that, your Windows knowledge will increase naturally because you'll learn as you go. The plan here is to give you four basic components: windows, keystrokes, menus and user interaction tools.

Windows components

We'll begin with a picture of a window and a description of its components (see Figure 1). The components are labeled on the image. Look them over, then we'll run through each labeled item.

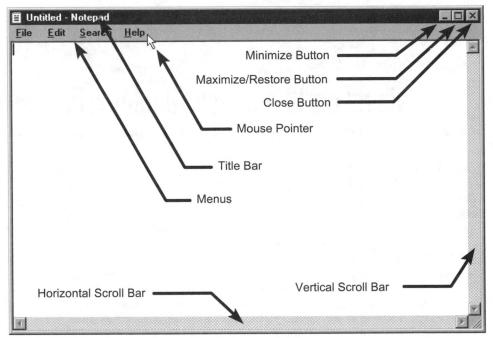

Figure 1 The basic components of a window

Mouse Pointer

When we tell you to **click** something, we mean to use the computer's mouse to move this pointer over the object, then quickly press (click) the left mouse button.

When we say to **double-click** something, place the mouse over the object and click the left mouse button twice in quick succession, *without moving the mouse* as you make the two clicks.

When we say to **right-click** something, place the mouse over the object and click the right mouse button, then release it *without moving the mouse*. A right-click will bring up a short menu of commands.

Beep! Beep!
Many experienced mouse users don't truly understand how to use a mouse pointer. When we say to put the mouse on something, we mean the **tip of the pointer** only. The rest of the mouse is there just to make the pointer visible. So, it's possible to put 99 percent of the mouse on an object, but to actually have the **tip** positioned on another object. If you think you've clicked on one thing and something else happens, try again and be sure you get the very tip of the pointer on the targeted object.

Scroll Bars

The horizontal and vertical scroll bars let you use the mouse to scroll through documents that are too large to fit on the screen. To scroll through a document, you use the mouse on the arrows at the ends of the scroll bars. Often, your cursor arrow keys or the Page Up and Page Down keys will perform the same function.

Minimize Button

When you click on the minimize button, the current window drops to the bottom of the screen. You'll then see either the desktop or any other windows that were open underneath the window you minimized. A minimized window is still open, and is quickly accessible through commands you'll learn later. In Windows 95, a minimized application remains visible as a button on the Taskbar.

Maximize/Restore Button

When you click on the maximize button, the current window expands in size to fill the entire area it's allowed to fill. Some people believe that maximize means to make a window fill the screen, but you'll see that that's not true. Once a window is maximized, this button changes appearance and becomes a "Restore" button. Clicking on a restore button, restores the window to the same size, shape and location it was before being maximized.

Windows that contain applications will generally fill the entire screen when maximized. Thus, maximizing an application window will generally cover all other open applications. (The other applications remain open, they're just covered by the maximized window.)

Applications have windows within them that are used to contain documents. These windows are called "document windows" even though they may hold a spreadsheet file or an e-mail message. Document windows cannot exist on their own; they only exist as children of an application. The application window is the parent, and the document window is the child. So, when a document window is maximized it cannot fill the screen—it can expand no farther than the size of its parent window.

Close Button

The button with the "X" in it closes the associated window. If the close button is on a document window, that document is closed. So, if you click on the close button of an e-mail "In" box, only the In box closes and the application remains open. When you click on the close button of an application window, the entire application closes. If any of the open documents within that application needed to be saved, you'll be asked to save them before the application closes.

Title Bar

This is the heavy bar at the very top of every window. The title bar includes the name of the application and the name of the active document in use by that application. You can use the title bar to drag the window around to different places on the screen.

If a window is not maximized, you can double-click on the title bar to maximize it. If a window is maximized, you can double-click on the title bar to restore it.

Menus

Menus are lists of commands that can be selected with the mouse or with keystrokes. To activate a Windows menu with the mouse, place the pointer over the word, then click. A list of commands will drop down. You then can click on one of those menu commands—and then, perhaps, another.

When we tell you to activate a menu command, we'll depict it like this:

✔ Click **File**.

When we tell you to activate a series of menu commands, we'll depict it like this:

✔ Click **File, Document, Properties**.

Keystroke commands

Most mouse operations have equivalent keystroke commands. We'll show the keystroke commands in bold and all caps. So, when we tell you to use a keystroke command (for example, to hit the Enter key), we'll depict it like this:

✔ Press **ENTER**.

Keystrokes that require you to use one or more keys together will be tied together with a plus sign. So, when we tell you to use a combination keystroke command (for example, to hold down the Control key and press the F4 key while you're holding down Control), we'll depict it like this:

✔ Press **CTRL+F4**.

A series of keystrokes will be strung together and separated with commas, like this:

✔ Press **ALT+F, O, ALT+V, ENTER**.
✔ Press **CTRL+SHIFT+F1, ALT+O, C, ENTER, ENTER**.

The ALT key

You can use the **ALT** key in lieu of clicking on almost any menu command. Notice that every menu command has one underlined letter (see Figure 2). You can activate a menu by holding down **ALT** and pressing the underlined letter. Once a menu has been activated, you perform the sub-menu commands by pressing just the underlined letter. For example, you could save a file with this command:

✔ Press **ALT+F, A**

Hitting **ALT** once a menu has been activated will cause the menu to close.

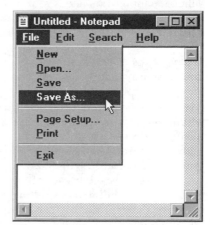

Figure 2 Using the **ALT** key

Right mouse button

Many experienced Windows users still are not in the habit of relying on the right mouse button to boost efficiency. Don't make that mistake! The right mouse button can save you hours of time that you might spend in aggravation looking for the correct menu. Instead you can quickly **right-click** an object and the menu items that you most likely need will pop up.

You must, however, <u>be very careful</u> to right-click **exactly** the correct spot. The menu that pops up is tied precisely to the spot that the mouse pointer is over. Your computer cannot read your mind. For example, if you have highlighted a file that you want to copy to a floppy diskette, you can place the mouse pointer over that highlighted area, then click the right mouse button for the menu item that will **Send To** the floppy drive (see Figure 3). But many people never use this handy shortcut because they highlight the file then move the mouse pointer, *then* click the right mouse button, which produces the wrong menu. Simply placing the mouse pointer *directly over the desired object* before the right click will produce the correct menu!

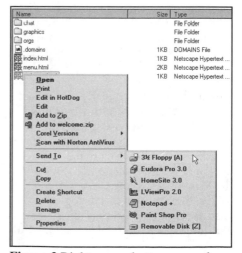

Figure 3 Right mouse button example

Beep! Beep!

The **Menu** key on your keyboard (next to the **Windows** key) also produces a menu of options for the object that is under the mouse pointer. You then can quickly activate the desired menu item by pressing its corresponding <u>underlined</u> letter.

Common controls

When an application needs to show you information or get information from you, it uses a control called a "dialog box" (see Figure 4). The name describes very well what's happening because the application uses a dialog box to have a dialog with you.

Dialog boxes can be as simple as just presenting a text message. But they usually present controls you can use to perform some action within the current application. Dialog boxes use a lot of different types of controls—we can't list them all here. Because there are so many controls and because they can be arranged in so many different ways, dialog boxes have nearly an infinite variety of appearances. Even though there is such a wide range of possibilities, we'll show you some of the basic dialog box controls.

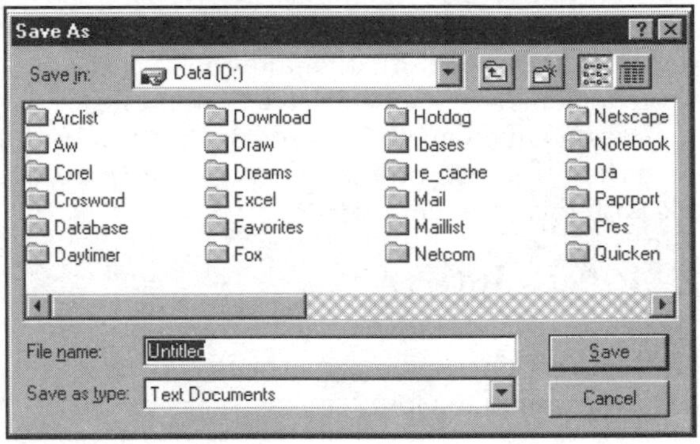

Figure 4 A commonly-used dialog box

First, let's continue with this very common dialog box. When using it to navigate through folders, many people have missed using the **Up One Level** control that's immediately to the right of the current folder name (see Figure 5). Clicking this button navigates you up to the parent folder of the currently-displayed folder.

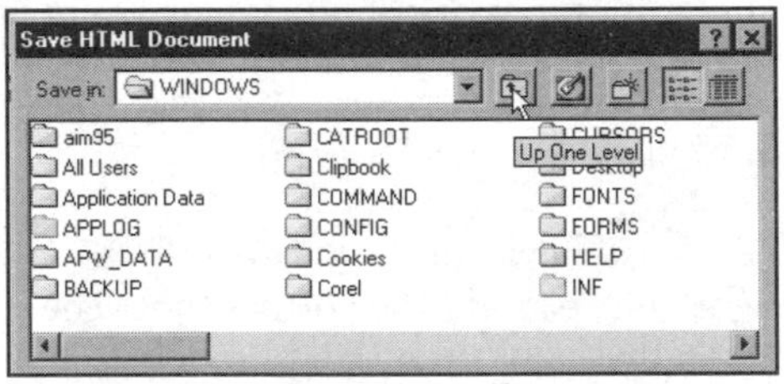

Figure 5 Navigate up to parent folder

One of the most frequently overlooked buttons is the **New Folder** button on every Windows file dialog box. Computer trainers report that many people will get to this dialog box (see Figure 6), realize they need a new folder, close this window, open the Windows Explorer to create the new folder, then reopen this dialog box. Instead, they could simply click **New Folder,** type a name folder and hit **Enter**.

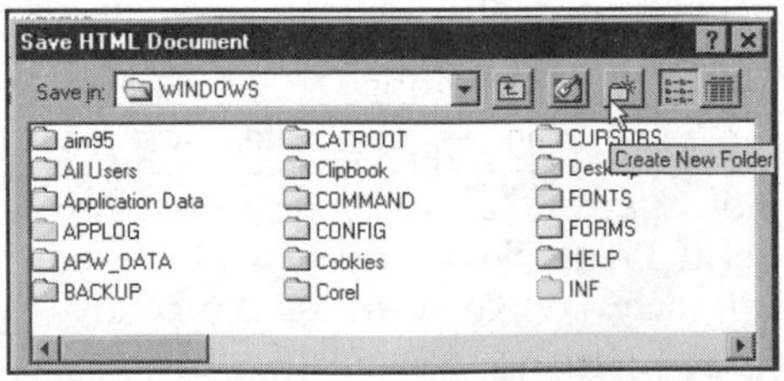

Figure 6 Create a new folder

Beep! Beep!

The standard Windows file dialog box also lets you perform nearly every file management function. You can perform simple, obvious tasks with keystrokes. For example, to delete any folder, highlight it and hit the **Delete** key. To rename a highlighted folder, press **F2**. For more options, right-click the desired file or folder.

Radio buttons

When a dialog box needs to give you a set of choices and you are only allowed to select one of the choices, they often use a radio button control (see Figure 7). In this example (taken from the Solitaire game), there are two sets of radio buttons. Each set is independent of the other.

If we tell you to make a radio button selection, we'll depict it like this:

✔ Under **Scoring**, select **Vegas**.

Check boxes

Check boxes are similar to radio buttons in that they present a set of selections. The difference is that marking one check box does not exclude other selections.

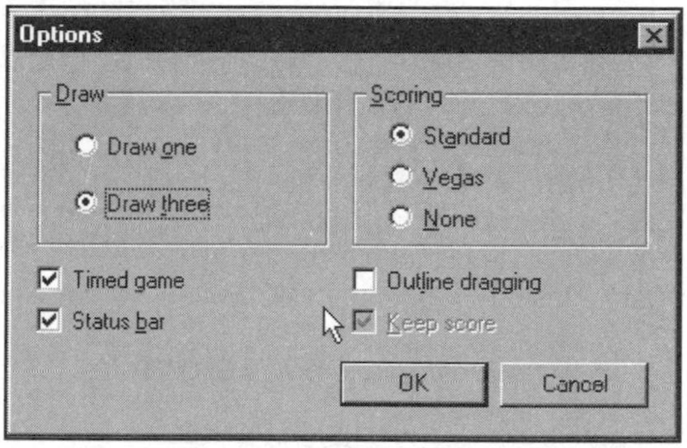

On a dialog box with multiple check boxes, you can check or uncheck as many as you wish. And you can change your mind as many times as you like because the selection doesn't take effect until you click the **OK** button. If you click **Cancel**, then all of the selections you've made will be ignored.

Figure 7 Radio buttons and check boxes

If we tell you to make a check box selection, we'll depict it like this:

✔ Check **Outline dragging**.

✔ Uncheck **Timed game**.

Beep! Beep!

You can use radio buttons and check boxes with keystrokes, too. Each control has one letter underlined. In the example above you could select Vegas scoring by pressing **ALT+V**. And, hitting **ENTER** is the same as clicking on **OK**. So, you could switch to Vegas scoring with: **ALT+V, ENTER**.

Spin buttons

Sometimes programmers use a tool called a "spin button" (see Figure 8) that lets you select a choice from a list. The spin button does the same thing as a radio button, but can only see the selected choice.

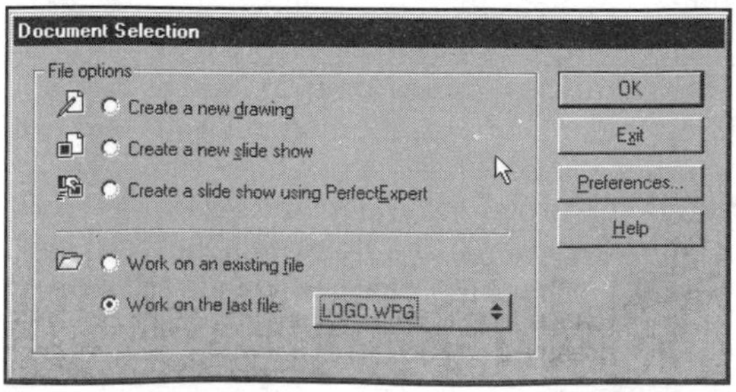

To use a spin button you must hold down the left mouse button on the spin button and then—while still holding down the left button—you

Figure 8 Spin button near the bottom of the box

highlight your selection. Releasing the mouse selects the highlighted menu item, and then you can click **OK**.

If we tell you to make a spin button selection, we'll depict it like this:

✔ Select **Iconic Symbols**

Text entry box

Text entry boxes let you enter information into an application (see Figure 9). After typing the information you can press **ENTER** to tell the application you're through. Of course clicking on **OK** will do the same thing, but when you're entering text, hitting **ENTER** will be much quicker than stopping to pick up the mouse and then moving the mouse pointer and then clicking **OK**. When we tell you to enter text, we'll depict it like this:

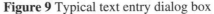

Figure 9 Typical text entry dialog box

✔ Type *a:setup* and press **ENTER**.

> ### Beep! Beep!
> You also can activate the **Run** dialog box, shown above, by pressing the **Windows** key, then pressing **R**. Many other basic Windows functions also are available through this key. For example, once you've pressed the **Windows** key, you can press **P** to launch a new program, **F** to find a file or folder, or **U** to shut down your computer. If you activate this menu by mistake, or change your mind when it's open, just hit **ALT** to make it disappear.

Congratulations for sticking with these lessons. You've learned enough now to get you through our Step-By-Step exercises. Go back now and do something fun.

Switching Windows

Remember, "Windows" is plural. You can have a lot of windows open at once, but you can only work with one at a time. So, you need to know how to switch between them to access the one you want. The techniques are different for switching between application windows and document windows.

Switching application windows

One of the best things about Windows is its ability to run many applications at once. Running only one application at a time and exiting each application before starting another is a waste of the power of Windows. At the same time, you can have open your Web browser, e-mail, newsgroups reader, word processor, contact manager and a game and then instantly switch back and forth between them. You can copy and paste information between open applications and use one application while another is busy downloading information from the Internet.

The key to using multiple windows is knowing the methods to switch between open applications. Let's start some applications so you can try these methods.

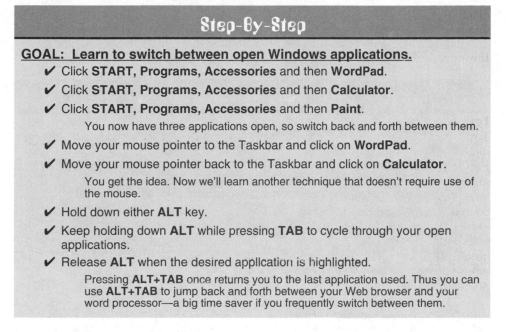

Step-By-Step

GOAL: Learn to switch between open Windows applications.

✔ Click **START, Programs, Accessories** and then **WordPad**.

✔ Click **START, Programs, Accessories** and then **Calculator**.

✔ Click **START, Programs, Accessories** and then **Paint**.

> You now have three applications open, so switch back and forth between them.

✔ Move your mouse pointer to the Taskbar and click on **WordPad**.

✔ Move your mouse pointer back to the Taskbar and click on **Calculator**.

> You get the idea. Now we'll learn another technique that doesn't require use of the mouse.

✔ Hold down either **ALT** key.

✔ Keep holding down **ALT** while pressing **TAB** to cycle through your open applications.

✔ Release **ALT** when the desired application is highlighted.

> Pressing **ALT+TAB** once returns you to the last application used. Thus you can use **ALT+TAB** to jump back and forth between your Web browser and your word processor—a big time saver if you frequently switch between them.

Here's a summary of the methods you can use to switch application windows:

* Click on any visible application window to make it active.
* Click on the desired application on the **Taskbar**.
* Use **ALT+TAB** to cycle through all open applications.
* Use **SHIFT+ALT+TAB** to cycle backward through all open applications.
* Press **ALT+ESC** to cycle between open applications. In contrast to using the **ALT+TAB** keystroke, this command cycles through applications in order and does not begin with your most recently used application.

Switching document windows

Document windows exist only under the control of an application window. Document windows may contain more than just documents. They may also contain database files, e-mail messages, spreadsheets, graphics images or sound files, but they're still called document windows and you use the same method to switch between them regardless of the contents. If your application window supports multiple document windows, it has **Window** on the menu bar. Here's a summary of methods for switching document windows:

* Click on any visible document window.
* Click **Window**, then the name of the file you want.
* Click **Window, Cascade**.
* Click **Window, Tile**.
* Press **SHIFT+F5** to Cascade.
* Press **SHIFT+F4** to Tile.
* Press **ALT+W**, then press the number of the file you want.
* Press **CTRL+F6** or **CTRL+TAB** to cycle through open document windows.

Taskbar Options

If you are hooked on using the mouse but tired of giving up screen space to the Taskbar, you may want to do the next Step-By-Step exercise. It shows you how to reconfigure the Taskbar so it will be hidden until you need it.

Step-By-Step

GOAL: Learn to hide the Taskbar.

✔ Position your mouse over a blank area on the **Taskbar**.

> The next step won't work correctly if your mouse is over any of the buttons on the Taskbar.

✔ Click the right mouse button on a blank area on the Taskbar.

✔ Click **Properties**.

✔ Make sure **Always on top** is checked.

✔ Make sure **Auto hide** is checked.

✔ Check **Show Clock**. (optional, but why not?)

✔ Click **OK**.

> The Taskbar now has been reduced to a thin line at the bottom of the screen. You probably can't see it because it's gray and the status bar on your current application is gray. With some applications, though, you'll notice the line.

✔ Move your mouse pointer to the very bottom of the screen.

> This activates the Taskbar so you now can use it normally. When you move the mouse away, the Taskbar automatically hides from view.

Beep! Beep!

The Taskbar doesn't have to stay at the bottom of your screen. Position the mouse over any blank area on the Taskbar and drag the Taskbar to another side of the screen. And if you touch the edge of the Taskbar with the mouse pointer, you'll see a double-headed arrow, which you can use to adjust the width of the Taskbar.

Customizing Your START Button

Click your **START** button, then let go of your mouse so that you can see what's on the menu. You'll see a thin line dividing the menu into two parts. Below the line, beginning with the **Programs** menu item, are items that you cannot control. But you can put anything you want above the line—and you can delete anything there now that you don't want.

Step-By-Step

GOAL: Learn to customize your Windows START button.

✔ Right-click **START, Open**.

✔ Delete any item in this folder that you don't want on your START menu.

✔ Add shortcuts in this folder to anything that you want on your START menu.

✔ Close the **Start Menu** folder.

ORBITING IN CYBERSPACE

Frank's World O'Windows
http://www.conitech.com/windows

This is one of the most popular sites on the Web for Windows information (see Figure 10). You'll find every version discussed and analyzed, along with tips and tricks that will help you master Windows and get the most from your Internet service. One of its most valuable features is its rich resource of drivers for nearly every type of hardware and version of Windows. This one-stop source of driver updates can keep your system running smoothly. And, this site is always an excellent resource for information that will help you decide when it's time to upgrade to a new version of Windows, when one emerges.

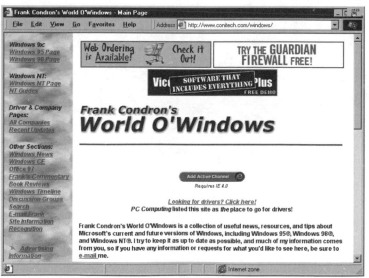

Figure 10 An excellent resource for keeping up with Windows

Tip World
http://www.tipworld.com

Each business day, Tip World will deliver free newsletters to your e-mail box. You can select a wide range of topics including Windows 95, Internet Explorer, Netscape Navigator, Microsoft Office, Internet tip of the day, Internet bug of the day, plus many more. Just visit this site, check the tips you want to receive daily and submit your request. You can come back any time and enter new selections.

PC World
http://www.pcworld.com/software/opsystems

Here's a good source for tips and news about Windows. You'll also be able to download software utilities and games as well as demo versions of new applications. There's an archive of past information and a local search engine that helps you zero in on the information you need.

Home PC Tutor
http://www.geocities.com/SiliconValley/Park/6645

Here's an online introduction to home computing! Help with PC Operating Systems, Software, and the Internet are all just a link away! Click on the site's links to sample what's available on the Internet. The <u>Starting Out in Windows 95</u> link can get you on track quickly if you're struggling with the basics of Windows 95.

Appendix

NOTES

GLOSSARY

anonymous FTP - Using the FTP function of the Internet anonymously by not logging in with an actual, secret login ID and password. Often permitted by large, host computers who are willing to share openly some of the files on their system with outside users who otherwise would not be able to log in.

Archie - An ancient Internet search tool, not used much since way back in the good old days of 1994. It's an archive of filenames maintained at Internet FTP sites. Don't pine its passing, you didn't miss anything—the Web is much more fun.

bandwidth - The transmission capacity of the lines that carry the Internet's electronic traffic. Historically, it's imposed severe limitations on the ability of the Internet to deliver all that we are demanding it deliver, but the high-speed cables of your Road Runner system will remove many of your bandwidth problems.

Bookmark - (see Favorites Folder)

browser - Software that enables users to browse through the cyberspace of the World Wide Web. Netscape Navigator and Microsoft Internet Explorer are the primary Internet browsers today.

cable modem - An electronic adapter that permits a personal computer to receive Internet data from the high-speed information resources of a cable television system. Cable modems permit personal computers to receive Internet information at rates of up to hundreds of time faster than typical, consumer market telephone modems. A cable modem attaches to a personal computer through a network interface card (NIC) installed inside the computer. The cable television system's cable brings the information into the cable modem and then the cable modem sends the information into the computer through the NIC.

CGI - Common Gateway Interface. A programming function used on Web servers that gives Web pages the ability to interact with Web visitors.

ClariNet - A commercial news service that provides tailored news reports via the Internet. You can access ClariNet news within Usenet newsgroups. There is a whole series of them, dedicated to a wide range of broad topics. In general, you can find them on news servers at clari.*.

dial-in - An Internet account that can connect any stand-alone computer directly to the Internet. The account is used by having a software application dial-in to an Internet service provider (ISP). The software connects with the ISP and establishes a TCP/IP link to the Internet that enables your software to access Internet information. The computer that accesses a dial-in connection needs either a modem to connect via a regular phone line or a terminal adapter (TA) to connect via an ISDN phone line.

e-mail - (Electronic mail) Messages transmitted over the Internet from user to user. E-mail can contain text, but also can carry with it files of any type as attachments.

FAQ - (Frequently Asked Questions) Files that are maintained at Internet sites to answer frequently asked questions so that experienced users don't have to bear the annoying burden of hearing newbies repeatedly ask the same questions. It's good netiquette to check for FAQs and read them. It's extremely poor netiquette—and a good way to get flamed—to post questions that already are answered in the FAQ.

Favorites Folder - A special feature of the Road Runner Browser that enables you to store the location of favorite Web pages in folders for quick future access. This is a powerful and important feature since many Web addresses are difficult to remember. When a Web site is added to your Favorites Folder you can give the site any name you choose and then return to it later by reference to that name.

Finger - An Internet function that enables one user to query (finger) the location of another Internet user. Finger can be applied to any computer on the Internet, if set up properly. For example, the most famous finger site of all was a Coke machine at Carnegie-Mellon that students wired to the Internet so they could finger it and track such important information as how many bottles of which beverage remained and how long the bottom bottle in each stack had been in the machine—so they wouldn't walk all the way to the machine and find it empty or purchase a warm soda. You won't use this, but it was fun while it lasted. Most sites have disabled Finger because it helps hackers crack a system.

firewall - A combination of hardware and software that protects a local area network (LAN) from Internet hackers. It separates the network into two or more parts and restricts outsiders to the area "outside" the firewall. Private or sensitive information is kept "inside" the firewall.

flames - Insulting, enraged Internet messages. The equivalent of schoolyard brawls in cyberspace. Unfortunately, a good schoolyard brawl would be preferable because at least then the only people who suffer are the dummies who fight. On the Internet, everyone suffers as resources are squandered on ridiculous, infantile behavior. But you won't be using flames, of course.

FQDN - (Fully Qualified Domain Name) The "official" name assigned to a computer. Organizations register names, such as "ibm.com" or "utulsa.edu." They then assign unique names to their computers, such as "watson5.ibm.com" or "hurricane.cs.utulsa.edu."

FTP - (File Transfer Protocol) The basic Internet function that enables files to be transferred between computers. You can use it to download files from a remote, host computer, as well as to upload files from your computer to a remote, host computer. (See Anonymous FTP).

gateway - A host computer that connects a network to other networks. For example, a gateway connects a company's local area network to the Internet.

GIF - (Graphics Interchange Format) A graphics file format that is commonly used on the Internet to provide graphics images in Web pages.

Gopher - A tool that organizes information by means of a hierarchy of menus. Gopher is now buried under mountains of WWW pages—don't bother learning how to use this directly. You sometimes will find a Web link that takes you to a Gopher site, but at that point, if you're using Netscape, its usage will be obvious and will look a great deal like the Web.

hacker - Anyone who tries to gain unauthorized access into remote computer systems. Though many hackers work simply for the challenge of cracking a difficult security system, many hackers tap into remote systems for malicious purposes such as theft of secure information, destruction of information, to disable a computer system, or to infect it with a computer virus (see "virus" entry).

host - A system that includes TCP/IP and runs applications, delivers files, provides computing services or shares the system's resources.

HTML - (Hypertext Markup Language) The basic language that is used to build hypertext documents on the World Wide Web. It is used in basic, plain ASCII-text documents, but when those documents are interpreted (called rendering) by a Web browser, the document can display formatted text, color, a variety of fonts, graphic images, sound, video clips, run programs, perform special effects and handle hypertext jumps to other Internet locations anywhere in the world.

HTTP - (Hypertext Transfer Protocol) The protocol (rules) computers use to transfer hypertext documents.

hypertext - Text in a document that contains a hidden link to other text. You can click a mouse on a hypertext word and it will take you to the text designated in the link. Hypertext is used in Windows help programs and CD encyclopedias to jump to related references elsewhere within the same document. The wonderful thing about hypertext, however, is its ability to link—using http over the World Wide Web—to any Web document in the world, yet still require only a single mouse click to jump clear around the world.

IP - (Internet Protocol) The rules that support basic Internet data delivery functions. (See TCP/IP.)

IP Address - An Internet address that is a unique number consisting of 4 parts separated by dots, sometimes called a "dotted quad." For example, 198.204.112.1. Every Internet computer has an IP address and most computers also are assigned one or more Domain Names that are easier to remember than the dotted quad.

IRC - (Internet Relay Chat) Currently an Internet tool with a limited use that lets users join a "chat" channel and exchange typed, text messages. Few people have used IRC, but it is going to create a revolution in communication when the Internet can provide the bandwidth to carry full-color, live-action video and audio. Once that occurs, the IRC will provide full video-conferencing. Even today, while limited for all practical purposes only to text, the IRC can be a valuable business conferencing tool, already providing adequate voice communication.

Java - A programming language that permits Internet sites on the World Wide Web to include computer applications that run on the computers of people who visit the sites. Java programs only work on computers that have Java-capable Web browsers, such as the Road Runner Browser that's included free with your service. Java programs can run games, create animation effects, drive database searches and permit user inquiries for information.

JavaScript - A simplified subset of Java that enables Web authors to include Java-like programming without needing to know how to program in the full Java language.

JPEG - (Joint Photographic Experts Group) The name of the committee that designed the photographic image-compression standard. .JPEG is optimized for compressing full-color or gray-scale photographic-type, digital images. It doesn't work well on drawn images such as line drawings, and it does not handle black-and-white images or video images.

kbps - (kilobits per second) A speed rating for computer modems that measures (in units of 1,024 bits) the maximum number of bits the device can transfer in one second under ideal conditions.

kBps - (kilobytes per second). Remember, one byte is eight bits.

listserv - An Internet application that automatically "serves" mailing lists by sending electronic newsletters to a stored database of Internet user addresses. Most lists let users subscribe and unsubscribe automatically, not requiring anyone at the server location to personally handle the transaction. But for a "reflector" mailing list, the request to join goes to a human being's mailbox who must manually perform the subscribe or unsubscribe transaction.

mailing list - An e-mail-based discussion group. Sending one e-mail message to the mailing list's list server sends mail to all other members of the group. Users join a mailing list by subscribing. Subscribers to a mailing list receive messages from all other members. Users have to unsubscribe from a mailing list to stop receiving messages forwarded from the group's members.

MIME - (Multipurpose Internet Mail Extensions) A set of Internet functions that extends normal e-mail capabilities and enables computer files to be attached to e-mail. Files sent by MIME arrive at their destination as exact copies of the original so that you can send fully-formatted word processing files, spreadsheets, graphics images and software applications to other users via simple e-mail, provided the recipient has a MIME-capable e-mail application (most of them today are).

modem - An electronic device that lets computers communicate electronically using regular phone lines. The name is derived from "modulator-demodulator" because of its function in processing data over analog phone lines.

netiquette - Internet etiquette. Good netiquette will keep you out of trouble in newsgroups.

network interface card - A card that is installed inside a personal computer that permits a personal computer to transfer data via a computer network. Commonly used in computers that are linked to office local area networks (LANs), a network interface card is required to connect to a cable modem. Some Macintosh computers and even some Windows computers have the functions of a network interface card built into the basic circuitry of the computer.

newsgroup - An electronic, community bulletin board that enables Internet users all over the world to post and read messages that are public to other users of the group. There are now more than 30,000 public newsgroups available and countless thousands of private newsgroups. All together, newsgroups collect many gigabytes of data daily. No one knows the actual count of current newsgroups because the number changes rapidly as new groups are added and unpopular groups are dropped.

NIC - (see network interface card)

NNTP - (Network News Transfer Protocol) An Internet protocol that handles Usenet newsgroups at most modern Internet service providers.

POP - (Post Office Protocol) An Internet protocol that enables a single user to read e-mail from a mail server.

PoP - (Point of Presence) A site that has an array of telecommunications equipment: modems, digital, leased lines and Internet routers. An Internet access provider may operate several regional PoPs to provide Internet connections within local phone service areas. An alternative is for access providers to employ virtual PoPs (virtual Points of Presence) in conjunction with third party provider.

protocols - Computer rules that provide uniform specifications so that computer hardware and operating systems can communicate. It's similar to the way that mail, in countries around the world, is addressed in the same basic format so that postal workers know where to find the recipient's address, the sender's return address and the postage stamp. Regardless of the underlying language, the basic "protocols" remain the same.

router - A network device that enables the network to reroute messages it receives that are intended for other networks. The network with the router receives the message and sends it on its way exactly as received.

signature file - An ASCII text file, maintained within e-mail programs, that contains a few lines of text for your signature. The programs automatically attach the file to your messages so you don't have to repeatedly type a closing.

SMTP - (Simple Mail Transfer Protocol) The simple, classic protocol used to handle the Internet's e-mail functions.

spam - Anything that nobody wants. Applies primarily to commercial messages posted across a large number of Internet Newsgroups, especially when the ad contains nothing of specific interest to the posted Newsgroup.

T-1 - An Internet backbone line that carries up to 1.536 million bits per second (1.536Mbps), which is very fast, but still far, far slower than the connections to the Internet that we deliver.

T-3 - An Internet line that carries up to 45 million bits per second (45Mbps). Some companies connect to the Internet with multiple T-3 lines so that they can enjoy the fastest possible service available without using a cable system.

TCP/IP - (Transmission Control Protocol/Internet Protocol) The basic programming foundation that carries computer messages around the globe via the Internet. Co-created by Vinton G. Cerf, former president of the Internet Society, and Robert E. Kahn.

Telnet - An Internet protocol that lets you connect your PC as a remote workstation to a host computer anywhere in the world and to use that computer as if you were logged on locally. You often have the ability to use all of the software and capability on the host computer, even if it's a huge mainframe.

Unix - The computer operating system that was used to write most of the programs and protocols that built the Internet. It is similar to MS-DOS that is at the heart of all Windows computers. The need to know Unix is rapidly waning and mainstream users will never need to use Unix directly.

URL - (Uniform Resource Locator) A crucial term. It's your main access ticket to Internet resources. It's the equivalent of having the phone number of a place you want to call. You will constantly use URLs with your Internet software to identify the protocol, host name and file name of resources you want.

Usenet - Another name for Internet Newsgroups. A distributed bulletin board system running on news servers.

Veronica - Archie's companion—not really, because Veronica actually helps you find information on Gopher menus. It's an acronym for "Very Easy Rodent-Oriented Net-wide Index to Computerized Archives." You will probably never use it, however, because Web searches are faster and more extensive and Veronica is now considered "ancient" technology on the Internet.

virus - A computer program that can automatically jump from one computer to install itself on another computer. Viruses are harmful because they generally damage any computer on which they're installed. The damage can be anything from simply displaying a message, to deleting files, to totally wiping out all data on the computer. There are many computer programs on the market that will monitor your computer for the presence of a computer virus and either alert you when a virus is detected or eliminate the virus from your system.

World Wide Web - (WWW) (W3) (the Web) An Internet client-server distributed information and retrieval system based upon the hypertext transfer protocol (http) that transfers hypertext documents across a varied array of computer systems. The Web was created by the CERN High-Energy Physics Laboratories in Geneva, Switzerland in 1991. CERN boosted the Web into international prominence on the Internet.

INDEX

Amazon 113
applet 56
ARPANET 63
attachment 73-75
Attachments 73
bandwidth 11, 12, 49, 59, 60, 74, 75, 85, 131, 167-169, 173, 203, 205
Beta test 55
binary file 73
Boardwatch Magazine 14
Bookshelf 121
bulletin board 77
cable modem 12, 91, 92, 117, 163, 167, 203, 206
caching 48
certified delivery 28
CGI 154, 159, 160, 164, 165, 173, 203
ClariNet 181, 185, 203
Common User Access (CUA) 189
Computer Literacy Bookshops 14
Congress 117, 118, 126, 131, 132, 145, 188
copyright . . . . i, ii, viii, 22, 62, 118, 145, 152, 156, 170, 174, 179, 181-188
Cox, Dr. Brad J. 28
credit card 24
cruft 70
Cyber Course 13
CyberCash 26, 31, 32
DejaNews 86, 108
Department of Defense (DoD) 6
DHTML 156, 157
DigiCash 31
domain name 65
double-click 190
Einstein, Albert 5
emoticons 20, 86
FAQs 61, 62, 84-86, 105, 156, 179, 204
Farcast 86
Favorites Folders 56
firewall 41, 204
flame war 16
Four11 directory 76
FrontPage 158, 173
FTP 9, 35, 38, 47, 58, 72, 118, 136, 163-165, 203, 204
GIF 54, 154-156, 168, 169, 171, 172, 174-176, 178, 204
Gopher 9, 47, 58, 118, 119, 136, 204, 205, 208
government . . . . i, 5, 27, 29, 32, 37, 65, 88, 119, 125-128, 130-133, 135, 136
hacker 24, 25, 33-36, 205
HotDog 157-159, 163, 173

hypertext ... 7, 8, 10, 47, 52, 53, 55, 119, 135, 143, 153, 154, 156, 157, 159, 205, 208
IAB 6
IETF 6
Infoseek 105, 106
InterNIC 69, 70, 186
Intranet 58
ISOC 6, 13
Java 51, 56, 154, 160, 162, 166, 205, 206
JPEG 54, 154, 168-172, 174-176, 206
Jughead 9
King, Martin Luther, Jr. 11
library 10, 30, 32, 66, 98, 101, 111, 116-124, 126, 132, 141, 165, 180, 188
Library of Congress 117, 118, 126, 132, 188
LView 174-176
Lycos 62, 139, 142, 146
mail server 68-70, 72, 74, 207
mailing list 9, 13, 149, 185, 206
micropayments 26
modem 11, 12, 59, 91, 92, 117, 160, 163, 167, 203, 206
MPEG 60, 61
National Science Foundation (NSF) 6
NetBill 29-32
netiquette . . . . i, 2, 15-18, 21, 22, 64, 83, 85, 86, 204, 206
Newbie 13, 18, 22, 84
news server 77, 78
newsgroups . . . . i, viii, 9, 16-18, 42, 44, 58, 77-81, 83-86, 96, 108, 146, 150, 183, 196,
                                                                                                203, 206-208
newsreader 77-81
NNTP 77, 207
NSF 6, 29, 32
Paint Shop Pro 173
PNG 175
Quicktime 61
RealAudio 58, 59, 165
right-click 190
router 4, 207
scanning 152, 168, 176-179
SearchAmerica 147
Secure Sockets Layer (SSL) 25
signature file 76, 82, 86, 207
SkiSoft 155, 156, 163
smileys 20
Smithsonian 90, 91
SMTP 69, 207
spam 18, 207
SSL 25
stocks 23, 141, 142
TCP/IP 5, 6, 46, 66, 70, 203, 205, 208
Telnet 9, 10, 35, 118-121, 135, 136, 208
Toolbar 48, 50, 51, 73, 78
UNIX 41, 42, 170, 208

UPS 137, 183
Usenet 42, 77, 81, 86, 108, 139, 183, 185, 203, 207, 208
USPS 128, 129
Veronica 9, 208
White House 145
Windows, close 191
Windows, dialog box 194
Windows, maximize 191
Windows, minimize 191
Windows, radio button 195
Windows, spin button 195
Windows, title bar 192
WinZip 75
World Wide Web 7
Yahoo! 97, 105, 107-110, 119, 128, 131, 132, 142, 146, 178
Zip codes 160

NOTES

NOTES

NOTES